Southside Kid

To order additional copies, please contact us.
BookSurge, LLC
www.booksurge.com
1-866-308-6235
orders@booksurge.com

L. CURT ERLER

SOUTHSIDE KID

2006

Southside Kid

TABLE OF CONTENTS

I Dedicate This Work To Kathy, My Devoted Wife Of Forty-six Years, And Our Three Beautiful Daughters: Cassandra Maria, Nicole Antoinette And Honey Colette. This Endeavor Would Have Lacked The Necessary Incentives Without Your Inspiration. You Are So Precious To Me In Your Individual Ways.

I Am Fortunate Enough To Have Three Great Sons-in-law: Charlie, Bill And Jeremy. You Guys Are A Blessing To This Family.

We Are So Proud Of Our Four Grandchildren: Brooke, Brett, Faith And Hannah-Rose. You Are Truly Gifts From God.

As I Write These Pages, One Individual Takes The Journey With Me. Ron, I Know That You're Watching As I Pen Each Line. You Are Sorely Missed In My Life. It Has Been Forty-six Years Since You Left Your Loved Ones, Yet Each Day Brings You Into My Thoughts. I'll Try To Be Good So That We May Continue Our Fun And Laughter On The Other Side.

(Ref: Ronald J. Laffey ~ November 25, 1938 / October 28, 1960)

In Memory Of My Wonderful Parents, Cash And Winona Erler

PROLOGUE

Take a little walk with me: to a place where this child learned to be a man. Where so many hard-working Chicagoans, both men and women, toiled at their daily labors. There were the wives and moms that stayed home to ensure their children a safe and secure home. There were the husbands and dads that worked at their trades. These moms and dads were the backbone of this wonderful country. We survived these difficult times with the efforts of the blue-collar workers, and of the fighting men and women of our militaries and their undying dedication to family, faith and country. I lived among so many dedicated folks who worked and fought to keep our future generations free. Those that sacrificed life and limb shall never be forgotten. Not only did these hard-working citizens protect our country, they also continued to build it and improve it.

Ever since I was a very young boy I have been curious about the ways of other people. There seemed to be so many different cultures, traditions and wonderful foods. A multitude of faiths had been carried over from many homelands. I wanted to see all that I could see.

The Southside of Chicago was such a large melting pot with so many languages and dialects. As you wandered its streets and neighborhoods, the cultures and ethnicities created a virtual world tour. You could "visit" Italy, Ireland, England, Scotland, Germany, Poland, Russia, Africa, Scandinavia—and who could forget Chinatown? You name it, we had it!

As you turn these pages you will witness no brutal murders, no felonious violence, no rapes, no torrid bedroom scenes. The language would rate a PG13 at worst. There will be one unsolved mystery. At least I have never solved it. If you will take this walk with me, I promise to take you to places you'll not soon forget. You'll meet some wonderful folks. This is simply a story of a young boy growing up on Chicago's Southside, a typical blue-collar working class neighborhood of those times. It's a book of true-life experiences. It was a wonderful time in our history and, in my opinion, the greatest place on earth. It was the perfect environment for a young boy to grow to manhood. Come along, walk with me!

It would be so hard not to be melancholy while reflecting on one's own life. The loves, lost and won. The friends that stayed and those that are gone, some way too soon! I'm not at all shy or apologetic about in-depth descriptions of my emotions and personal experiences during these two decades. It was, in fact, my life!

Some names and places have been changed for various reasons. However, if it's in this book, it happened!

BIG CITY, LITTLE BOY

Kid on His Trike! ©

CHICAGO, SPRING OF '42 – The world was at war and I was a three-year-old boy in my new neighborhood. On this warm and breezy morning, I sat there on my new red tricycle. Santa had brought this three-wheeled treasure last Christmas morning when we still lived in our old house at 80th Street and Dorchester Avenue. This was the brown stucco bungalow with that big parlor where Mom and Dad always let me play with all of my Tootsie Toys. Boston, the bull terrier across the street, gave me his sad-eyed look. He knew that he was at his territorial boundary, and I knew that the curb was as far as I dared travel. My home and family were just one hundred feet or so to my rear. With every little move that I made, Boston's little tail would wag vigorously, sweeping the concrete sidewalk below. This was 83rd Street and Harper Avenue, where it all began. As I looked to my right, beyond the red fire hydrant (actually, we called them "fire-plugs"), two rows of trees shrouded the long black street all the way to 82nd. These trees—elms, maples, oaks, mulberries and more—would always be there, watching me grow.

"Mornin', Whitey!" a big man with a large leather bag flung over his shoulder called to me. This giant of a man was our mailman and always called me "Whitey." My Mom said that it was because I was a towhead. Now which is it, I wondered, am I Whitey or a towhead? In any case, I was always happy to see him. I twisted and turned to get that little red trike aimed to the east. "Ya' gonna keep me company, Whitey?"

I just nodded my head up and down and started to peddle. He hesitated as he began his 83rd-Street trek. I caught up and rode alongside of him until we reached the stoop of Dad's camera store. I jumped off the trike and walked in with him. He always seemed to be carrying some kind of surprise.

My Dad was busy making pictures in his mysterious darkroom. My brother Percy was always at the counter ready to serve the multitudes of folks as they passed over the threshold that we called "the stoop." "Hey, Percy, looks like you hit the jackpot today," Mr. Mailman said as he hauled out what seemed to be a hundred pounds of mail.

Percy said, "Yeah, mostly bills, I'll bet!"

With that, Mr. Mailman turned and tapped me on the head and said, "Will I see you again this afternoon?" I just shrugged my shoulders, not knowing what that meant. Back in those days there were two mail deliveries a day, but I had no idea. It seemed that I was always taking a nap at the later time, which was normally around two-thirty PM.

I asked Percy why the mailman had asked me that. "Well, Curt, your friend comes back again later with more mail, but you'll be napping."

Hearing that, I climbed the stairs, all nineteen of them, and made a beeline for the kitchen. That always seemed a sure place to find Mom. *"Don't sit under the apple tree with anyone else but me"* were the words coming from Mom's Philco radio perched atop our Coldspot refrigerator. She really loved music and seldom worked without that radio serenading her. "Mom, do I have to take a nap today?"

Having no idea what prompted that inquiry, she said, "Would you like a glass of milk?" as she pondered my question.

"Okay, Mom, but can I have some Obiltine in it?" You remember, that famous drink that ensured that we would live forever—Ovaltine!

"Sure, Curt, sit down and I'll make you some Obiltine!"

At this point of my growing up days I had been promoted to a regular big-people chair. I loved the shiny white enameled one with the zoo-like bars across the back. I positioned myself on my knees for this event. I had to show how big I was for my special request. "Mom, the mail guy is coming back later and wants me to help him." I felt it necessary to add some importance to this unusual mission.

Mom kinda rubbed her chin and said, "Would you like to take a nap now so that you will be rested for your job?" Mom knew approximately what time he'd be back and wanted me to have the chance to help my new friend.

"Okay, Mom, I'll drink my milk and go right to bed. Thanks, Mom!" It was probably ten AM, and I had only been up since about eight. That didn't matter to me as long as this nap would satisfy my need for sleep. I never did understand those afternoon naps. I never did sleep much anyway.

"All right, Curt, but just today, so don't ask again tomorrow. I'll turn the radio down and you tuck yourself in and close your eyes."

Needless to say, I just lay there for an hour or so, wondering what my mail friend might have me do. I really wanted to help him this afternoon. I finally called into the kitchen, "Mom, is my nap over yet?" I could hear someone singing about some gal in Kalamazoo. It was Mom singing along—she often did that. I figured that this gal must have been visiting the animals in some zoo.

"Okay, Curt, you can come out now." What a waste of time that was. But who cared, I had done my time.

Sure enough, about two-thirty PM, as I sat on my trike looking north down Harper Avenue, I heard my friend call out, "Hey, Whitey!" What's this, he's coming from Stony Island Avenue? What's goin' on here I wondered, is he already done for the day? I peddled toward him as fast

I could go. As I approached the door, I could hear Percy telling him that I would be able to help him.

Percy said, "Curt took an early nap so that he could see you again on your afternoon run." Mr. Mailman handed Percy a few letters and asked if I could do Harper Avenue with him if he walked me back. "Sure!" Percy replied, "I'm sure that he'll be a good helper."

Apparently, he ran the afternoon route in reverse. This time the trike stayed home as I walked by his side. First stop was 8249, the Hudnuts. Nope, no mail for them this afternoon. I had been this far just a few times, either with Dad or Percy. I remembered that the next house, 8245, was where the big parrot screeched from the enclosed porch. As we approached the only driveway in the neighborhood that went downhill to the garage, the large jungle bird began yelling at us. Later in life, this would be the home of my buddies Sean and Casey. Today, it was the home of a dentist.

Mrs. Dentist came to the porch door, "Shush, Rainbow," she called to the parrot. "Well, who do we have here? Is this your little boy?"

"No ma'am, this is one of the Erler boys from the Kodak shop around the corner," Mr. Mailman replied.

"Gee, it must be nice to have a helper."

This remark stayed with me until I returned home. I couldn't help thinking, "Mom will be proud of me now that I really am a helper." As we continued north, we reached the corner of 82nd Street. Now Mr. Mailman had to cross the street to do the west side of Harper.

"Hold my hand, Whitey," he said.

Man, what a hand. This guy was a giant. Not even Dad's hand was this big and strong. It was a sure thing that I had nothing to worry about with the mailman as my bodyguard. After reaching the curb on the other side of the street, he released my hand and handed me some important mail to carry. Wow, this was getting better and better. I was a kid mailman. Wait 'til I tell Sis, Luke and Todd, and Dad too! We began our trek south on Harper. All of a sudden something came to mind. "Do you think that Boston will be home?" I asked.

"Who is Boston?" my friend asked.

"Boston is my favorite dog. He lives on the corner, way down there." I pointed toward 83rd Street.

"Well, I don't know, but we'll see when we get there."

Now all I wanted to do was get all of this mailing business done so that we could look for Boston. When we got there, the mailman knocked on the people's door as an extra favor. Immediately we were greeted with, "Woof, bark, yap, woof!"

Boston seemed excited. His owners must have been at work. This did not please me very much. I got down on my knees and called through the mail slot. "Boston, it's me, it's me. Hi, how are you?"

He knew I was there. He whimpered as though he wanted to come out and lick my face. I thought, "Gee, I guess I'll just have to wait until another time to pet my buddy, Boston."

Mr. Mailman walked me home and thanked me for all of the help. I was so proud. I could hardly wait to tell Mom and everybody else of my big day. The very next morning, as I returned to my regular post on the corner, there was Boston, smiling at me. At least it looked like a smile to this three-year-old. While I knew the temptation was even stronger than usual, he just sat on the very edge of the curb. This time, though, he was kind of whining to me. I thought, "Someday, someday for sure, I'm going to hug that puppy. I just know it!"

Dad had worked at the store on 83rd Street for several years. Mr. Schultz, the previous owner, had sold the business and the property to Dad in early 1942. It was a big two-story brown brick building. Dad soon became a franchised Kodak dealer. This was most appropriate, with Dad having been born in Rochester, New York, the home of Eastman Kodak Company. It was without doubt a great investment for Mom and Dad. They now had a camera store and a photo-finishing plant downstairs. Upstairs, there was a two-thousand-plus-square-foot house and a great big yard. It was the largest yard in our neighborhood.

I still recall the first day that we were there. Todd and Luke were all excited because there was a boat in the yard. Luke was shouting, "We can play Sinbad the Sailor and everything! This is going to be great. Just think, we'll be havin' sword fights like Errol Flynn and Douglas Fairbanks, Jr." A few days later some men came with a large truck and hauled the treasure away. I guess that Mr. Schultz still wanted it. "That's all right, we still have the biggest yard in the world!" Luke exclaimed.

Now the big store below our new house had a new name, "Cash Erler Photos." Dad sold cameras, various kinds of photo equipment and supplies. He hired additional employees as he strategically planned his new business venture. The darkroom was now staffed with experienced men and women. It seemed so odd to me that people could spend their days in this very dark environment. There were little red safety lights allowing the folks to see what they were doing. Dad provided his photo services to hundreds of the drugstores and other stores throughout the city, the Southside and the Northside! The route guys would pick up and deliver on a daily basis. Percy, Buck, Cary and other employees took their turns at the different routes. Percy used to take the Morgan Park route because it kept him closer to home. Actually, if my memory serves me correctly, it was a piece of cake! The B route was the largest and Dad's big-money route.

Dad was a rather large man, more than six feet tall with big shoulders and hands. He had pure white hair, almost! On the right side of his head the hair had a streak of golden brown. Mom said, "That's from the developer that he has his hands in all of the time. When he's in the darkroom, he throws his hair back with his right hand. That makes his hair look that way." I really liked it. I thought that he looked like a movie star.

I know that people liked Dad a lot because when he wasn't in the darkroom, he was always talking to someone. I'd hear him talking about the war, politics, theology, cameras, sports and much more. They were always asking him questions and for his advice. Luke said, "That's because Dad knows so much. He was going to be a lawyer before he married Mom." A lot of people that came in would ask, "Is Cash in?" Percy would always get a sour look on his puss when that happened. He liked to think that he was the boss. We all knew who the real boss was—it was Dad!

Dad served in the U.S. Army in WWI. I understand that he started out as a cook. Shortly thereafter, he was loaned to Canada's Royal Flying Corps. This was called "TDY," which really meant that he was on temporary duty with that organization. While there, he taught aerial photography to the Canucks.

It's May and that means gardening time! Mom and Dad have tons of flowers in our new yard. Even though Dad works a million hours every week, he still loves to grow things. I just love those red and yellow tulips in the flower beds. With empty flower pots and flats strewn all over the yard, Mom's soft voice declares, "Cash, let's get these snapdragons planted and then we'll call it quits for today."

Mom has these snapdragons in several different colors. My very favorites are the yellow and white ones. Now, most boys in the neighborhood might not be willing to express this type of love. Tell ya' what, if they think that it makes me a sissy, let 'em come and tell me about it. As we finish the planting, weeding and watering, Mom says, "Let's go kids. I'll make us some liver sausage sandwiches and we can all have a Coke." The work is over and Dad is already lighting up his Camel cigarette. It seems like the tough guys always smoke Camels. I don't know why, though—they smell terrible to me.

"No mailman today, Curt!" Mom told me that Sunday was my friend's day off. Mom says that he needs to spend time with his family on Sunday. This will be a fun week because my baby brother, Junior, will be having his first birthday on Tuesday. Everyone will be here for this big day. Mom tells me, "Gramma and Aunt Selma will be coming for the party, Curt. Won't that be nice?" Now I begin to picture one of those big white cakes with all of those sugary flowers on the top and nuts all around the side. There will be ice cream and root beer, too! Mom says that there will be a ton of people here and that I have to be a good boy. What else could I be with all of those goodies at stake?

Sis let me walk down to the streetcar corner with her on Tuesday, the birthday party day. Sis is my only sister and everyone just calls her "Sis." She is two years older than me. That's old enough to go all the way to Stony Island Avenue where the streetcars are. We always climb into the big tree on the corner.

"This must be the biggest tree in Chicago, Sis."

Sis replies, "Yeah, it just might be. I guess that's why we call it 'the big tree.' It's probably a hundred years old!"

Pretty soon my brothers Cary and Buck will be coming by after work. Percy and Dad will close the store about six o'clock, Sis says. My other brothers, Luke and Todd, are in their rooms doing homework. Todd is more than seven years older than me and almost a grown-up. He's usually playing baseball or listening to baseball on the radio. Luke is four years older than me. He loves to look at his comic books and then draw the funny-looking people in them. He told me that he was going to be a cartoonist, whatever that is. Baby Junior is taking his nap. He's always taking a nap or drinking milk.

Buck is really old, and I know that he is tough too, 'cause Dad told me that Buck "popped some guy in the kisser" at work the other day! Buck works on the railroad and he works for Dad, too. He loves work, I guess. Cary works at a place called "Southworks" and makes a lot of money. He must work a lot because he has a great big Buick. He also works for Dad when he wants to make some extra money. Dad has the best car in the family. It's a dark green Lincoln Zephyr. We kids just call it "the Zephyr." It's gigantic inside, and the doors open with a big round white button on the inside.

I can still remember last year when Mom said that she wouldn't be coming home for a few days. I cried and cried. How could my Mom not be here for days? She told me, "I'm going to bring you a new little baby."

Well, sure enough, a few days later Gramma and I waited at the front door for Mom to come home. "Here they come!" shouted Gram as Cary's Buick pulled up out in front. There he was—my baby!—just as Mom had promised. I was sure proud to have my own baby. I was very glad to see my real Mom too, 'cause Gramma was from Dresden, Germany, and had some very strict ways. She poured boiling water on my head when she washed my hair in the bathtub. I would tell my Dad, but he'd just say, "Oh, she doesn't mean it, she's just old-fashioned". I couldn't see where that mattered, that hot water still hurt.

Well, let me tell you, from that day on, if anybody said to my Mom, "Your little baby is sure cute," I would interrupt and tell them that he was *my* baby. I wasn't going to hear any more of that. What did they know? Well, now my baby is one year old and I am ready to celebrate with cake 'n' ice cream. I know that I am a lucky boy. I have five big brothers, a big smart dad, my baby brother, and a pretty mom and a pretty sister.

As the year of 1942 grows short, I begin hearing Bing Crosby more and more. *"I'm Dreaming of a White Christmas, with every Christmas card I write."* It's coming from Mom's radio and the radio in Dad's car. Percy also has the phonograph record. I love that because he plays it for me while I lie on the floor remembering last Christmas when Santa brought all of those Tootsie Toys and my red tricycle.

"What do you think Santa will bring me this year, Percy?" Percy says that I need to tell him what I want so that he can drop a line to Santa for me. He adds, "Santa might not be bringing as much this year because America is fighting in the war." I didn't really understand as I nodded with an "Oh!"

Little did we know that next Christmas Percy would be fighting in the war over in Italy and Africa. Buck would also be in the Army next Christmas.

The Washington Redskins beat the Bears 14 to 6 for the football title on Sunday, the thirteenth of December. I didn't even care. I didn't even know!

"Curt, guess what?" Sis exclaims. "Next Friday is Christmas and Dad is going to put up the tree on Wednesday night. He told me that all of us kids could help decorate it if we're good all week."

"I'll be good, I promise. I'll be real good! I asked Santa for a fire engine. Think I'll get it?"

"I don't know, Dad says that Santa doesn't have as many toys this year 'cause the war people need our metal and other stuff. We'll see, we'll just wait and see."

"Sis, aren't you kinda worried about all of this? I sure am!"

FAST FORWARD TO SEPTEMBER 2005

Before we continue, let's take a step forward in time. As I returned to this magical neighborhood in the fall of 2005, so many thoughts came rushing back. Could it really have been sixty-plus years since this all began?

Today, as I stroll down Harper Avenue, I can hear the sounds of yesterday. These include "Yer too bleddy cheeky, young man" coming from Mr. Glassbrook as he rants and raves from his little concrete porch. "Bleddy cheeky," this meant that I talked back a bit too often to this ol' British chap. He did, however, have two faces. One was the front porch face out of which he yelled at the neighborhood kids for playing ball, riding their bikes and scooters, flying a kite and any human activity that didn't meet with his approval. Then again, there was the kind side of the old gent. Many times, as we walked or rode our bike down the alley, he would be "visiting" his garage full of memories. It seems he had owned a store of some kind in his younger days. He would often stop us to offer a piece of Wrigley's gum, usually spearmint, and always as hard as a popsicle stick. We would accept our gifts and go on our way with seldom more to say than "Thanks!"

As I continue down this incredible street of memories, I can still hear the sound of a baseball bouncing on the tar-coated surface. Our side streets were, for the most part, covered with softer tar, rather than the asphalt, which came later. The tar-coated streets seemed softer and more inviting, almost rubber-like in texture. Oh, what fun it was when the tar truck would come down Harper Avenue with its bed laden with the neat-smelling cargo. It was hot and so versatile. We would grab a handful, roll it and shape it. Some kids even chewed it, but I never did! The truck would dump the licoricey substance as it slowly made its way down our street. This procedure was followed, closely, by the formidable steamroller. The next morning we had a brand new softball field, racetrack, roller rink or whatever we willed it to be. Now the bat really danced on the rubbery surface as we threw it and headed for the first base sewer. Yes, the sewers served as home plate, as well as first and third bases. Second base was often someone's hat, or even a T-shirt. Oh, how our moms loved that on Monday (y'know, wash day!).

More sounds come rushing back, the whirling sound of the hand-driven lawnmowers, the sprinklers with their "wish, wish" sounds, so many dogs barking and horns honking in vain attempts to chase the little monsters from their path. Actually, it was our path! There were sounds of kids yelling and screaming in every octave and parents screaming even louder!

Just one door south of our moody Mr. Brit, stood a lady on her porch soliciting some boy, any boy, to be her messenger. She always had the same need. "Would you please go to the store (Julie's candy store on 82nd Street) and get me two packs of Tareytons?" She was referring to her Herbert Tareyton cork-tipped cigarettes. You see, in those days anybody, any age, could buy cigarettes, Ask me, I know! Once inside of Julie's, a kid would have a hard time thinking of Herbert Tareytons. There were so many other features within those walls. I usually gravitated to that beautiful glass candy counter full of penny candy and the vast array of nickel candy bars—Old Nick, Oh Henry, Denver Sandwich, Tango, Whiz, Powerhouse and on and on. A real favorite of mine were the candy swords that came in such tasty flavors as cherry, lime, licorice and lemon. Just to my right was that tempting gumball machine attached to the wall.

I would dig down deep in the right-hand pocket of my brown corduroys. "Great, I still have two pennies from yesterday's pop bottle refund. I'll see if I can get a winner." As luck would have it, one of those red-striped yellow balls came down the chute. "I won. It's a nickel candy bar winner." I opted for a Powerhouse. I loved those nutty caramel bars. "Hey, I had better get those cigarettes before the ol' girl has a nicotine fit."

The reward for this little mission was usually enough to choose your favorite bottle of pop from that ice-filled cooler. Anyone knows that on the southside of Chicago we didn't buy soda in aluminum cans. We drank pop from glass bottles! Soda was something the local soda jerk, or in many cases the pharmacist, concocted for you. A tall, frothy drink made from ice cream and the syrup of your choice—cherry for me. Then our local chemist would shoot some seltzer water into that tall glass so that it would fizz up and become a cherry soda. In any case, it was always neat returning to the gang with an icy cold bottle of Old Colony Lime, Hire's Root Beer, Old Dutch Cream Soda or some other local brew.

A little further down this sidewalk, now etched with so many cracks, I can hear another mom as she screams, "Close the door before you let all of those green flies in," as her boys rush to join in the daily mischief. Funny thing, I had never noticed that flies came in colors! This was one sweet lady, and a good mom, but apparently she had had some nasty experience with flies in her earlier days— green ones!

One sound we were all familiar with was the call to supper. We never called it "dinner"! Dinner was for the folks over west, in Beverly Hills. Yeah, we had a Beverly Hills too. In our little world there were three times a day to eat. Breakfast was one, but only when we felt like wasting time at home in the morning. There were so many other promising activities on our agendas. When we did stop long enough for this AM inconvenience, it was normally a bowl of Rice Krispies, Kix or puffed rice. But never Wheaties! Geez, how I hated those Wheaties—just a bowl of mushy goo.

Lunch, more often than not, was a peanut butter and lettuce sandwich. Yep, peanut butter 'n' lettuce, still a dynamite sandwich today. Then, as the day wore on, sometime between five and seven PM, we would hear the call for supper time. That meant wonderful aromas of pot roast, fried chicken, hamburger patties frying in onions, and there was always some loving mom simmering her spaghetti sauce. Of course, each of us was convinced that our mom was the best cook on the block—as it should be! While many of the kids had a set time to be home for this evening event, our cue was that call from Mom. In her sweet, soft voice, Mom would call out from the kitchen window as loud as she could, "It's supper time!" For her that was not too loud, but we were in tune with her frequency.

Smells, oh yeah, we had smells! Each season had its catalog of smells. Oh yes, I can still remember the smell of a well-worn sixteen-inch Clincher softball. It was kind of an earthy, sweaty smell. As you'd prepare to pitch it to the kid at home-sewer, you would bring the ball toward your face. There it was, that odor of dirty old leather. Just think of the many trips that it had taken, and God knows where. That ball carried with it the essence of summer! Spring and summer had some of the most memorable scents. Who can forget the smell of a big pitcher of Kool-Aid? There always seemed to be some enterprising kid selling this sugary treat, usually at two cents a glass. Once again, cherry ranked way up there with this consumer.

We were fortunate enough to have access to our Dad's backroom stock of six-ounce Cokes. You see, he had a nickel Coca-Cola machine in his camera store. So, when we got that entrepreneurial itch, we would set up a two-cent Coke stand right at the streetcar stop that later became the bus stop. I guess that even at that age, we had a feel for demographics. This was a sure winner on those "ninety/ninety days," Chicago talk for degrees and humidity. Folks exhausted from their nine-to-five day with no such thing as air conditioning came pouring out of their crammed coaches. Yeah, it was a pretty easy sell, and the tips were great too! It took three of us to man that station. We had a server, a cashier and a runner. It was a half block run to the backroom! We had to take special care opening those warm and sometimes shaken-up bottles. Gee, we would hate to see any of that precious liquid hit the hot pavement. *Poof,* there goes a bit of our profits. Speaking of profits, Dad finally pointed out the fact that his net profits were not exactly attractive in the Coke biz. So that little scheme came to an end posthaste!

There was that unmistakable smell of fresh paint. This was before latex, so it was just that good, old-fashioned, oil-based stuff! The local dads were performing their annual rituals. Some were busy painting the fence while others were up on their ladders perking up the gutters. Garages needed a new look every few years, and there were those combination screen-storm windows to keep up to snuff. In the evenings, the men would be out watering their new crop of Kentucky bluegrass. This seemed to be the choice of these wise ol' horticulturists. Besides, Sears always had big sales on this commodity, every spring. Some of the dads would simply set up the sprinkler and sit on their stoop (y'know, the concrete step) with a cold iced tea or something else cold! Soon after, when the house was back in order, dishes done, etc., the moms would come out to share the day's events with dad and some of the neighbors.

Zap! A crackling bolt of lightning rips through the evening clouds. *Bang*! is the next sound as thunder rolls through the sky. *Zap*! again. This time with a rolling thunder just seconds behind. If what they say is true, that bolt of lightning struck somewhere very near. We had always heard that each second that transpired between lightning and thunder represents a mile. There's no doubt then, this bolt struck close by. The rain comes pouring down and for a moment nobody budges. You see, it's been a mighty hot today, and this is even better than that expensive commodity, air conditioning, and it smells so good. The kids dance in the streets barefoot while the parents casually look for cover. Just another summer evening on Chicago's Southside!

Injun Summer brought that wonderful aroma of burning leaves. The kids, at least the bunch that I knew, would race through these little bonfires on their bicycles, Schwinns, Roadmasters and J.C. Higgins. The dads would yell as the leaves and ashes were scattered into the middle of the street. I'm not sure how much concern there really was for our safety. I would guess that they were so well-tempered to our ways that the fire was not their primary worry, just the mess!

Of course fall, or autumn, whichever pleases you, brings much more than smoldering bonfires and multicolored leaves. It brings football, Halloween and so much more. Oh yeah, there's school too, but let's not even discuss that now, please! Football always seemed to be prefaced by two words, "Notre Dame." Frankly, I always pulled for the other guys, their opponents. You can get up to your neck in this local idol worship. The Fighting Irish? It always seemed to me that there were a whole bunch of Polish guys playin' there too. There were likely a few Germans and probably an Italian or two on the squad. Let's not forget the Frenchmen, the Greeks and all of the rest. Fighting Irish? Don't be silly! Anyway, I was a Northwestern fan and just didn't care about those guys from some other state. What else would you expect from a Southside Cubs fan? I was so accustomed to pulling for the underdogs!

Next came winter at 83rd and Harper Avenue and, I would assume, everywhere else. First things first: winter meant snow, ice, hockey and Christmas. Let's see, what else was there? Few folks in our area had, or used, fireplaces. That was for the other kind of people, not the Avalon Park population. So, let's just think snow, ice, hockey and Christmas, that's it. We'll have much fun with these topics as we roll through the years.

Our Avalon Park community may not appear to be very large on a map, but it's four times larger than the Monarchy of Monaco—and one hundred times more fun! There have been so many colorful and unique characters that have dotted this life. These include the wide spectrum of personalities within my own family. I recall both the grouchy and the sweet neighbors, the acquaintances from all walks of life and from the four corners of this earth.

There was Luther, the mystery man in my life, and that wonderful gang of kids that helped to paint the canvas of my early years. This three-year-old boy could not have imagined the journey that was yet to come. If you'll keep listening, like a child by an open fire listening to his favorite ol' uncle, I'll tell you all about these real life experiences and adventures. We'll begin in this humble, hard-working neighborhood on Chicago's Southside and romp through this amazing land that we all so lovingly call "Home."

THE WAR HITS HOME!

As the year of '43 gets rolling, most big people are talking about "our boys over there." And about the Japs, Hitler and the Nazis, stuff like that. I may be young, but I sure know about that kind of talk. Percy is now eighteen and Mom says, "He's old enough to go to war, and that scares me." Mom is very worried that the Army will come and get him soon. I hope they don't! A lot of dads and brothers in our neighborhood are already in the war. I heard that some of them would not be coming home. I know what that means too, that they were killed by those terrible Nazis and Japs. Some of the houses down the street have stars in the window. That means that someone in that family is over there. If the star turns to gold, they will not be coming home.

Now Mom had the news on her Philco radio almost as much as our music. As the guy on the radio was saying that we need to be brave and all of that, I said, "I miss the music so much, Mom." Immediately, she turned the dial for me 'cause the news didn't seem too good that day. Mom didn't want me to hear all of that war talk. I knew that Glenn Miller sound when I heard it, and I loved it. "What kind of music is that, Mom?" I asked.

Mom said, "Why, that's Glenn Miller, Curt, and that's 'String of Pearls' they're playing now."

"Does Percy have that record, Mom?"

"I don't know. Why don't you go and ask him?"

Well, Percy had so much music by Glenn Miller that I stayed in his room for an hour listening to it. He had more of those big band records too. We listened to Artie Shaw and Benny Goodman and others that I hadn't heard before. Percy said, "Mr. Goodman used to live here on the Southside down in Hyde Park." Wherever that was.

Buck, another of my older brothers, had joined the Army and was in Georgia. Buck was a lot older than me. He was twenty-seven years old. He didn't write much, so we really didn't know how he was doing. He just wasn't the writing type. Big brother Cary was twenty-eight and was not going to be in the military. There was something said about his feet, or back or something. He wasn't the fighting type anyway. Maybe he could help right here in America. Dad would always comfort us by saying, "Don't you worry about Buck, he'll be just fine." Then one day Dad gathered all of us kids into the living room. He tried to tell us in his deep but quiet voice that everything would be okay, but that Percy was going into the Army. There was no way that we could stop from crying. I think that Todd was kinda' biting his lip, but he would not cry out loud. Mom was sitting next to Percy, squeezing his hand. Percy didn't say too much. We all knew that he was very upset inside.

Soon after this unpleasant day, Percy was gone. He was off to the war with all of the other young American boys and girls! Yes, there were a lot of girls and ladies at war too. Many of them served in the WACS, WAVES and SPARS. Someone had to take care of this great country so that we could all stay free. Dad really missed Percy in the store. There was hardly a week that Mom or Dad weren't making up some kind of package to send to him. They would buy him Heath bars, Hershey bars, Forever Yours, Tangos, Wrigley gum and all of his favorites. When Dad was down in the store after closing, he'd be busy packing up one of these surprise boxes. Sometimes we'd split a candy bar while he was making up one of the packages. He'd say, "Don't tell your Mom, 'cause she doesn't want me spoiling your appetite."

I remember that Sunday after Percy had gone to war. The mood around our house was very somber. Dad had a solution for just about anything. He called out, "'Anybody here wanna' go for a ride?" With that offer, we all piled into the Zephyr, ready for the unknown. We all had learned that on occasions such as this, Mom would be along shortly. First she had to powder her face and splash on some Muse, her very favorite fragrance by Coty. Mom slid into the front seat with Junior between her and Dad. Now smelling like a combination of a candy store and a fresh spring bouquet, she looked back for her roll call. No way was she going to leave any of her gang behind. After driving around the southwest side awhile, Dad and Mom decided on White Castle hamburgers for dinner. This pleased their audience and saved poor Mom from the kitchen mess for that day. As we pulled into the lot at the White Castle restaurant, Dad turned to us kids in the back seat for a hamburger count.

"Let's see. Two for Curt, Sis can eat three, Luke's good for five. Todd, how many can you handle?"

Todd answered politely, "Can I have six, Dad?"

"That's fine big guy!"

It was decided that Junior would be fine with just one. "Wow, sixteen back there. These kids are sure growing up fast." So Dad took Todd, Luke and me in with him. "We'll take two dozen, please, and we better have five Cokes, a cup of coffee with cream and sugar, and may I please have a cup of water?" Dad never drank coffee and, for that matter, never chewed a piece of gum. Don't know why, I guess he just never wanted to. Now we began the short trip to the Dan Ryan Woods for our in-car picnic. Dad found a way to ease the pain, at least for a few hours.

Percy Home on Leave – '43 ©

One afternoon I was in the dining room on the floor and, as usual, I was playing with my Tootsie Toys. There was this song playing on the Philco, and I could hear Mom crying. I went in to see if she was okay. She reached out and grabbed me, squeezing me with all of her might. *"When the lights go on again, all over the world,"* the lady on the radio was singing. Mom was crying so much that my T-shirt was all wet.

"Mom, Percy is okay, isn't he?"

"Oh yes, Curt, he's okay, he's okay I'm sure. I just miss him so much"

Now we were both crying like babies. I said, "It's a good thing that Sis isn't here, 'cause she'd be cryin' too."

Mom smiled and gave me a kiss on my forehead and then patted me on the shoulder. "Go on back to your Tootsie cars; everything's going to be all right."

Curt - Christmas '43 ©

Jan 31st 1944 – After a great birthday on Saturday, things were going downhill fast. I was now five years old, and that meant school! Cary drove Mom and me to Avalon Park School so that I could be "registered." I didn't care for that term, even at this very young age. It sounded too much like I was going to belong to someone other than Mom and Dad. Even as Cary pulled up in the Zephyr, that big brick building looked extremely humbling to this kid. By the way, Cary always preferred using Dad's cars on these family errands. He explained that this was only right.

"Why should I use my gas on family or business trips?" This stuck with me for years. If any of us kids would ask for a ride, anywhere, his response was always the same. "Sure, if Dad will pay for my gas." I couldn't figure out why he was so cheap.

Mom and I walked into that cavern at the southernmost door on Kenwood Avenue. It was a monstrous red brick building. I had been there before, but only as a witness to my sibling's torture. I often took the ride with Cary. As we entered the hallway, the first door on our left was the kindergarten class. The door was open and I could see all of the little prisoners in there. On to the office we marched.

"Oh Mom, can't we wait 'til next week?"

"No, Curt, we want to be sure that everything is going to go smoothly when you start classes on the seventh."

All I could think was that it was never going to run smoothly for me at that prison. After meeting with the principal and doing all of the things that Mom wanted to do, I grabbed her hand and tugged. We were about to escape, at least for a week. Here was that open prison door again. Then out popped this very pretty teacher lady. She wore a bright red dress (always my favorite color!).

"Well, good morning," she chirped. "I'm Mrs. Colefall, the kindergarten teacher. Would you like to come in and say 'hi' to our students?"

This time Mom began tugging at my hand as I was exit-bound. "Why sure, we'd love to come in. Curt will be starting first grade next week."

We walked in. The kids were all playing and seemed to be having fun. My mind was telling me, "These kids will be promoted to first-grade and in my room next week. I'd rather meet them then, not now, not this week."

Mrs. Red Dress asked if Mom would like to leave me and let me spend this week with her and the kids. Mom looked down at me as though to ask me. "No thanks, not today, but thanks." I was going home to do what I wanted to do! I still had a full week of freedom and boy, would I play, I thought. I'd play every game, and with every car and truck that I owned.

Cary was sitting patiently in the Zephyr listening to the radio: *"Mares eat oats, and does eat oats, and little lambs eat ivy. A kid'll eat ivy, too. Wouldn't you?"* "What a dumb song," I blurted out as I jumped into the rear seat. I was a bit tense after the close call with the warden and the guards. During the ride home, the music became more appealing as Louis Jordan was wailing away with "G.I. Jive." One song that completely baffled me was when Bing Crosby sang about "Perry Moonbeam's home in a jar." I thought that this Moonbeam guy must have been some famous actor or something. I just couldn't figure out why this guy was in a jar. It was years before I figured out that someone was carrying moonbeams home in a jar. Even that never made much sense to me!

Avalon Park School aka "The Jail" ©

Monday, the seventh day of February, came too soon, much too soon. This was the beginning of my long and unpredictable sentence. Mrs. Davis wore a black dress just like my Gramma's. It had that dumb-looking, lacy, doily stuff around the collar. "Just what I expected, an old grouch!" I thought. After her rather unemotional introduction, it was right to the rules. "Rules, who needs all of these rules? I wanna go home." My thoughts were not helping me a bit during this first of thousands of days yet to come.

"Percy has been hurt, hurt real bad!" It was Tuesday, February the 15th, and Dad and Mom were trying to explain this to us. Percy was in the 36th Infantry Division and had been badly wounded in the battle of Mount Cassino in Italy.

"Abraham Lincoln's birthday was the day that Percy was hurt. He will be sent to a field hospital in North Africa," Dad told us. "He was hit with a lot of shrapnel and his legs were hurt. Don't worry, kids. He'll be okay, I'm sure."

I didn't have any idea what this "shrapnel" was, but I sure hated that word. Todd told us about the battle and that the Nazis were using a Catholic monastery as a fort. We couldn't bomb them because it was a sacred place. As it turned out, the Allied Forces did bomb it on that very day, February 15, 1944. If only they would have bombed it the last week, Percy would have been okay.

None of us kids went to school on Wednesday. We were too sad and didn't want to have to talk about it at school. Mom told us kids, "Buck is very mad at the Nazis for hurting his baby brother. He is going to ask to be shipped overseas. I sure hope they don't do that. Dad's going to try to reach him down in Georgia. He'll listen to Dad, I'm sure."

V-Mail from Percy arrived at last. His first letter was written by none other than himself. Dad detected a certain feeling of optimism from this writing. He told Mom, "Now I know he's going to be all right. It's just a matter of time. We'll be seeing him soon, I know!"

Soon after this first letter, many more followed on a regular basis. He was in a full body cast with serious damage to both legs and some kind of wound to his left wrist. He was transferred to White Sulphur Springs Hospital in West Virginia. Dad made arrangements for Mom to take a train to West Virginia. The best medicine a guy could have was Mom at his bedside. The prognosis was that he would be able to walk again, but he'd be in a hospital for a long time. From this hospital Percy was transferred to General Gardner Hospital right across the parkway from the Museum Of Science and Industry on our own Southside.

Curt in the Big Tree – Waiting for Mom's Streetcar ©

For several months, I survived Mrs. Davis with her rulers and pointers. Whenever I was asked to stand up and read aloud, I'd just freeze. I was not much of an orator and saw no need to read to the other kids. "They have their own books, let 'em read to themselves." That's what I wanted to say, but didn't dare.

Then there were the times when this lady with Gramma's dress instructed us to go to the blackboard for some silly spelling thing, or something. The same response: I'd just stand there and do nothing. It seems that this old gal was pretty perceptive. She said, "Priscilla, why don't you show Curtis how to do it." (Oh, that always hurts—I'm not "Curtis"!) She apparently had observed us; we were often chatting on the playground. This method did help a little bit, but did nothing with any longevity. I survived that semester and was promoted to 1-A, which would begin the next fall. "Oh, I can hardly wait for the next dose of this poison. I wonder which witch I'll have to put up with when September rolls around," I thought as I said "good-bye!" to Priscilla and my other new friend, Virginia.

I met with Sis and Luke out in front of the prison. Todd was big now and walked home with his buddies. They would probably be playing catch all the way home. Right down the middle of the street. Some day, I thought, I'll be doing that! Our daily ride was late. I moaned to Sis, "Of all days to be late, why today? I wanna get home and change clothes and throw all of these papers away!"

Luke prophetically proclaimed, "That's okay, Curt. It's the last day of school. We can wait. Cary will be here in a minute or two." He was dreaming of his comic books, bugs, guns and his neat prairie forts.

Soon we were safely out of reach of all of those Grimm's Fairy Tales ladies. We were laughing and sticking our heads out the windows of the Zephyr. We were yelling and sharing the joy with each bunch of kids that we passed.

This summer vacation was going to be just great. I could get back to Tootsie Toys, the yard, my friends and all of the fun stuff.

One summer afternoon Todd asked if I would like to go to Mitch's house on Woodlawn Avenue. This would be great because Virginia lived right down the street. If it weren't for this opportunity, I'd probably have to wait until September to see her again. Virginia was one of my favorite classmates at the jail. She was taller than me and had reddish-auburn hair and freckles. Sis told me that she was a Scottish dancer. All I knew was that I liked her and I was about to look for her on Woodlawn. I knew the house and I knew that Todd would go to her door with me.

I jumped on Todd's handlebars, and off we went. We went straight down Harper to 81st and then west. We passed by Blackstone, Dante, Dorchester, Kenwood, Kimbark, Avalon and finally reached Woodlawn Avenue. It seemed that someone was waving to Todd on every block. Todd belonged to the Woodlawn Warriors. This was a gang of buddies that played ball and had fun together. Not a gang of bad kids, just a gang of kids! Just think of the classic old song, "That Old Gang of Mine." On the way there, he handed me a stick of gum and said, "Here, kid, you can give this to Virginia. She'll be impressed and like you even more!"

We walked up to the front porch at Virginia's house. Todd made me knock. "Softly, ya' wanna be polite," he told me. A very friendly mom answered. Todd explained who we were and that he'd be down at Mitch's house for awhile. She knew Mitch's family and other members of the Warriors. She immediately called for Virginia.

That cute little redhead came to the door with a shocked look on her face. "Uh, hi, Curt. Uh, what are you doing here?"

Her mom told her that I had come to visit for awhile. "Now, you kids stay right here in front, and I'll bring you something cold to drink."

"Wow, what a nice mom you have—she's just like mine," I proudly stated to Virginia. After we drank the lemonade, I broke out my little surprise treat. "Here, I brought this for you. Here, it's yours."

She quickly unwrapped the little stick of gum and began chewing it, when all of a sudden she let out a scream. "What is this? It's terrible. It's hot, it's really hot. What is this stuff?"

Todd had tricked me. It was a stick of hot gum from Riley's Trick Shop on 79th Street. Now Virginia would hate me forever and ever, I just knew it. Her mother came out as Virginia was screaming and yelling at the top of her lungs.

I explained to her mom what had happened, and she seemed to sympathize with me as well as Virginia. She calmly said, "Well, we'll take care of your big brother. We'll fix him. I've been to Riley's shop too, and I have just the thing for him." I was so glad that her mom had a good sense of humor.

By now, Virginia had calmed down a bit. "Here he comes, your brother is coming. I'll tell my Mom."

Her mom came out with a very special lemonade for Todd. "Here, Todd, have some cold lemonade." She had dropped a fake ice cube in the glass. It was plastic and had a big yellow bee inside.

Todd just gulped it down, never noticing the bee. "Thanks, ma'am, thanks a lot. Come on, Curt, we gotta be headin' home now."

Virginia actually gave me a bit of a smile as we turned to go. I still felt just terrible. Of all people to trick, my poor Virginia! Just a couple of weeks later that little star was featured in the magazine section of the Sunday edition of *The Herald American* newspaper for her Scottish dancing. Am I ever glad that she didn't stay mad at me.

Someone once asked me, "Curt, if you could be anything, what would you like to be?"

"A young boy in love!" I responded without a second thought. I believe that this all started when I began going to school. Frankly, it seemed that I was always in love. I found a certain comfort in knowing that I had someone to care about. Yep, first grade was my first exposure to a virtual plethora of girls. They always seemed much more responsive to me than the guys. Sure, I always had buddies at school and around my neighborhood, but they surely weren't pretty! The guys were just someone to play cowboys 'n' Indians and baseball with. The girls, with their flirtatious ways, had a way of keeping me on my best behavior, and Mom kinda' liked that trait in me.

"You have to put on your best face and always be polite for these young ladies," she told me. "A girl appreciates a gentleman, just like your Mom does."

A lot of the guys would deny themselves really knowing these walking dolls by acting tougher than they really were. I had noticed that the girls usually liked guys who were polite and not acting the part with every action. Some of these passing loves will come along as I tell you more about my trials and tribulations at Avalon Park School, and beyond.

This young-boy-in-love thing should not be misconstrued. Yes, I always did have an eye for the girls. It wasn't always a case of being in love, but of loving and being loved. I consider my relationships with certain people a reason to love. These relationships are often fleeting but nevertheless very affectionate, each one in its own way. There were my mailman friend, Mr. Johnson, our hard-working and always smiling Hunding milkman; Mrs. Kraft, a favorite neighbor; the kind black man that came to my aid on the highway; Sister Nila, and all the people that touched me with their loving ways. This young boy was in love with life and still is. It's as simple as that!

CURTIS wasn't lost, just asleep in mom's clothes basket

"Curtis wasn't lost…" ©

CHICAGO DAILY NEWS AUGUST 31, 1944

leeps as 50 Hunt Him" that's what the *Chicago Daily News* was telling their readers with the following copy:

"*CURTIS wasn't lost, just asleep in mom's clothes basket. The next time 5-year-old Curtis Erler vanishes from sight, his mother, Mrs. Cash Erler of 1540 E. 83rd St., is going to make a beeline for the clothes basket in a closet in her home. For three hours yesterday while his father and mother and a posse of about 50 neighbors combed cellars, alleys, backyards, neighbors' homes and empty houses. Curt was sleeping peacefully in a basket with soiled clothes as his blankets. Exhausted from her hunt the mother opened the closet door on a hunch and found her son sound asleep. She said she had left him at home with her other children, Todd 13, Luke 9, Sis 8 and Jr. 3 while she was visiting her older boy, PFC Percy Erler 20 who is recovering in General Gardner Hospital from wounds suffered in Italy.*"

The reporter scribbles some brief notes at the scene. Back in the office, he fabricates his story in time for the next press run. This is not atypical of how the media has always worked. This news piece would lead one to believe that Mom just ran off to the hospital leaving her brood alone. The truth is, Dad was always right there. He was working in his camera store. While Todd was only thirteen, he was very capable of monitoring his siblings. We were always welcomed at Dad's side as he worked. He loved it! Dad was very composed as he worked. He was doing what he loved, making pictures that made folks smile. I spent many hours in that darkroom while Dad worked at his Pako printer or souping prints. "Souping" was photo slang for developing prints. Those smells of Kodak chemicals and photographic paper were as familiar to us kids as the smell of summer rain. Now, if you want to know the real scoop, here's what really happened that day. I may have been very young, but I know what really transpired—I was there!

My mother had already returned from the hospital before this "missing" thing started. Mom usually took the Stony Island streetcar to and from the hospital. In fact, many times I'd wait for her in the big tree on the corner. We were all out playing when she returned. I had come in the house to say "Hi, Mom" as Cary and Mom were in the kitchen having a late afternoon cup of coffee. Mom loved the view from her kitchen window. She could enjoy her cup of coffee with a view of her garden and her kids as we played in the yard. As I entered the kitchen and began to speak, Cary gave me a negative wave with his hand and said, "Go on, this is big people talk!" He was almost twenty-five years older than me, but he was not my dad!

This big brother had a trait that became obvious as I grew a bit older. If he was in a situation that he could control, he was big and tough. We kids were perfect victims for this type of treatment. If it was some imposing adult, he became very subservient. If he was unhappy with someone's driving, he'd call them an S.O.B. or some other name, unless the guy had a big beefy arm hangin' out the window. In this case, the driver's bad driving was acceptable. As most guys know, that's called "picking your target." Yeah, I still loved him a lot, but I was always aware of his mean streak. I was always fairly emotional as a kid, and actually I still am.

His loud yelling at me hurt this thin-skinned kid. My bedroom was right off of the kitchen. I was not having any more of this treatment, so I hid in the closet. At one time during the search, Mom poked her head into the closet. I was wide awake but mad at the world. When I heard her footsteps, I buried myself in the dirty clothes so she wouldn't see me. Several hours later, Mom had a feeling about that closet. She opened the door once more and did find me there, sound asleep.

So, that's how this saga really happened. That evening, after I had really gone to bed, I heard my Dad coming up the stairs with this reporter guy. He was a regular in Dad's photo shop, as he always took pictures of his story subjects. He almost always wore this big black wool overcoat and always smelled of nasty cigar smoke. I do remember his name, but I'll leave him nameless for this little story. As he and Dad approached my bed, ol' stinky breath was holding his big press camera. "I want you to get into the basket where your mother found you so that I can take your picture." My only response was "Nope." After several reruns of my answer, dragon breath settled for a picture of me just where I was.

This little saga had been noted in other areas as well as Chicago. I've heard that there were news stories as far away as Wisconsin and Michigan. Slow news day, I guess. The *Dixon Evening Telegraph* reported the following:

Dixon, Illinois, Friday, September 1, 1944.

"HIDEAWAY" – Chicago – *"Some 50 neighbors joined Mr. And Mrs. Cash Erler in a hunt for their 5 year old son – Curt – but he wasn't lost. Returning home after a three hour futile search, Mrs. Cash went into a closet – found Curt asleep in a clothes basket."*

September brings more than autumn. It means back to school at Avalon Park. It's time to see who will be the Ring Master this semester. My siblings have been telling me that it will be Mrs. Westfall. Not to be confused with that pretty Mrs. Colefall that greeted Mom and me last winter. I really don't have much hope for a sweet loving teacher. I simply say, "We'll see, we'll just wait and see. Tuesday will be here soon enough!"

Our Sunday ride was very special today. Mom 'n' Dad let us kids go to General Gardner Hospital for Percy's birthday party. We drive through Jackson Park. This is one ride that never lets us down. Dad drives north on Stony Island Avenue. Just as he passes 67th Street, he turns right into Jackson Park. This beautiful park is our shortcut to the hospital. Once inside the park, the scenery begins to change dramatically. There are areas for picnics, boats to row, fishing in the lagoon and much more. There is even a wooded island where some lucky folks will spend this Sunday afternoon. Dad orders a whopper-size cake from Koch's Bakery. This was soon to become Steffens' Bakery, a landmark in our beloved neighborhood. Dad says, "Percy has a lot of soldier friends that will be celebrating with him. We'll need to keep them all happy."

It was quite a thrill to see Percy again. He had a little surprise for each of us kids. I remember having fun with some of his buddies and the pretty nurses, too. See, there I was again, falling in love!

There was now something very special at the northwest corner of 83rd Place and Stony Island. It was a large memorial and American flag reflecting the names of our fighting men and women that had been wounded and those that had lost their lives in the war. This type of recognition was seen in most communities throughout the Southside. There was great respect and patriotism shown, everywhere. We kids took our friends there to show them Percy's name. We are so very proud of our brothers! While Percy did return home in 1945, his injuries were permanent. He was never able to bend his left knee or his right ankle again.

Here we go again, another unfriendly schoolmarm and another failed attempt to get Curt to read aloud.

This type of scenario continued until early 1945. At this point, the school principal called Mom to advise her that "It's just not going to work out," or similar verbiage. Oh, sure, I definitely share the blame. I didn't care, nor did they. There always seemed to be a cold, impatient and indifferent attitude toward me. It may have been simply the luck of the draw—I just don't know. I believe that maybe I had caught these ladies near the ends of their careers; I'll call it "burn-out." However, my siblings did have some great and lasting relationships with a couple of the teachers at the school.

Mom and Dad were in a bit of a quandary. "Where will we send Curt?" seemed to be the burning question. My life changed dramatically after a little conversation between Father Walsh, the pastor at St. Felicitas, and Dad. It so happened that they were having one of their theology talks in our backyard. Dad was explaining that I was the sixth Erler to attend Avalon Park School. He told "Father" that I was struggling with shyness and that something had to be done soon. I can still see them sitting in those big Adirondack chairs. Father Walsh suggested that I enroll at St. Felicitas. Dad said, "Curt's not a Catholic!" That was fine with Father Walsh. He knew that they would convert me. At least he thought so! This decision would be a great move for this shy kid.

Goodbye Avalon Park, hello St. Felicitas!

SCHOOL DAZE

"World's Greatest Parish"

St. Felicitas School ©

Mom walked me to school this morning. I was very anxious, if not downright scared of this new environment. After all, school has not been kind to me in the past. What would make things any different here? We walked up the short flight of concrete steps into yet another big red brick building. As we entered, a look to the left and there it was: "The Warden's Office," I thought. My experience at the other school had strongly affected my mind-set. Mom and I were greeted by a kind lady in a nun's habit. This "warden," as it turns out, is not a warden at all. She is a kind and loving woman whose life is dedicated to God and teaching young children.

"Sister Regina Maria will introduce Curtis to his new classmates." This was Mother Celeste's briefing to Mom on this, my first day at St. Felicitas School. As I had requested, I entered the classroom alone. Sister used the term "non-Catholic" as she told the kids a little bit about me. In retrospect, I realize that she was simply trying to soften the blow. It was her way of getting me off the hook as this subject was bound to come up at a later date. I will be the only student here at St. Felicitas with this prefix added to my identification. Unaware at the time, just the opposite will be my burden from some other folks. It won't be long before I begin hearing personal descriptions like "cross back", "holy roller" and "church mouse"!

I knew, in a moment, that this new kind of teacher was going to be much more like Mom than those grouches at Avalon. She immediately demonstrated her loving way as she reached out for my little hand. "Come on, Curtis, we'll find your desk. Here, now this will be your desk from now on."

I was still in somewhat of a euphoric state but was able to smile as I walked with her. I believe that Sister was very strategic in choosing my assigned desk. Close enough to monitor, yet leaving a bit of a buffer zone for the new kid. This allowed me to get acquainted with the other children and not be right under her nose. It certainly worked for me.

At the end of this school day, I walked home with Francis, whose desk was across the aisle from mine. I knew Frankie somewhat, as he lived right up the alley from me. Frankie was a nice-looking kid of French descent. It wasn't long before I realized that he was a very intelligent kid. He and his mom and dad lived in a basement apartment on 83rd Place. Their sub-level kitchen window was at the same level as the concrete gangway outside. Many times, as we would walk to Koch's Bakery (later Steffens' Bakery), we'd see his folks having their breakfast, lunch or coffee. There was always a smile as we nodded or waved.

Soon after this first day, I would often head over to 83rd Place to visit a pretty little girl from school. Some days Sis would go with me. This always seemed to ease the shock of my rather impromptu calls. Sis would play "Teacher" with us on Katie's front steps. Teacher was a game where the teacher would hold a rock in one of her hands and the "students" would start on the bottom step. The students would then guess which hand the stone was in. If you guessed correctly, you were promoted to the next grade and moved one step up. As the school year rolled on, I became friends with several of the guys. I remained enamored with little Katie for quite some time.

May 8, 1945 – The Nazis cry uncle! Today, the world celebrates the fall of the Nazis' brutal war machine. After more than five years of bloody war across the continent of Europe, it's over! Hitler had taken his own life just days before. Now the newspaper headlines read, *"Victory In Europe as Germany Surrenders," "War in Europe Finally Over."* Percy is still recovering from his war wounds at General Gardner Army Hospital. However, today he and his buddies all have reason to celebrate. Most of the world is celebrating, but the war in the Pacific is far from over!

Once again, it was time for every boy's favorite subject, summer vacation! There would be the familiar sounds of "Rags-O-Lyon," the fascinating sounds coming from the scissor and knife sharpening man. Once again, we'd be grabbing those cold clear chunks of ice from the old wooden-floored ice wagon. This big strapping man would always find it convenient to leave some of those refreshing nuggets available as he turned his head.

There were so many events to anticipate. Each day seemed to bring a new surprise. If we were lucky, the organ grinder, with his pesky little monkey, would be by. This little monkey was quite the beggar. The squatty little Greek man with silver hair and raggedy pants would turn the grinder on his music machine as his monkey ran around soliciting pennies with a tin cup. The monkey wore a bright red shirt, green shorts and a red velvet cap that was fastened by an elastic strap that he continually adjusted under his fuzzy chin. He was a grabby little devil. Not a shy bone in his wee little body!

Mr. Johnson, our Hunding Milk driver, would be making his daily visits. His big milk wagon was propelled up and down our streets by Tony, his big brown horse. The world's very best chocolate milk was packed in ice-filled crates. Sixteen cents would get ya' an icy cold pint bottle of that healthy brown nectar. Now, isn't this Southside of ours one big slice of heaven?

"Gonna take a sentimental journey,
Gonna set my heart at ease.
Gonna make a sentimental journey,
to renew old memories."

Doris Day and Les Brown had the number one song on the charts. Oh man, did I love that tune—and the pretty wren that sang it!

August 6, 1945 – On this day, a U.S. bomber, the Enola Gay, dropped an atomic weapon of about 15 kilotons on the Japanese city of Hiroshima. Three days later, on August 9, a similar bomb was dropped on the city of Nagasaki. The bombs devastated both cities. For all practical purposes, the war was over. I was with Mom as she was doing the laundry in the basement when Dad called downstairs with the news.

"I thought that I felt something!" was Luke's scream as he tore down the stairs. As the good news of world peace reached our friends on Harper, there were more claims of feeling the bomb. Hey, young boys have incredible senses!

"V.J. Day!"

There are parades on every main thoroughfare. Today, August 15, 1945, has been declared V.J. Day. The Japs have officially surrendered! There doesn't seem to be a lot of conversation, just noise everywhere. You can hardly hear yourself think. It is a mass celebration with folks singing, dancing and yelling, horns honking, and there's a lot of kissin' goin' on! Mom let us kids grab anything that would make noise. We're lined up along Stony Island. Luke has chosen his toy bugle, Sis is waving Old Glory and I'm banging a big spoon on the bottom of one of Mom's big pots. Mom is keeping Junior at home. He's just too young to be running around in this hysteria. Some of Dad's employees have come over to join in the fun. An endless procession of cars and trucks are streaming by. Some have taken time enough to decorate their parade vehicles. Most simply fly the stars and stripes.

I spot a big yellow convertible coming down Stony from the north. Actually, what I have spotted is a beautiful blonde lady also sporting yellow! She is clad in this canary yellow gown. It is much like those worn in the Technicolor musicals that I have seen at the Avalon Theatre. I run toward her, and then along with her as she sits up on the back of the rear seat. I just know that she is waving at me. I realize that she is much older, maybe twenty or twenty-one, but this surely appears to be love at first sight. This six-year-old boy is in love again! Within minutes, my new-found love is gone forever. I'm totally exhausted. I retreat to the somewhat quiet confines of Mom's kitchen. This nets me one big, cold glass of milk and a couple of Salerno Butter Cookies.

The Cubs go to the World Series this year. It's now sixty-one years later and there have been no repeat performances. Gee, this baseball addiction of mine can be very painful! Maybe next year?

"What's the real name of that song?" I ask Luke while Perry Como is crooning his big hit, "Til The End of Time" on Mom's Philco. "I'll betcha' a nickel that I know it!"

Luke isn't having any of this. He knows my love for all kinds of music. "No, I ain't bettin' ya' no nickel. If you know it, I'll give you a penny. Okay, what's the real name of it?"

"It's Chopin's *Polonaise*. Ya' owe me a penny!"

Luke begrudgingly reaches into his front pocket and digs out a penny. "Here, genius, it's an Indian head, too!"

"I'm not a genius Luke. I just listen to music all of the time and I remember this stuff. Thanks for the penny!"

Music has been a love of mine ever since I first heard Mom's Philco radio way back on Dorchester Avenue. I listened to all of the words to the pop songs. I was sure that "Rumors Are Flying" was about people being thrown out of their hotel rooms. Just like I had thought that Perry Moonbeam was home in a jar when Bing would sing "Swingin' on a Star"! The big bands and the great vocalists all had my ear during these times. I cried my eyes out when they said that Glenn Miller was dead and would not be coming home again. That was around Christmastime back in '44.

Thanksgiving Day was great, as Mom did her usual baking of bread and pies. Dad stuffed and roasted a thousand-pound turkey. At least it looked that big to me. Gramma and Aunt Selma brought some treats from Hillman's Market at 63rd and Halsted. Hillman's always seemed to have stuff that we had never seen, some good, some not so good. I took the ride with Cary to pick them up. They lived at 63rd and Green, a neat neighborhood that was predominantly populated by Germans, Polish and Irish. We had a total of fourteen people for this annual event.

Rhoda and the girls showed up just in time to eat. Rhoda brought some terrible-looking cookies that none of us would eat. Cary brought his own beer that no one else dared to drink! He loved his Pabst Blue Ribbon beer. Luke and I had a secret method for eating the ripe olives without a trace of larceny. We knew just how to restock them so that Mom didn't miss them. At least, that's what we thought. A few years later, I caught Mom restocking them. She looked just like an olive fairy. As usual, she was taking good care of her "kidlets," as she often called us. There was one person, however, that was unable to attend. Percy was making the best of it at the Army Hospital.

AND NOW, THERE IS LUTHER

Luther ©

I had been asleep for several hours when Mother Nature called. It was Saturday, November 25th. The other kids were all sound asleep. I walked through the dining room in my Superman pajamas. As I reached the hallway, with the bathroom just to my left, something made me peek into the living room. I was immediately scared silent. I was petrified by the sight of a large man sitting on our mantle. I turned away quickly and hurried back to my bed while crying the wettest cry that I had ever cried. This just didn't seem possible. There really was a man sitting on the far left side of the mantle. My heart was pounding as

I recounted what I had just seen. I wet the bed rather than attempt the bathroom again.

As I awoke, the bright sunny morning gave me newfound courage. I jumped out of bed knowing that I would be in trouble for my accident. I hurried through the dining room and spotted Mom sitting in the living room reading her morning newspaper. I took one step into the room and immediately jerked my head toward the fireplace and mantle area. There was no man, no monster this morning. I also wanted to see if Mom had any knickknacks on the end of the mantle. There was nothing on either end.

"So, a big man could have been sitting there," I thought. "He'd have enough empty space." This was just more evidence that it did happen and wasn't a dream.

"Curt, what are you looking at?" Mom quietly inquired. I told her that I had had a terrible dream and that it had made me wet the bed. Mom didn't look too pleased with me, but she began to ask me about the dream and this "monster man." She consoled me and said something like, "You were just real tired. Sometimes that will make you have bad dreams."

I tried to explain this whole incident to Luke. "Of all people, he'll believe me," I thought. I knew that Luke loved reading about monsters and other scary people. I think that he wanted to believe me. But the trouble was, it just seemed too unbelievable, even to him.

Not more than a week later, same scene and another "accident"! At this point, I was forced to convince Mom that this monster man really did exist, and that he was really there last night and last week. I described the man to the best of my recollection. "Mom, I've only seen him twice, and as soon as I see him, I run away. He is real scary, and I don't want him to get me. He's really big and doesn't smile. I think that he had a reddish shirt on." That was the best I could do from the two brief encounters. Needless to say, I was quite the topic around our house for quite awhile.

I remember thinking, "Luther, why do I call him Luther? I don't know why, but I know that his name is Luther! He's Luther. I know that for sure!"

Todd & Curt ©

Christmastime came and went with no further sightings of the mystery man. I tried to forget him, but I couldn't. I had repetitive nightmares in which Luther would be sitting in that same spot on our mantle. There were no vocal sounds, no movement other than the dangling movements of his legs and arms. From this time on, I was never comfortable in the living room at night unless Mom, Dad or Todd were with me. I hated those middle-of-the-night calls from Mother Nature!

Santa brought me a great big brown teddy bear, and Mom and Dad bought me a navy peacoat just like the real sailors wore.

Car Fare

"Car fare" is the common term used for describing the money needed to commute on one of Chicago's great-looking streetcars. These big red streetcars run up and down Stony Island day and night. They are used to shuttle our hard-working neighbors to and from their jobs. Kids take them to school and to their friends' homes. You only know one way to get to the museums, parks and beaches. Anywhere that you need to go, you just grab a street car—that is, if you have car fare!

Sis is on the phone with our Gramma. Mom interrupts for a moment: "Tell Gramma that Dad will pay her car fare when she gets here." This offer is used on a regular basis when you need an incentive to ensure someone's presence for one reason or another. You will often see this term in the classifieds. There will be the daily salary as well as the additional bonus of car fare.

Many times, on many rides, my car fare is momentary. Dad once employed Steve as a printer in his darkroom. He is now a motorman for the CTA, and he often has the Stony Run. Luke and I jump aboard this gorgeous red coach. We're heading for Cary's house down at 91st. Steve's hand turns over, as his habit dictates. I drop my car fare into his open hand. Within a spilt second, he reaches for my hand, turns it over and returns my cash. Steve was often the motorman when we laid a couple of stones on the track just to watch them turn to sand. He'd shake his finger at us as if to say, "you better be careful." This is another wonderful personality who still has a special spot in my heart.

With the war over and most of our guys back, Dad's store is busier than ever. Some days, there's a line all the way around to Harper. People are waiting in these long lines just to buy Kodak film and Brownie cameras. Last Sunday, at dinner, Dad was explaining to Mom how he was going to sell these Brownie cameras for a buck apiece. "I've ordered a gross of them from Rochester. When they arrive, we'll do a window display in red, white and blue. I'm going to have Buck do his art work with the colored crepe paper. Then we'll fill the window with these new little Brownies and sell them for ninety-nine cents each. That's about what I pay for them. They'll be limited to one to a customer. By selling out all 144 cameras, I will have gained 144 new photo-finishing customers. If they go fast, I'll reorder. We can fill the background with packs of flashbulbs—number fives, some blue fives and few press size bulbs scattered throughout the display. Buck will make it look good, I know!"

I can see that Mom approves by her big smile. She jumps up and dumps an extra helping of spuds on Dad's plate.

Cash Erler's has more employees than ever before. "Mom, I'm tryin' to count all of Dad's helpers. I don't know if I can even name 'em all, there are so many!"

"Yes Curt, Dad's business is really doing well. People are happy with the war over and all of the soldiers and sailors back home. With Easter right around the corner, it'll just get busier, probably busier than ever!"

Mom looks absolutely beautiful on this Easter Sunday. She's wearing a cotton candy pink coat with a white fur collar. Geez, I sure hope that the fur isn't rabbit! Our yard is full of tulips, snapdragons and other colorful spring flowers. I may be seven years old now, but I love my gold and brown bunny with his bright green vest. All of the Erler kids got big full baskets this morning.

"What's shoe fly pie and what's apple pan dowdy, Mom?"

"Oh, you mean that song! Well, I know what apple pan dowdy is 'cause your Aunt Selma makes something like it. She calls it 'Apple Josie.' You've eaten it and loved it. It's like my apple pie, only it's kind of all mixed together and full of cinnamon. I'm really not too sure what the shoe fly thing is. I think that it's something from Down South. Just ask Buck. He'll know."

Buck wrote it down for me on Monday morning. He knows how much I love song lyrics. "Here, Curt, this is the way it looks when you write it down: shoo fly pie and apple pan dowdy. The shoo fly thing is made with tons of brown sugar. They make it Down South. It's easy to make and cheap, 'cause they raise a lot of sugar down there."

The newest member of our family is almost as cute as Boston. Our Patsy is a fox terrier, or at least mostly fox terrier. Percy got her late last year from a lady on the Northside. That's so far away from here—heck, she's almost like a foreigner! Actually, Patsy is Percy's dog, but I know that she loves Mom best!

"Let it snow, let it snow ...." Vaughn Monroe was ensuring that we were all in that Christmas spirit—not that we needed any incentives.

"This is going to be the best Christmas yet!" Luke was forecasting our holiday future. "I've seen Dad, Mom and Percy sneakin' stuff into the house for weeks. I already know one thing you're getting'!"

"Shut up, Luke. I don't want to know anything that I'm getting!"

As it turned out, this big surprise was the saddest Christmas present that I have ever received. I had hinted at a pair of ice skates for months. The first thing that I looked for on Christmas morning was there, right up front under the tree. "My ice skates!" I exclaimed. But as I got closer to my big gift from Santa, I was devastated. They were double runners. This was more than I could hide.

Mom chimed in quickly, "Maybe Santa doesn't realize what a good skater you are."

Nothing else mattered to me for at least three minutes! Lying on the floor, I spotted a "real" FBI tommy gun. What could have been better? Junior got a real Indian tom-tom drum and a cool car that looked like something from outer space. It was bright blue with a big domed roof. Luke got a baseball game called "Push 'em Up Charlie." Sis got everything that she wanted, and more!

"Merry Christmas to all!"

My future bride with Santa at Marshall Field's – 1946 ©

ONCE, THERE WAS A CANDY STORE

Julie's was once a magnet for every kid in the neighborhood
– gone forever! ©

Every neighborhood had its own little corner store. We were lucky enough to have Julie's, simply the best! If Julie didn't have it, you just didn't need it. It was an oasis, a meeting place and a place where kids were (almost) always welcomed. The "almost" accounts for the times that one might have been "suspended" for some act that did not meet with Julie's approval. It had to be pretty bad, though, 'cause you were, in fact, a customer. Customers had something to do with her eating and paying the bills. I can hear her now: "Curt, Sean, Junior, you better stop that or I'll have to ask you to leave. That was usually enough to end the horseplay for awhile.

When a delivery came in, you just couldn't leave until she had unpacked all of the stash in those boxes.

"Sean, look. Those new disc caps are here, and I see some gangster cap guns too. That one might be a 'Snub-nosed' 38."

Sean eyed it immediately. "Yep, it's a snub-nose for sure. How much for that one, Julie?"

"I don't know yet. Can't you kids wait until tomorrow? I'll have everything priced by then."

Sean and I weren't havin' any of that. "'Yeah, wait until tomorrow when it's already sold!" we both blurted out, almost simultaneously.

"Can I please have a bottle of Nehi cream soda?" I said as I reached, deep into the pocket of my corduroys. "Here's my six cents Julie. Mind if we stay and watch you unpack the rest?" Now, we were home free; we were customers again.

"It's going to be priced $3.99 boys. That's what my invoice says."

So much for the new "gat." Neither of us had that kind of cash, here or at home.

"Hey, Sean, I'll tell my brother. There's a chance Luke will rush down here after I tell him about it. That would make me kind of a part owner."

Julie continued unpacking: Hi-Flyer kites, Revell models, both planes and cars. There were some dolls from Japan, but who cared? Gliders, baseball cards, wax whistles, bean blowers (pea shooters to some kids) it was endless pain. We were both officially broke now.

"Here, guys. Have a couple of these little licorice babies." Julie's was a very important part of our lives for many years. The last time that I stopped there, after the Army, I didn't know a soul. Life goes on, I guess.

Another school year comes to a close as third grade ends. I very much regret that my favorite nun, Sister Nila, will no longer be administering her special care to this non-Catholic kid. She has shown so much compassion during the past school year. No doubt about it, I'm still very averse to reading to the class. "Why won't they just let me read and study? I know that I'm as smart as most of the kids here. In fact, I feel that I am much smarter than many."

The fact was, I was not a bit shy in any other facet of my daily life. I have always loved learning but I sure hated the demonstrative act of reading aloud.

Now, with Sister Nila not there demonstrating her patient ways, what will I do? Will my next nun be harsher on me? What will happen to me come September? Thank God for summer vacation! At least for awhile I'll be able to relax, play ball and enjoy kid things.

"Cleaning garages and basements can net us a fortune, Curt." This was Luke's entrepreneurial brainstorm of the day. "Just think of the bottles and stuff that we will find. We'll probably find all kinds of treasures."

He was twelve years old but quite shy. He knew that I would knock on some doors to get this project rolling. I was eight and ready to find these "treasures." Heck, I knew that the bottle thing was already a proven winner. Why not expand?

A lady in a house down near 81st asked if we would clean her shed and basement. She would pay us each two bucks. She said, "There is sure to be some of my junk that you boys can use."

This basement was amazing. There was even a boat down there. It looked like a rowboat with a flat bottom. Luke looked at it for a minute, "How did they ever get this down here? There's no way. It couldn't fit through that door."

The little vessel was loaded with junk. There were old tools, cleaning supplies, chains, you name it! We continued to haul junk up to the alley for an hour or so. Mrs. whatever her name was called down, "Would you boys like a root beer?"

We accepted and sat down on the stairway outside. Just moments later, Luke said, "He built it down there, that's it. He built it and couldn't get it out!" He laughed so hard that the lady heard him and came out to investigate. Sure enough, she confirmed this twelve-year-old's assumption. Her late husband had done just that.

Another hour or so of hauling boxes and barrels out to the alley and we were whipped. The afternoon was over. We had decided that this was too much work for the rewards received. It was time to retire from this trade. Luke netted a microscope and some other science junk. "Gee, I'll bet that you can hardly wait to check out some bugs with that thing."

I did okay myself. I now had a vice for my workshop and three more Tootsie Toys—and in great shape, too. Hauling our newfound treasures in Luke's clunky lookin' red wagon, we made a stop at Julie's on 82nd. The deposit money from the bottles was enough to buy us each a brown bag full of candy. Those bags were full of Jelly Swords, Red Dollars, Heidi Bananas, Walnettos, Kits, B.B. Bats and some candy cigarettes. We each had a bag full of dentist's delights. What's a dentist, anyway?

Curt & Luke ©

Another summer activity for Luke and me was playing pilot on the old trainer planes at Chicago Vocational High School, more commonly called "C.V.S." This had been a training school for WWII pilots. The planes remained there for many years after the war. It was a great place for a boy to get his kicks, and it was free.

We'd take turns. One day I'd say, "Luke, you can be Tokyo Joe, and I'll be John Wayne."

Another day, Luke would say, "Okay, Curt. You're a Nazi Messerschmitt pilot, and I'll be an American ace!"

One day as Luke was jumping out of his plane, he scraped his leg pretty badly. It just kept bleeding and bleeding. "Don't worry, wingmate, I'll get ya' back to the field hospital," I told him, as though he had been wounded in action. Southside kids knew how to have fun, anytime, anywhere!

Todd is often assigned tank room duty in the evenings. This is where the rolls of film are developed. There are several deep ceramic tanks where the rolls are developed for a specific amount of time. The tank room is situated about three feet above the floor level. There is a short stairway leading up to a plywood door. Once inside, with all of the exposed film, there will be no light until the film is processed. Well, there is some light—a small, red safety light is casting its strange effect on the small area.

On many evenings when Todd had this duty, it would usually go like this:

"Hey, kid, 'wanna keep me company while I do the film?"

This was always a tough decision because once in there, you had no choice but to stay for the duration. Todd would set a timer and begin his tasks. Compounding the loss of my freedom were the ghost stories that Todd would tell once I had been imprisoned. He could spin these scary tales with the adeptness of the ghost himself. His favorites were the stories of the Rats in the Graveyard, the Swamp Man and several others that would raise the hairs on the back of my neck. Let's not forget: I was the only Erler that knew "the other one" who lived there with us! Never wanting to be a chicken, I'd go for Todd's famous lure: "No scary stories tonight, kid." I knew that my fate was in his hands.

Sometimes, he'd just make up hockey or baseball stories. I loved his tales that talked about a rookie on the Blackhawks. His stories would always end up with his famous call, "A shot ... and a goal!" The "Rats in the Graveyard" saga would scare the wits out of anybody, even old folks. When he talked about that Swamp Man, all I could think of was Luther. He described the Swamp Man's moves through a mossy swamp on some sort of a raft. He'd bring his voice way down and deliver his disturbing account of the man's every scary move. "All that you could ever see was his shadow as the murky water sloshed beneath his oaken raft. He was up to no good. But where, what, who?" My thoughts were, "Oh, great. This is all I need—another strange visitor!"

"I'm only nine and a half years old, Mom, but I'm gettin' pretty good at making things from old pieces of wood. Old Lazy Bones, Dad's janitor man, always seems to burn the hunks of wood that I like. For some reason, he doesn't like me. I think it's because I'm a little smarter than him, Mom. I know how to make a fire in the hot water furnace, and that irks him 'cause he thinks that he's Einstein when he does it. He kinda' likes Junior, but he's always pickin' on me."

Mom doesn't know it, but I've come up with a trick that drives him nuts. When he's not around, I take the hose and turn the water all the way up. I then force the nozzle into the ground in the yard. The water pressure digs this snake hole as I keep forcing it as far as I can. When the dirt in the snake hole gets dry, you can't pull the hose back out. It's fun to watch from the window. He has to dig a big hole to get the hose back out. Good for him. He deserves it! Dad doesn't pay much attention to his snitches anymore, 'cause he has too many complaints. Dad's always too busy for such nonsense. Besides that, Dad hates snitch people!

It's a boring evening upstairs, so I decide to go down to my workbench and try to make something out of my wood scraps. My workbench is at the bottom of the basement stairs, facing the south wall. There is a hanging light with a pull switch over the bench. Before I even have a chance to turn on my little Emerson radio, I start to feel scared, real scared! I can smell something very odd. It smells like wet grass, or sod. As I turn to look toward the rear of the basement, my blood curdles! Luther is sitting on the wall of the coal bin about forty feet away. I am so frightened my body is goose-bumpy all over, my arms, legs and face. I am petrified! He is very much in the same pose as he was on the fireplace upstairs. He is sitting on this short wall with his head down. I can smell that smell even stronger now. It makes me think of the smell when Mom and Dad are digging in the garden. He is a grim-looking man, and again wearing a reddish-plaid shirt and blue jeans just like that first night on the mantle. Suspenders again, these seem to be a part of his regular outfit. His feet seem to dangle and his arms hang loose like a Raggedy Ann doll. His hands are immense and his feet the same!

I was shaking all over, probably crying, I can't remember. This was really happening. No dream, no nightmare, he was down there with me! I struggled to reach the light string. I yanked it as I began to run up the basement stairs. My legs felt like rubber bands. I darted to the top of the steps. I ran through the dark store and, without slowing down, I did my little three-step up the next flight. As I approached the upstairs hall, I don't know why, I darted straight to my bed. I was still shaking as I tried to fathom what I had just seen. I fell asleep exhausted!

Unfortunately, Luther would continue menacing me for many more years. I'd go to bed some nights and he was there, waiting for me, in my dreams—or were they mares? When I couldn't muster up the courage to look around the corner into the living room, I just assumed that he was there, sitting on the mantle, whether I could see him or not. Big and quiet, but very assuming! He remained part of my life from the time that I was five years old until the ripe old age of nineteen. Amazing, but so it was!

Dad had this little tradition. Whenever a silver dollar or a two-dollar bill was noticed in the brass register, he'd hand it to one of us kids: "Bring that up to your Mother." I used to love emptying Mom's little gray strongbox. I would dump all of its treasures on the bed. I loved counting those big heavy circles of silver. The feel and sound were fascinating to me.

Mom and Dad had been thinking about trading in the Zephyr for a new car. Mom came up with a brilliant idea. "Cash, let's see how many silver dollars I have in that box."

"Mom, let me do it, please?"

"Okay, Curt, but be sure to stack them in tens. Do it on the dining room table. That will make it easier."

"The final count is eight hundred and thirty-six bucks, Mom!"

Those silver dollars were the down payment on our new, baby-blue, four-door, 1948 Buick Super. We were one proud family on our next Sunday ride to the Karmel Korn shop way out on Western Avenue

"Holy cow, Luke, do you see what I see?" An immense blimp was heading north at a very low altitude. This was the Stagg Beer blimp, and it was nearing our house. Closer, closer and, believe it or not, it was now virtually right above our heads as we looked up. We were actually waving at the crew in the cockpit. We sensed some tension in that cockpit from our vantage point. There was definitely no waving back from these guys. Something was wrong, and we knew it. Until this exciting moment, the only blimp that we had ever seen was the world-famous Goodyear blimp. That blimp, of course, was always seen at a much higher altitude.

As Luke and I stood on the old wooden landing, or porch if you wish, the massive balloon was casting its large shadow over the entire area.

"Curt, listen to that sound. And do ya' see how it's kinda wobblin' from side to side?" The loud humming was downright threatening. "I've never seen anything fly this low. Must be a mistake. I sure hope it's gonna be okay. It's full of gases. This could be a disaster! There are electric and phone lines just a few feet away."

It just kept moving from side to side as it hovered over our heads. We just stared, riveted by its swaying. By this time, Junior was on the scene with us. "Yeah, it's very scary. I'll be glad when it's gone."

As I look back, this event must have been a mistake of some kind. Midway Airport was about nine miles to the west and three miles to the north. Some miscalculations had to have been the reason for this close call. For a nine-year-old kid, it was an immediate thrill. But in just a moment it became very threatening to all three of us. The sheer size and the overwhelming sound of the ship will be forever etched in my mind.

Home for a Coke! ©

HAPPY BIRTHDAY, AMERICA

Air Raid sirens are shrieking throughout the city! It sounds like London during the blitz. I must have overslept. It's Tuesday morning and 10:30 AM. All is well; it's just the weekly air raid test. It's somewhat like the fire drills at school. With the whole world in constant fear of nuclear attacks, Chicago has implemented this weekly routine.

Last night was just fantastic with its skyrockets, Roman candles, aerial bombs and more. It was the Fourth of July! Todd and Percy just had to compete as they placed their respective fireworks orders. Percy ordered Spencer's Display Package. This set was chock-full of the prettier stuff. While this was a cool package, it also included some sissy items like lady fingers. Lady fingers are these little bitty firecrackers that go *poof* instead of *bang*! Todd, on the other hand, ordered his from Banner Fireworks. Todd's set was more like an arsenal, with cherry bombs, two-inchers, whistling bombs and big, fat, Roman candles! It also had a lot of Todd's favorite, zebra firecrackers. These little guys could take out the average Tonka truck.

We younger boys were allotted an arsenal of the smaller and somewhat safer explosives in the morning. "Hey, Curt, hey Junior, come on, get up!" Luke was calling into the bedroom.

I jumped up and threw on my brown corduroys and my Indian moccasins. I didn't need a shirt. It would be hotter than Hades today, and what a day it was!

The three of us pounded down the back stairs. I stopped just long enough to scatter some toys on the floor. "Let's see, which ones are ready for demolition? These little plastic trucks from Japan are great for blasting. This red tanker hasn't had all four wheels in years. I'll blow it up!" Junior grabbed some expendable cars, trucks and airplanes.

Between the three of us, we had a virtual city to wipe out. The war had a major impact on most young boys. There seemed to be an acceptance of guns, tanks and other weapons that could and would destroy anything that needed destroying. Luke was more into tin cans and other items that he would blow sky high.

Luke, being four years older than me, was deemed more responsible. Yeah, right! He was armed with a handful of those red two-inchers and a couple of packs of zebra firecrackers. He said that he was setting up a "Nazi camp." Green bean cans made great oil reservoirs. There were those big Manor House coffee tins and those wax milk cartons. It was a virtual war zone. He had a knack for placing all of his explosives strategically, then lighting multiple items and yelling, "Run like hell, it's an attack!" *Bang, boom, ping*—the sounds would vary as the plastic and tin were now airborne. What a thrill it was to smell all of that gunpowder. As the sounds and smells subsided, we were already planning our next attack.

Luke ran into the house knowing that Todd was still asleep. He snatched a few cherry bombs and hurried back downstairs. He had borrowed a bottle of Sis's red nail polish. This time he said, "We're attacking this Jap airstrip." He painted the Rising Sun on the sides of a few old planes. "I'm lighting 'em all at once!" This was not an easy task, but Luke had a way with matches and fires. Sure enough, he had four wicks going at once. "Get back. Hurry, get back!" As he was running backwards, he tripped and fell. As any good soldier would do, he buried his head in the ground and covered up. This little mishap cost him the visual effects of his attack. However, those four cherry bombs, all going off at once, could be heard down at 82nd. This was tantamount to a WWII block buster bomb on a mini-scale. Yes, there was no doubt about it, although it was seven years later— we still remembered Pearl Harbor! It was awfully hard not to.

Mom heard the "block buster" and suddenly appeared in the kitchen window. "All right boys, enough is enough! Come on upstairs for some breakfast." Mom did not like any of this type of play. Oh, that dreaded breakfast ceremony again! I settled for a bowl of Kix with a big fat banana sliced up on the top and drowned in Hunding milk, whole milk! While this was a thirteen-minute delay, it gave the troops newfound energy.

As the day darkened and the hot dogs and potato salad disappeared, it was time for the night show. Neighbors who were in the know had begun to gather outside of the white picket fence. Soon, the midday dragonflies gave way to the evening lightning bugs. These little critters were in for some strong competition!

Special guests Sean, Casey and a few of the older neighbors were in the yard with us. Dad had spent most of the day pounding away on his Pako printer. No customer of Cash Erler's was going to be disappointed at not having their snapshots ready for viewing tomorrow if that was the day that they were promised! As tired as he was, he still managed to try out one of those red, white and blue Roman candles! Dad made sure that there were plenty of Cokes, and Mom had made plenty of her famous iced tea with big chunks of lemons. The picnic table was spread with Jay's potato chips, Fritos, and non-melting candies such as Necco wafers, Charms, Mary Janes, Chuckles and more. Sis and Junior had set up some pinwheels as the evening session began. Luke, Junior, Casey, Sean and I grabbed some sparklers and handed some over the fence to friends. There was even some hazard with these little guys. You haven't lived until you've picked up a recently expired, and still hot, sparkler. They become part of your anatomy as the hot wire sticks to your thumb, index finger or both!

Now, the big stuff was in the hands of the big guys. Todd and Percy had the sky afire for at least a couple of hours. The skyrockets seemed to cause most of the "Oohs and aahs!" from the crowd. Personally, I loved those menacing-sounding whistling bombs! You could hear every dog in the neighborhood barking, and I'll betcha', not one of them was a purebred! The main thrust of this event was to celebrate the birth of the greatest nation known to mankind, the United States of America, and celebrate we did!

While we were blasting everything in sight, the Pirates were blasting the Cubs as they took both ends of a double-header at Forbes Field!

Buck & Cardboard Kodak Friend ©

Luke and I spent many afternoons at the Avalon Theatre. Today, it was *Joan of Arc,* starring Ingrid Bergman, along with a good pirate movie. It's 1948 and I've been attending a Catholic school since 1945. This documentary type of film taught me so much. Perseverance, sacrifice, tolerance and understanding, they were all expressed in the story of this great woman. Most importantly, Joan of Arc showed so much faith!

We crossed over the Pennsylvania Railroad tracks on the way home. We always hurried when we got near the Hobo's shack on the south side of the hill. We never knew too much about this hermit guy, but we never took any chances. Many years later, Casey told me what a nice man he was. We just didn't know, and he seemed to be kind of scary.

Once we were back on Stony, walking down the CTA tracks, I told Luke how much I liked Joan of Arc. "She sure was brave, and she was really beautiful too! The sisters will be glad to know how much I love her. I hope that I see them this summer. The sisters walk down Stony once in awhile. Mom said that I can walk with them as long as I don't go past 83rd Place. I guess Mom doesn't know that I've been all the way past 87th all by myself! Sister Noel always holds my hand as we walk. I'll bet ya' that she was born on Christmas Day!" ... "No, Luke, not Joan of Arc, Sister Noel!"

September is here and this means just one thing to a kid— school! Maybe it was the little pewter statue of Jesus in his beautiful red robe, I don't know. We had a special day at school last year. We were allowed to bring money for the purchase of "holy items." My attention was immediately drawn to this particular statue. With Jesus in plain view, I said many prayers over the summer. Somehow, my prayers have been answered. I will be in a split class this year. We'll be sharing a classroom with third graders. Our nun will be Saint Nila. Oops, I meant Sister Nila. Incredible, absolutely incredible! I'm entering this school year with much less anxiety. I feel that I will do real well with Sister Nila mentoring me again. I like the split class deal too. Now I can be an upper classman right in my own room.

October 4, 1948 – Our Cubs surprised and disappointed a lot of fans today as they traded power-hitting Bill Nicholson to the Phillies for Harry "The Hat" Walker. I'm learning that these baseball heroes are not really ours—God just loans them to us for a little while. Todd and I are gonna miss ol' Swish!

As we stepped out onto the sidewalk in the front of Dad's store, there was something new—the smell of snow, the first snow of 1948. Who cannot recall the special smell of that cool, pleasant winter air? Dad would soon be freezing the yard for us. Up at the break of day, Dad would run the hose oh so gently so there would be smooth ice for us kids to skate on. He'd cover the lawn with several coats of ice. After a couple of days of his careful treatment, we'd be scooting all around the yard. If we didn't have any windy mornings, this ice would freeze up nice and smooth. I would have to stuff cotton in the tips of Todd's old hockey skates so that they'd fit me.

"Hey, Curt, want my figure skates?" Sis had just obtained a brand new pair of Planet figure skates.

"Sure, I want 'em, but they're white. I'll have to get them black somehow."

Sis had a plan: "We'll just keep coating them with that black Shinola. You know, the stuff that you guys use on your boots. That'll make them look like boy's skates."

Curt Pitching a Snow Ball, 1948 ©

There it was, that familiar sound of Dad's steam heat making its way up to the radiators. He had been down in the basement stoking the furnace. Sometimes, Dad would be down there as early as 4:00 AM, ensuring a warm home for his family. He would build a bank of coals that seemed to last for most of the day. This was an art that so many dads had learned to perfect. We needed to have the house warm all day today—it was Christmas morning! As always, between Mom and Dad and Santa we would all have plenty of great gifts.

As we arrived in the living room, Mom was still snoozing in the bedroom. It was about 5:30 AM. They should both be sleeping! I'm sure that they had been up late preparing for this morning. Dad was now stirring around down in the store. Luke crawled behind the tree and plugged in the lights. "Now, it's officially Christmas!" he stated very proudly. "Let's wake Mom and call down to Dad!"

After we had convinced Mom that it was late enough to get up, she joined us kids while rubbing the sleep from her eyes. Dad plopped himself down in his favorite chair. Luke was so excited with the first gift that he spotted with his name on it. "Holy cow, I got my own camera! Look, it's a Six-Twenty Brownie just like Dad's!"

Immediately, Dad jumped up, remembering that there was no film with this special gift. "I'll be back in a minute." He came lumbering back up the stairs with a couple of rolls of 620 film and a sleeve of number 12 flashbulbs. "Now, Pickle Puss, you're a real photographer!" Dad often called Luke "Pickle Puss" because Luke loved sweet gherkins!

Sis got just about everything that she wanted and more! I was fortunate enough to receive two great gifts right off the bat. "Look what I got—a soda fountain and my own 78 rpm phonograph and some records!"

As that last week of 1948 rolled by and 1949 rolled in, I drove Todd nuts with a record called "Laugh, Laugh, Phonograph." He hated it, and I loved that!

New Year's Eve 1948
Mom – Percy – Sis – Dad – Curt ©

Cash "Dad" Erler 1949 ©

I'm just ten years old; and I'm a president! The president of the newly formed Wild Cats. Our club consists of several of the kids on our block: Junior, Sean, Teresa, the Kentucky Boys and myself. We are still recruiting for more members. New members will have to pay their initial twenty-five cents and then a weekly membership fee of ten cents. Big Bro' Percy now has his own garage in the back. First it was a brand new '47 Caddy, then a new '49 Caddy and now a new '49 Packard Convertible. So many of our nice neighbors just drive their Fords, Chevrolets and Plymouths. What is Percy trying to prove? Who cares anyway—we're moving into his old Crosley garage. It's just the right size for us. "Wild Cats" is now boldly painted on one of the double doors.

With our first week's treasury money, we invest in a padlock. Only the president and vice-president have keys. Of course, Junior is the Veep! As the petty cash grows, we'll have candy and popsicle parties. What else could a bunch of kids do with a couple of bucks?

Percy now had a real Hi-Fi phonograph. He ordered it from "Monkey" Wards with his newly acquired credit card. It was a Montgomery Ward's Airliner Three-Speed model. Along with it were his first three long-playing record albums. He and I listened to them together on the day that the Railway Express guy delivered them. They were "Miss Liberty," "Kiss Me Kate" and my favorite, "South Pacific." I used to love those guys when they sang *"There's nothing like a Dame; …What ain't we got? You know damn well!"* I felt all grown up being allowed to hear those "damn" lyrics.

Before spring was over, Percy and Todd had purchased a TV set. It was a twelve-inch Muntz, with knobs the size of hockey pucks!

"Here's the deal, kids. Only Mom, Dad, Todd or myself can turn the set on or do any adjusting. No kids, everybody understand?" This was the subject of a family meeting called by Todd and Percy. The TV came with a metered cash box on the back. They had to insert quarters in this box before they turned it on. This way, they would have enough cash for the monthly payments.

"I'll bet that Dad ends up putting plenty of money in that box, too." This was the consensus of Luke and Sis.

Now, on Tuesday evenings, our living room was packed. Relatives and a few special friends and neighbors would arrive early so that they didn't have to sit on the floor. We kids didn't care if we had to hang from the ceiling, because we had a TV and nobody else on the block did! Milton Berle would come on, and Mom would have the coffee pot perkin' away. After Uncle Miltie, it would be much less entertaining for the kids. *Fireside Theatre* was next, and that was not too hot for us guys. Junior would have to get one of those privileged adults to turn the TV on after school. He never missed *Howdy Doody* or *Judy Splinters.* Later, in early 1950, *The Small Fry Club,* with Big Brother Bob Emery, was his favorite.

Everybody seemed to have their favorite shows. I never missed *Walt's Workshop* on Friday evenings. Walt Durban, the host, would teach me something new each week. Dad, Todd, Luke, Junior and I loved being able to see the Cubs on our new twelve-inch screen. As much as we enjoyed Bert Wilson and Bob Finegan on WIND, we just loved actually watching Handy Andy Pafko and the Cubs.

Mom and Percy watched all of the sissy stuff like *Lux Theatre* and other live drama shows. Saturday mornings meant *Burn 'em Up Barns, Flash Gordon,* cartoons and so much more!

Mr. Muntz—I hope that you live forever!

SOMETIMES A TRUANT!

Todd & Curt "Home from the B-Route"! ©

Todd would often say, "Hey, kid, if ya' ditch school tomorrow, I'll take you on the B route with me." It was almost time for summer vacation, and I hated the thought of getting caught now. "We'll be back before school lets out." Of course this came with great risk to both of us because if Dad found out, we'd both be doomed!

"Todd, tomorrow's Wednesday and we only have a half-day. The publics come in for their religion classes and were off after lunch."

Todd, always quick on his feet, retorted, "Big deal. Just tell Mom tonight that you'll probably be going to Avalon Park to play ball after school. That'll be even better!"

The rewards were always pretty neat. The B route went all the way to the North Side, and that was quite an adventure. It was almost like another city to us Southsiders! As we traveled through different neighborhoods,

Todd would announce what "country" we were in. "Comin' up to Poland in a couple of blocks! After that, we'll be entering Ireland for awhile." Todd would always make sure that I got at least one treat during that long day. I always prayed for a big chocolate malt from a place called "Roman's Drug Store." Nobody could mix chocolate, malted and vanilla ice cream like that big round man! If not a chocolate malt, I'd settle for a Forever Yours or a 5th Avenue, both great candy bars.

The first thing that Todd grabbed was the morning *Tribune's* sports page. It was at Roman's that Todd and I read of the tragic shooting of former Cubs player Eddie Waitkus. Waitkus had played for us until last year when the Cubs traded him to the Phillies. Todd and I both loved this guy. He was a war vet and a good guy. We got Dutch Leonard and some other old-timer in return. Eddie didn't know it, but he was being stalked by some obsessed female admirer. She shot him with a .22 caliber rifle on the 14th of June. Eddie did come back in '50, playing all 154 games and hitting in the .280+ range. He played until 1955. The movie *The Natural* was loosely based on Eddie's life.

On his wilder days, Todd would play this little trick on his kid brother. In retrospect, I had to have known what was going to happen each time. He'd say, "Wanna ride on the fender for a block or so? I'll drive real slow. Just hang on to the hood ornament."

"Okay, ... but promise, not too fast!"

"Don't worry, Curt, you'll be fine."

Things would seem all right for a bit, and then he'd pick up the speed with me hangin' on for dear life. He'd laugh his fanny off while I screamed. Once stopped, he'd have the windows up and the doors locked. I had to promise not to tell on him before he would let me back in. Of course, I wouldn't tell on him anyway.

Back in the safety of the front seat, I'd turn the volume up and ignore him for awhile. The radio was constantly playing our favorite songs. Todd loved "Mule Train," but my favorite song those days was Vaughn Monroe's hit, "Ghost Riders in the Sky": *"An old cowpoke went ridin' out one dark and windy day ..."*

With some coaching and whining the next morning, Sis would write an excuse note for the nun at school. "Please excuse Curt from school yesterday. He had a sore throat, blah, blah, blah." This always worked. She could sign her real name at the bottom, 'cause it was the same as my Mom's. So, actually, it was a note from my sister, but nobody ever questioned these notes.

Curt in Percy's '49 Packard ©

Luke comes bursting into the yard. "Curt, Dad 'n' Mom said that we can go to the Railroad Fair tomorrow. Here's the deal: you gotta get the lawn cut, and I'm doin' the downstairs windows. No more baseball today. Come on, we gotta get workin'!"

"Great news, Luke. I'll get us each a Coke first so we can talk about it, okay? My treat, 'cause you're gonna be spending some of your money tomorrow, I know! Then we can both start gettin' our jobs done."

"Okay, but let's get things done so that we can get to bed early. We're gonna take off real early. Dad says that we can take the I.C. and walk to the lake from there."

The Chicago Railroad Fair was held on the Chicago Lakefront in 1948, 1949 and again in '50. There were 39 railroads represented, offering nothing but fun for two young boys! It was referred to as "The Last Great Railroad Fair." We had a blast that day! Luke's big reward was one of my homemade rings. I took a big one-inch machine nut and filed it out to fit his finger. Then I rounded all but the top two edges and polished it. I sure as heck wouldn't want to get punched by anybody wearing one of these hunks of steel.

Halloween: trick or treat time has arrived. There's that overwhelming smell from a pile of crackling leaves smoldering at the curb. Yep, Injun summer is here.

Like most neighborhoods, ours had a wide spectrum of folks. There were those that were very friendly, and many that were totally scary! As important as the goodies to me was the prospect of seeing inside all of the old bungalows in our neighborhood. As each door opened, I would immediately check out the décor, the smells, etc. There were brown brick, yellow brick, stone, stucco and frame homes. The architecture on our Southside was as fantastic as anywhere in this country. All year long we'd see the lights go on at night and wonder what was goin' on in this house or that house. Some of the darker and spookier houses were simply off-limits to most of us. We never even considered approaching them, let alone knocking on their door, for any reason. One location that was always on our off-limits list was the professor's house. We used to lie in the bushes at night and take notes of his strange ways. We would take shifts with our pencil and a Scripto pad in hand. We would then share our findings. Some of us thought that we had it figured out: "He has buried someone in his yard!" He very often would be digging in his yard in the evenings. As we grew older, we tried to rationalize and concluded that he may have been burying his garbage. We'll never know, I guess.

We wouldn't be crossing Stony Island this Halloween evening. While this was a little neighborhood in the big city, it had its own little cities within its boundaries. For example, some folks that lived east of Stony assumed that we were different, and vice versa. Folks from Chatham would likely tell you that their neighborhood was very different than that of Avalon Park. The truth was, we were pretty much all cut from the same cloth. We were simply middle-class Americans!

Our favorites were the homes where the ladies made popcorn balls or taffy apples, and we thought that money was pretty cool too! There was one old girl that baked these horrible cupcakes. I tried one the year before and almost lost it! I have a feeling that the frosting was actually colored Crisco. This year's little cake looked much better after a '42 Hudson inscribed the frosting with its B.F. Goodrich stamp of approval!

Many of the older folks anticipated this day almost as much as we did. "Come on in, kids. Let's have a look at your costumes. Now, what are you, young man?"

My answer was usually the same as the year before. "I'm a hobo, ma'am. I like being a hobo! It's easy 'cause all I have to do is look in my big brothers' closets and there it is—my costume!"

Luke liked to dress up like an idiot. That always worried me a bit! Once inside of these foreign environments, we would detect strange and intriguing sights and smells. Most smells were that of cooking and baking. Cabbage and sauerkraut always seemed to dominate the evening. I guess that's what you would expect in this European-American neighborhood. I can still remember one house that always smelled as though they had fried chicken in varnish! The lighting varied drastically from home to home. It seemed that the older the folks were, the yellowier the lighting; don't know why. While on this "older" subject, it also seemed to me that many of the older people had funny looking dogs!

Our parents were void of any worries when it came to us entering these homes. You see, we were living in this little heaven on earth, the Southside of Chicago! The biggest worry was crossing the streets with masks on, etc. I loved my hobo outfits because they didn't encumber me in any way.

The lucky kids, like myself, who attended St. Felicitas School had an ace in the hole. The day after Halloween was All Saints Day, and that meant one thing—no school! While my siblings were trying to figure out what 23% of something was, I was sorting out my brown bag full of sweet stash and counting my cash.

And now ... the red, gold and brown hues of autumn have given way to a beautiful white canvas. Oh, how we loved that first

step into a newfallen snow. All at once, it was time to start thinking of the fun that we would have this winter. There'll be snow forts, snowmen, snowball fights, just endless fun.

Sis says, "It's just right for snow angels, Curt. Come on, let's head for the yard." As we flew through the gate, we could see Mom smiling out the window. Mom loved watching all of her kids from her little perch in the kitchen. As the daylight began to disappear and the fun was about over, we were usually frozen solid. Mom would be ready with some hot cocoa. She needed to thaw out her little Eskimos.

Christmas shopping was done by each of us kids. Dad always had this very simple formula. "You'll each get one dollar to spend on each of your siblings and three bucks for Mom's gift." He didn't consider himself in this plan. That's okay, we all knew the routine and had saved a little extra so that Dad could get his Bay Rum cologne and some of his favorite candies. He loved it when I got him a box of candied ginger. I think of Dad every time that I taste that stuff today.

Sis has obviously discussed this year's plan with our banker—Dad! "It's going to be snowing a lot tomorrow Curt. Wanna go to Sears and start our shopping? We can walk there and take the streetcar home."

"Okay, starting tomorrow it's gonna be the Christmas season, Sis. We'll be shopping, wrapping and making our homemade ornaments. I'm gonna ask Percy if I can get the Christmas 78 rpms out. Hey, Junior, we're goin' shopping at Sears tomorrow, right after school. Santa is already at Sears, and I already know what he's giving out this year, but I'm not tellin'!"

Dad got his Bay Rum and Mom got her Evening in Paris, some Coty's face powder and tons of bubble bath and candy. Patsy received her own Christmas stocking this year. It was fun watching her rip it open. There were some Milk Bones, doggie candies and a chocolate flavored rubber ball. Santa was good to all of the Erlers!

After hanging out at Lou's Drug Store on 82nd Street one night, I was walking home down the alley. This meant passing the dreaded delivery door behind Ryan's Funeral Home. We all knew what was delivered there. I hated that place.

This little journey can be bad enough on its own. Even worse tonight,

I have to go to the basement when I get home. I have a real love-hate thing with our basement. It's not just downstairs, but downstairs twice. The store separates me from my little workshop and my home and family on the second floor. I really love spending time down there. I've set up a nice workshop with drills, saws, all of my tools and my Emerson radio. God knows, this young guy needs his trusty radio for security. I'm a long way from home! I need to finish that jewelry box that I'm making for Percy. I'm in no mood for Luther, no mood at all! I just hope that he isn't there.

"Please, don't be there tonight, please! This Luther thing has to end someday. I am glad that Dad had the new knotty pine bedroom added to our home, but I don't like going the back way anymore because it's all closed up now. Luther could be there anytime that I turn that dark corner downstairs. What's his mission anyway? Why me? Does he hate me or is he trying to be my friend? I wish I knew. He needs to show up when I'm with Dad, Todd or Buck. Then we can get to the bottom of this, once and for all."

As I continue down the alley and get closer to home, I keep thinking about that dark hallway. I decide on entering through the front door. I run up the stairs to let Mom know that I'm home. "Hi, Mom, I'll be in the basement. I gotta do some woodwork. See you in awhile, okay? I'll be up by nine."

With a little support from Patti Page and Nat "King" Cole, I finish my woodwork. I pull the light string and do my three-step special: up the stairs, three steps at a time, and then I dash through the dark store. Now, I do the three-step again. With no sightings this evening, I'm elated as I arrive upstairs, winded from my escape.

Mom says, "Would you like to have a cup of coffee?"

"Sure, Mom, I'd love it!" Mom and Dad let me have coffee once in awhile as long as I add plenty of sugar. Can you imagine—plenty of sugar? I went to the cabinet and dug out my secret stash of McLaughlin's Manor House instant coffee. If I didn't hide it there, Cary would be drinking it, and that ain't fair. I bought it, and it's mine!

Another summer and one more exciting air sighting! Junior and I were having a grounder game in the yard. He was Roy Smalley and I was Dee Fondy. I'd have to imagine that the Cubs were losing! Coming from the southeast was the largest airplane that we had ever seen. It was heading our way.

"Curt, look Curt, look behind you, you won't believe it!"

I was stunned: "What in the heck is it? Never saw any plane that big, or that low. Hey, remember the blimp, Junior?"

Junior hadn't moved a muscle. "Yeah, but this looks like a bomber. It's bigger than those B-29s, I know that!"

"Look, Junior, the engines are on the back of the wings, not the front. The props are backwards and there's six of 'em."

The plane was casting its shadow as this massive roar passed overhead. "It seems like we're in a war movie, doesn't it, Curt?"

"Yeah, this is amazing, just amazing!"

Peacemaker Bomber

This was a memorable but somewhat tense event for two Southside kids and, I'm quite sure, for every kid in the neighborhood. I don't think that we realized the proximity and magnitude of Midway Airport. It was, at that time, one of the largest airports in the United States. As it turned out, the plane was the B-36 Peacemaker bomber. This was an extremely large plane to be flying as low as it had been. The aircraft was 162 feet long with a wingspan of 230 feet. Its height was equivalent to a five-story building. Fully loaded, it weighed 410,000 pounds, or 205 tons!

Jr. and Curt beside Todd's '47 "Red Rag-Top" Plymouth at the
Rainbow Ice Cream Shop on South Western Avenue ©

THE "KID" GOES TOM SAWYER

This summer's big chore was to paint the outside of our picket fence. I'd paint the inside the next summer—maybe. I had mixed emotions about this fence. I loved it because it protected the place where I pitched and hit. It was also where we had our great Fourth of July parties and so many other good times. It was eighty feet from east to west and a hundred feet from north to south. That sounded like 180 feet to me. I figured that there were approximately 370 pickets to be painted. This would take some delicate balancing of my baseball schedule.

Dad sent Cary to Sears to buy the paint. I went with him so that I could pick out the brushes that were easiest for me to work with. I'm sure that Cary bought a little something for himself while holding Dad's bankroll. Here was Cary once again greasing the wheel so that I could work. He was great for saying to Mom, "Curt's big enough to do that now. Let him do it." Now, if it was something that he could profit from, he'd grab the job. He knew that I was free help on this one, therefore he couldn't compete.

I didn't care. It was a challenge, and I'd be proud when it was done. Whether big bro' Cary thought so or not, Dad and Mom would be treating me with some kind of a reward when I'd completed my job. I had my eye on a first baseman's glove at Sears. That would do just fine!

We bought the paint and the other necessary supplies. Mom fixed pork chops and her famous milk gravy tonight. She knew that this was one of my favorites and that I'd be working hard all day tomorrow.

"First thing in the morning I'll grab my engineer's cap and hit that fence with a few thousand strokes, Mom!" Mom laughed, knowing that I loved my old blue and white striped hat. It was the kind that the railroad guys wore.

I had to wrestle with the choice, because this was also one of my baseball caps. After just a moment's thought, I said to myself, "Yeah, I'm gonna wear it to keep the paint out of my hair. It ain't any fun combing

that turpentine through my hair!" I always had the bill turned all the
way up. This allowed me to see the pitches comin' when I was at bat. "I'll
just try not to get too much paint on it."

After my first day on the job, I had a little system worked out so
that I could squeeze in a little baseball too. I would first paint the sides
of about three sections of pickets. This was the toughest and slowest part
of the job. I'd hang the ol' railroad cap on an unpainted picket. This
would give the appearance that Curt was workin' hard over there on
Harper Avenue. I'd check to see if I could stir up any baseball action on
Harper. If not, I'd take a quick ride to Avalon Park. After satisfying my
baseball needs, I would attempt to enlist the help of a friend or two, when
possible. I'm quite sure that this little trick was gleaned while watching
The Adventures of Tom Sawyer several years earlier. Upon my return to the
job site, we'd slap the fronts of those pickets with that white paint. With
my hat back in place, I'd head for the yard to do my daily paint brush
cleaning. This way Mom could see how hard I was working and likely
note the time. Looking like a hero, and verifying my presence, I'd head
in for a moment and request permission for a cold Coke.

Family dinners on nights like these were always neat. Dad and Mom
would discuss the events of the day. Mom would say to Dad, "Sis did a
lot of ironing for me today, and did you see how far Curt has come with
the painting?"

As I neared the end of the project, I was working on the 83rd Street
side of the yard. Suddenly, I saw Peggy Sue coming down 83rd on her
blue bike. This was a rare sight, for sure. My heart began to pound as
she approached. I was thinking, "Geez, she lives about a mile from here.
I have never seen her anywhere but school or a school event." She was
wearing a red sweatshirt and Levis. Not a parochial school jumper or any
other uniform. All I could think was, "I have never seen her looking so
much like a movie star, or at least a starlet. She looks absolutely beautiful,
a bit like Jeanne Crain!"

I, of course, was wearing "the hat" and some old worn-out pants.
"Oh well, I am working," I thought as she came closer. I waved her to a
stop.

"Hi, Peggy Sue. How's your summer going?" This was a rare opportunity for me. It was the middle of July, and I hadn't expected to see her again 'til September. I began to explain to her how much fun it was playing Tom Sawyer while painting the fence. We talked for a few minutes as I continued to glorify this wonderful and fun project. She considered going home and changing, then returning to share in the fun and have a cold Coke with me while enjoying the music on my Emerson.

I like to assume that her parents would not allow her to return, but I'll never know! In any case, this was a big blow to my ego. I kept telling myself, "You should have jumped on your bike and rode alongside of her all the way to her house. You should have tried harder!" I can still hear the song that was playing as she began heading west on 83rd, "*Music, music, music—all I want is loving you and music, music, music.*"

However, there were a couple of girls to whom I needed to pitch the reverse side of this horrible chore. There was the mess of getting paint in your hair and on your hands, face and clothes. Let alone that terribly strong smell of the enamel. I explained the pain of having to rub the turpentine all over your arms and hands. Then there was that nasty smell after the process, and on and on! You see, these girls would have driven me nuts!

Did Somebody Say Baseball? ©

Great big raindrops began pounding down, creating that special scent in the air. This hot and muggy day had suddenly become most refreshing. Baseball outside was not possible this afternoon. As for baseball, Luke and I knew how to handle the situation. We pulled out our Cadico Ellis All-Star Baseball Game. From Todd to Junior, we all loved this game. However, it was Luke and I that were most involved at this point in our lives. With the big canvas awning over the dining room windows to detour the downpour, we were able to leave the windows wide open. There has never been an air conditioner that felt quite like this. The fresh, cool smell and feel are beyond description. Suddenly it was as refreshing as a night game in Boston. "Nothin' like it anywhere!" I stated to Luke as we began to choose our teams.

Luke and I each had one constant. He had to have Stan "The Man" Musial on his team. I had to have "The Splendid Splinter," Ted Williams, on mine. So, first choice was an unnecessary exercise. Then it was on to the rest of our choices in an attempt to build our dream teams for the day. These were to be exhibition games because our regular season had already ended. Each little player disc was about 3½" in diameter and represented the player's actual statistics.

We usually ended up with certain favorites. Luke would have Del Ennis, Yogi Berra, "Puddin' Head" Jones, Marty Marion and other big names of the day. My team wouldn't be complete without Andy Pafko, Vern Stephens, Gil Hodges and Bobby Thompson, and I always vied for Warren Spahn. He was my choice for the all-time greatest lefty. For our regular season schedule, which began in conjunction with the majors, we followed most of the league rules. We would draft our teams, and we honored the trade deadlines and followed an actual big league schedule, usually that of the Cubs. Today, it was simply a respite from the rain. Even before the first pitch, Mom showed up with iced tea for both managers.

This is summer as it was meant to be!

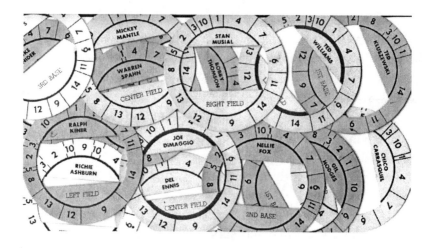

All-Star Player Discs

The summer was rapidly coming to an end. Cary suggested that we all take a trip to The Dunes State Park in northern Indiana. "I'll ask Dad and Mom if you kids can go with Rhoda and me to Indiana this weekend. It'll be fun with the whole gang of you kids, Sis, Luke, Curt, Junior, Carol and Renee." Rhoda, not known for her generosity, stated, "If your Dad buys the hot dogs and pop, we'll take you kids." I wanted to tell her that she was a mooch, but Mom 'n' Dad had taught all of us guys to be gentlemen.

Carol and Renee were our cousins, and their two kids! Of course, Dad and Mom approved. There was never an opportunity for family vacations due to Dad's business. So this would serve as a bit of a summer vacation. "Sure, Cary, just grab some money from the cash register and go to the National Tea and get plenty of everything for you guys and the kids."

Oh, did Rhoda love this: her chance to shop with our money. We all went to the store with Cary. Oscar Mayer wieners and bacon, ground round steak, Jay's potato chips, Butter Nut bread, mustard, ketchup and on and on. Cary took a run to Bubble's Liquors at 91st to grab a case of Pabst Blue Ribbon beer. I'm quite sure that Dad bought that too! Dad had plenty of Coca-Cola in the back of his store for us kids. He and Mom gave us each spending money because they knew that there was a general store at the park.

The trip was exciting. The females all camped out in Cary's big '36 Buick. He fabricated a lean-to tent from an old Cash Erler Photos awning. We stuck the top in the door openings and closed the door securing that portion. Cary staked the bottom into the ground. We now had a tent for the four guys. We loved cooking our own dinners over a campfire. None of us had ever camped out, so this was just great. We roasted our wieners on sticks, over the burning logs. After dinner, we all toasted marshmallows. Luke told ghost stories to scare the girls. Luke was a great one for telling weird and scary stories. Actually, he scared this little brother more than he did the girls. Once again, Luther was uppermost in my mind as I put my head down to sleep that night. Here I was, in the middle of some pitch dark forest, not knowing what to expect between now and dawn. Luke and I were lying there whispering long after all the others were asleep. It was eerily quiet when a skunk came wandering by our tent. Luke motioned with his hand to stay still. He knew that one wrong move and we'd all get sprayed.

"Thank God, Luke knew what to do last night. I saw my first skunk!" I told everyone as we were having our bacon and eggs breakfast. That afternoon, we all walked down to the park's general store. Luke was exclaiming, "Wow, look at all the different kinds of pop in this cooler." We all searched through the icy water and each grabbed something that we had never had in Chicago. There were some odd ones all right. Cowboy Cherry was my choice, 'cause I just loved anything that was cherry flavored. The bottle was really neat too. It depicted a cowboy with his lariat. There were many more for the kids to choose from—Jones' Fruit Punch, Grape-Ola and some goofy-named root beer that nobody could pronounce.

On the drive home, with all of us kids fried to a crisp from the sun at the beach, we sang and laughed. *"Irene goodnight, Irene goodnight, goodnight Irene, goodnight Irene, I'll see you in my dreams."* By the time that we reached the Lever Brothers plant, some of the girls were sound asleep. As Cary pulled up at 1540, we were all glad to be home!

Now, summer was officially over. There were just a few days left before school would start. Vacation time seemed to have rolled by quicker than its sudden thunder storms. So, it's back to readin', writin' n' arithmetic at good old St. Felicitas.

Sometime during the first week of school, I proclaimed, "I can't wait for Christmas vacation!"

As Johnny Cash once said, *"Christmas came and Christmas went. Christmas that year was heaven sent."*
Christmas, as always, was good to the Erler kids.

IT WAS A VERY GOOD YEAR

Monday, January 29th, means birthday cake and ice cream. I'm twelve years old and almost a teenager!

"Cary, take this and run Curt over to Art's Cycle Shop on 75th. Let him pick out the bike of his choice. Make sure that it's the one that he wants!" Dad was emphasizing the fact that he wanted Cary to allow me this freedom of choice.

"It's a C-note, Curt. What did you do that deserves this?"

"I guess that Dad and Mom think that I'm worth it. How's that big bro'?"

With little hesitation, I moved toward the Schwinn-Cadillac. "Cary, come here. This is it, this two-tone green one. I love those red pinstripes too. It's got a leather seat, and look at that tank with the horn in it and the streamlined headlight. This springer fork feature is great for flyin' over bumps and curbs! Do we have enough for this one?"

"Yeah, Curt. It looks like we have just enough! We'll get some rope and cardboard and tie it to the roof."

This special gift cost Dad and Mom ninety-six bucks plus tax. Mom and Dad, like so many other families, had their financial ups 'n' downs. Fortunately, for this kid, they must have been experiencing an up on this birthday!

"Hey, Mom, I received my Wee Folks gift certificate in the mail. I guess that I'll just have to peddle over there later this week. I also got several bucks from the kids at my party. I think that I have enough to buy that Jerry Mahoney dummy at Mr. Lazar's. What a great birthday this has been. We had Felicitas kids here for my party. I have my new bike, some birthday money and my new favorite shirt, the yellow- and white-striped polo from my dream girl, Peggy Sue!"

My mentor Todd left us this morning. It is a day that I'll never forget. He has become a Marine, and I'll bet that he'll be a great one! Its Tuesday, March 1st, 1951, a proud but sad day for this family. Mom is really down in the dumps today. She has already had her share of seeing her boys go to war. Dad is, as usual, busy in the darkroom. After school, I'm going to go in there and sit with him for awhile because he's gonna be lonely too. Dad always calls me "Hawk-eye" because I always find the negatives that drop on the floor in that very dark room.

Ted Williams is Todd's sports idol. "The Splendid Splinter" was a flying leatherneck in WWII as well as the war that now rages in Korea. Todd sure knows how to choose his idols, doesn't he?

Dad and Todd have taught me to check the news now and then. Dad says, "There's more than baseball goin' on out there, Curt!" Dad will be glad to know that I'll be doing that more than ever if Todd goes over there. I do know that the port city of Inchon was recaptured this week as the First Marine Division continues to show its mighty force.

Each day, as Dad finishes his darkroom work, he heads for the newspaper. I do peek at the front page once in awhile. Dad can discuss anything with anybody. He loves it when certain customers chew the fat with him. He lights up his Camel cigarette, slides his hand into his back pocket, rests his leg on the bottom shelf of the sales counter and talks their ears off!

I can't wait for Todd's first furlough so that he can tell me all about his training and all of his new buddies. I'll write to him as often as I can after my dumb homework every night. Maybe I'll be able to write and send *Tribune* sports pages a couple of times a week. As I hit the sack this night, I think to myself, "Gee, come to think of it, who am I going to pitch to? Who else can handle my fastball?"

I was very proud of my ability to make other kids say "Ouch" when I threw my heat! Only Todd could handle my newest pitches. Heck, he could handle Hacker, Minner, Rush, even Warren Spahn, any of 'em!

I had recently learned how to make a hickory stain for my baseball bat. This clever formula had been shown on the *Walt's Workshop* television show last Friday night. I always watched this show because it was about woodworking. I would go down in Dad's store so that I wouldn't have to beg the other kids to watch my special show. I knew that it was boring to them. With Mom's new blonde wood Motorola in the living room, Dad had the old Muntz down in the store for his Cubs games and wrestling. Because it was on Fridays, I would get to fry some shrimp for my special event. Mom and I usually didn't eat meat on Fridays. Mom seemed to like it when I cooked for the two of us. I would go down to the National Tea grocery store and buy a box of breaded fantail shrimp. They were expensive at seventy-five cents a box. I would whip up my own cocktail sauce. It was real easy. A half cup of ketchup, a dab of horseradish, some Lea & Perrins worcestershire sauce, a touch of lemon and a splash of Tabasco. Nothin' to it!

Now some people might ask, "Why would this kid want to work in that basement? This is where Luther seems to have appeared in recent times." While this may not seem to be a logical reason to many, it was simple to me. It was my basement, where my woodshop was. It was where I could skate and listen to my music, and I wasn't giving it up!

A couple of weeks after learning how to make my hickory stain, I decided to stain one of my bats. I'm thinking to myself, "If this turns out well, I'll do one for Junior. It's really pretty easy. Last Wednesday, I broke up that old 78 rpm record. It was some opera thing that Percy never listened to. He'll never miss it, I hope! I put the pieces in a jar with some alcohol just like ol' Walt Durban said. It should be hickory stain by now."

As I began to sand the bat, things were looking good. I was able to remove the shine while still leaving the famous Louisville Slugger lettering. I had my Emerson on, and once again Mr. Monroe was belting out his big hit record, "Ghost Riders in The Sky." All of a sudden, that wet sod smell was now stronger than the old varnish that I was removing. It was hot and dry down there from the blasting iron furnace. It was not at all wet down there. I dropped my sand block and turned to the rear of the basement. This time Luther was there; and just as quickly, he was gone! Now, let me tell you, he *was* there, exactly where I'd seen him in his previous visits. Sitting on the coal bin wall and wearing the same clothing as before. It was that farmer-looking outfit of jeans and the plaid shirt. He looked just the same from what I could see with the brevity of his appearance.

With one pull of the string, off went the radio and the light bulb. I ran like hell up to and through the store. In a moment I was flying up the nineteen stairs to safety. As usual, my heart was pounding. I grabbed a baseball manual and flopped on my bed. Still not over my most recent sighting, I could only think, "Not another soul, excuse the expression, in this damn house, has this problem. Why me? Here I am, twelve years old, thinking that I'm a tough guy and still running away. I'm running away from someone that no other member of my family has ever seen.

It doesn't seem to matter how many years go by. Luther always looks just as he did that first night on the mantle. It's been over five years since that scary night. I'm still very frightened at each appearance. If he wants something, why doesn't he talk? If he is someone that I should know, he should tell me. If he wants, or is able, to hurt me, why doesn't he?"

This was definitely something between him and me. As the years went on, I'd sometimes make sure that I had company when I needed to go down there but had a feeling that someone was waiting for me. Not once, when I was accompanied by another person, did Luther show any sign of being there. As I look back, I should have had Patsy come down just to see what the results might have been.

This was to be the Christmas that Junior and I would become hooked on Dinky Toys. These little four-wheeled gems from England were even neater than most of our Tootsie Toys. Percy had come into some extra money due to the profit on the sale of his Olds 88. He knew that the Wee Folks toy store had a display case full of these tiny vehicles. He used some fine judgment in his choices because we both considered this haul our best presents of the day. Junior and I each received nine Dinkys. My everyday car was an Alvis roadster. My favorite car for robbin' banks was a blue Triumph sedan. It adorns my office windowsill as I write these words!

We played with these cars and trucks for millions of hours, maybe less! I still have a few that survived many years of play, as does Pepsi.

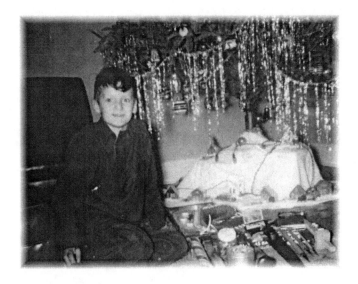

Christmas '51 – Tools & First Baseman's Glove ©

T.V. STAR FOR A DAY

Patsy Beggin' for some Coke ©

One day in May, Percy called to me as I returned from school at lunchtime. I was about to dart up the stairs, all nineteen, in just six leaps, as usual! Mom probably had a can of Heinz mac and cheese heated up for my short stay. I was the only kid in my family that was close enough to come home for lunch. When I didn't go home, I'd go to Steffens' Bakery for a cream horn. I just loved those flaky pastries filled with gobs of creamy meringue. I have always remembered Todd's big dare: he said, "If it's a horn, why don't you blow on it, Curt?" Always willing to oblige my big bro', I gave it a good honk. The meringue flew across the dining room table and some of it caught Todd's face! While he may have been upset, he just had to laugh. Mom did not!

Percy called out again, "Curt, come here, I want to show you something." It was a letter from WGN-TV saying that I was chosen to be the guest emcee on a television show called *Photo Quiz*.

"What, why me? I ain't no TV star."

Percy explained that he had sent little notes and photos of Luke, Sis, Junior and me. For some reason, I was the loser. At least that is how it appeared to this rather shy kid. Actually, I was far from shy with my family or neighborhood buddies. I was simply not an orator at all. Put me in front of more than four people and I clam up!

Now, I was supposed to return to school and tell Sister Josanne that I would not be coming to school on that date. "No way," I thought. "If I do that, everybody will be watching that show, including Peggy Sue and my buddies. Nope, I'm not telling. I'll just have Sis write me a note after I miss school that day."

Sis was prompting me to get out of bed, as she called, "Come on, get up Curt. It's your special day. You're going to be a TV star!"

That dreaded day had arrived and I was ready to throw up. This whole event was not very funny to this twelve-year-old, not funny at all! Mom and Sis were just dying to tell me what to wear—probably some clunky-looking shirt and tie.

"Not so fast!" I thought. "I'm the one sufferin', so I'll pick the wardrobe. Hey, I know what I'll wear. I'll dig out that cool yellow- and black-striped polo shirt that Peggy Sue gave me at my birthday party. "Most of the kids had tucked a buck inside of a card, but Peggy Sue gave me that neat shirt. It'll be just perfect and it's probably loaded with good luck! Now, I'll feel more confident and I'll just make the best of it."

Sis just had to mess with my hair; she always did! "Wait, Curt, let me fix the part. I'll push that wave up a little too."

"When do we leave? Who's taking me downtown?" I asked. Todd was home on his first leave, what luck! Betty Lou, Todd and his new Marine buddy Tug were taking me downtown. Now, things were really lookin' better—I had the Marines to back me!

"Hey, Curt, there's the *Tribune* Tower," Betty Lou said from the front seat. I spun around to my left.

"Yep, there it is. Do we hafta go?"

Todd said, "Sure, buddy. You're gonna be a star!"

Tug just kinda winked at me. I knew that he was feelin' bad for me. As we parked the car, I gave it one more shot: "Let's just go home and tell Mom and the rest that I didn't feel good."

Betty Lou had the cure, as she said, "Curt, you'll probably get a nice prize. Maybe baseball stuff, maybe a new bike."

"I already have my neat Schwinn from my twelfth birthday. But ya'know, I sure would like to have a trapper's glove like Todd's."

Up the elevator we went. If anyone thinks that a twelve-year-old boy doesn't sweat, they just don't know! We were greeted by some friendly old lady. She must have been at least thirty. Now we had to part company. My escorts had to sit in a little grandstand area, which made me smile. It made me think of the *Howdy Doody Show*, and now the Marines were in the Peanut Gallery!

Sue Topping was the hostess, and Frank Sweeney was the real emcee. They told me what I had to do when the red light came on the camera. I was now sitting behind this big desk with the host and hostess. The red light was on and the camera was aimed at me: "It's too late!" My first chore, and it was a chore, was to call some kid whose name I pulled from a box of postcards. Great, it's a girl, Delores. That's a heck of a lot better than some guy named Sluggo. I had to ask this girl one simple question.

"Hello, Delores. My name is Curt, and I'm calling from WGN's *Photo Quiz*. Are you ready for today's question? I need you to name any state in the union that borders an ocean." This chick just froze. She was in worse shape than I was. I don't know why, but I blurted out, "You're right, New York!" I think that it was because she sounded cute!

Well, now my job was over, I thought! I've done my phone thing, and now Delores and I would collect our great prizes and Todd can buy me a Coke—I needed one! As I was beginning to catch my breath, I remembered that I still had the cookie commercial to do. While emcee Frank laughed and giggled, they reapplied this sissy tan makeup to his face. "How can a man let them do that?" I thought.

Sue handed me a glass of milk and a box of Zion chocolate chip cookies. I followed my instructions: "I sure love these Zion cookies!" I said to the camera as I dunked one in the glass of milk. I felt as if the whole world was in my Mom's kitchen at lunch time, yet I maintained my composure.

The red light was out, I was off camera! "Whew, I'm done, right?"

Not a chance. I had to sit there next to these two for another ten minutes. Finally, all of the cameras were turned off and my job was finally over. Now it was time for my rewards. Sue Topping was talking to Todd and Tug. Sure they were Marines, but what about my stuff? Betty came over to console me, followed by that old lady that we had met earlier. She really dropped a notch or two when she said, "Curtis, we have something for you." She knew that I was Curt; that was the name on the letter, not Curtis! The last time that I had accepted this "Curtis" thing was when Peggy Sue had dotted the letter 'i' with a great big heart on my valentine. Who cares, anyway? I'm about to collect!

My big surprise was a cardboard wallet and a cheap brass key chain. No money, just a lousy cardboard wallet! It looked like something from F.W. Woolworth's. It wasn't over yet. Now she hands me a box of the now infamous Zion chocolate chip cookies.

"Let's go," I said to Todd, "Come on, let's go!" I said goodbye to Sue Topping. Heck, it wasn't her fault. Besides that, she was beautiful and we had been TV stars together. She gave me a little peck on the cheek and said, "Bye bye, Curt."

As we hurried to the elevator, I handed the stupid cookies to Betty Lou, stating, "I'm never going to eat another Zion cookie again. I never heard of 'em anyway, 'n' I hate 'em!"

As we began driving south on the outer drive, good ol' Lake Michigan never looked better. "Jezebel" was blaring from the radio. "Man, I love that Frankie Laine!" I exclaimed. We were finally headin' south, yeah, to the Southside, where we belonged.

As we were going through Jackson Park, Todd looked toward the back seat and said, "Good job kid, you were great. Did you remember Delores's number?" He knew that I had scribbled it on my hand. I just grinned shyly, 'cause Betty Lou was there. The real reward was coming soon. Todd promised that he'd take me to Super Burger on Stony Island. I could smell those curly fries already. I think that Todd actually wanted to show off his turf to Tug. Tug was from down south and had never seen anything as cool as our kinda neighborhood.

After chowing down on double cheeseburgers, curly fries and malts, we cruised by South Works. That's part of the U.S. Steel Mills where Todd had been employed before joining the Marines. "See those rail yards, Tug? That's where I worked." Todd was proud of our Southside. Me too!

Mom and Dad congratulated me for my performance. Luke, Sis and Junior also gave their reviews of my TV career. Now, I had to think of an excuse for yesterday's absence. "I'll just tell Sister the truth. It's too late now, and they'll never see me on TV." This seemed like the right thing to do. I may fib about certain things, but I sure ain't gonna lie to a nun.

Sister was somewhat upset with me. She thought that I should have tipped her off. "Curt, I would have asked Mr. Stepanik to bring the television over from the convent. The whole class could have watched. You know, like when the Yankees are in the World Series."

Did she really think that the thought hadn't crossed my mind? Yep, I was right; I knew what I was doing all along. It wasn't over yet. Sister made the announcement that we had a TV star in our class. For the most part, the kids were pretty neat about it and asked me a lot of questions. I really wanted to tell Peggy Sue what I had worn for this occasion, but I chickened out at the last minute.

It always seems that the nuns are easier on the girls than us boys. We all know that girls are never bad and they're always smarter than us guys. This is what Gramma would call "a bunch of malarkey!"

"St. Patrick's Day will soon be here. You children will begin practicing next week for this year's play." Sister is preparing the class for the annual three weeks of torture! At least it will be torture for most of the guys. There are a few that seem to enjoy this silliness. Not me! As the next week rolls around, we are assigned our parts in the play. I don't know why, but it seems that the guys that will likely offer the most resistance are being told that they will be little elves. Oh, ain't this sweet? Naturally, Curt is one of the chosen few. It figures! We are told that our parents will be picking up the tab for our green elf costumes. I'll tell ya' right now, it's just a waste of money, 'cause I am not showing up on that day! No normal guy wants to run around on his tippy toes lookin' like Peter Pan!

For the next couple of weeks, I seem to be having a lot of sore throat problems, toothaches and other common maladies. On the big day, March 17th, I seem to be very, very ill! I told you, just a waste of good money!

I'd be willing to bet that I'll be very sick again next year about this time!

It was time for Todd to return to the Marines. Mom, Carey and I drove him to Lexington, Kentucky in the Buick, where he caught a flight back to base. Mom just wanted to spend a little special time with him—thus the drive to Kentucky! Todd was being shipped to what they were calling "the Cold War" over in Korea. The only thing "cold" about it was the winter weather that we had all read about. We bid adieu to Todd as he climbed aboard a little puddle jumper plane.

Mom and I were not in very good spirits as we drove through Cincinnati. My mood was somewhat revived as we crossed a bridge and, to my wonder, Crosley Field was in full view. The Reds were playing a night game. The only big league parks that I had ever seen were Wrigley Field and Comiskey Park. It was already evening, and the ballpark was glowing with lights. I could hear the sounds of baseball. By this time, I had my head out the window looking from left to right as Cary slowed down for me.

Mom asked, "Curt, what are you looking for?"

"Oh, I was just wonderin' if I could spot that Chinese laundry where Hank Sauer always breaks the front window with his prodigious homers." That brought a smile from Mom as we drove on.

Many Saturday mornings, I'd grab the Stony Island bus and head for the Jackson Park Lagoon. This was the ol' fishin' hole to many. I started out with a bamboo pole. After weeks of frustration, I knew that I had to change my style if I was ever going to catch a perch, or any kind of fish. I earned enough money cutting lawns to buy an aluminum casting rod and reel at Morrie Mages sporting goods on Halsted Street. I tried everything, but nothing seemed to work.

"Sears may have the right magic. I'll buy some Eagle hooks and a couple of spinners like the old guys are using." After purchasing my fishing supplies, I was heading for the side door as I passed through the toy department, two black men with their little kids were heading toward me. As they approached, in a kidding way, I zigged and zagged, finally passing between the kids with a smile and a "Hi!" A few steps later, I heard the little girl ask, "Can he come to our house?" I can still picture those two kids as they looked back with their big smiles!

One Saturday as I sat there with my bobber bobbin' and still no bites, I asked the old black man that was a fixture there on most summer mornings, "Sir, I notice that you always seem to have a lot of fish on that string." He would sometimes have perch, carp and catfish on his lifeline, which hung in the water next to him.

"Well, son, today I'm usin' dough balls. Other days, I may use crawfish tails. Just never know what they lookin' fer."

That was really not much help, but he was one helluva fisherman. I tried his suggestions, as well as minnows, canned tuna and worms. I never did catch a fish there, or anywhere! I donated my gear to a neighbor kid down around 82nd and Harper.

Today, June 15th, was not a good day for a Cub kid like me. We lost one of our all-time heroes, Andy Pafko. Todd is going to be very surprised and upset with today's baseball trade. Todd is now in infantry training, and it's unlikely that he'll be reading any sports pages. More than likely, he's on some rifle range and catching an hour or two of sleep each night. I believe that he really wanted to support his country in this so-called Cold War. When we were younger, he was always right on top of the action in WWII. He knew where each branch of the military was and could always recount the week's events at the asking. I think that the Marines at Iwo Jima on Mount Surabachi have always been emblazoned in Todd's mind. Dad (WWI), Percy and Buck (WWII) were all veterans, so Todd was not going to stay home and play. He left his best girl, Betty Lou, the boxing ring, his baseball glove and his snazzy '47 red Plymouth convertible. I just know that every time Betty Lou hears Nat "King" Cole singing "Too Young," she's going to cry her eyes out, 'cause that's their song.

The Cubs and Dodgers made a four-for-four trade prior to today's game. We lost our favorite Cub, Andy "48" Pafko, along with Johnny Schmitz, Rube Walker and Wayne "Twig" Terwilliger to da' Bums. Our end of the deal seems, somehow, insignificant. Losing Handy Andy and Schmitz, with his big jug-handle curve ball, is just unforgivable to Cub fans throughout the Windy City. Our new guys are Bruce Edwards, Gene Hermanski, Eddie Miksis and Joe Hatten. All eight of these players appeared in their new uniforms this afternoon. Andy wore his number 48, but it just didn't look right, because it wasn't right! The Cubs got the best of it today. Bruce Edwards knocked in four runs, three of them on a homer off Carl Erskine. Eddie Miksis looked okay at second base, but I miss Twig already. Andy hit his thirteenth homer in a losing cause against his old mates. He was also injured, and will be out of their lineup for awhile. If the stupid Cubs' bosses hadn't traded him, he'd still be okay. From this day forward, when Andy comes home to Wrigley Field, I'll pray for a walk. This is my only option. I surely can't pull for him to drive one on to Waveland Avenue anymore. Those days are gone forever, darn it!

I tended to be a bit of a truant in my younger years. When I couldn't hide anywhere else, I would head to The Swamp on 83rd, or I'd sneak into Gill Stadium. (Okay, Southsiders, do you remember where that diamond was located?) I loved taking little naps in that dugout. Like a lot of young guys, my dream was to be a big leaguer, and that dugout was heaven to me. Having my books, paper and pencil, this was a great time to write to Todd.

"Dear Todd: By now, I'm sure that you have heard that Handy Andy is with the Bums. I cried that night when I went to bed. He was our favorite Cub, ever! Dee Fondy is still hittin' around .300, but the Cubs just don't seem to win when he hits. In fact, they just don't seem to win very many games at all. Without Andy, we might end up in the cellar. I ditched school this morning. I'm in the dugout at Gill Stadium writing this note to you. I wish we were goin' on the B route today. Love, Your Buddy & Bro, Curt"

"Curt, wanna take your new bike on an adventurous journey?" Luke had a plan; he was going to lead the two of us all the way to the Lever Brothers plant in Whiting, Indiana. "We'll have to tell Mom that we're gonna be gone most of the day. I'll just say that we are goin' on one of our Saturday field trips. We can make some sandwiches and take some money for pop. Let's get up real early. I think 5:30 will be good."

"I have no idea how to go there, Luke."

"Don't worry, Curt, that's my job. Just promise that you'll do just as I say and be careful all day!"

By 6:00 AM, we were heading south on Anthony Avenue. Somehow, we ended up going east on 119th. After a pop stop in some strange neighborhood, we arrived at Indianapolis Boulevard. Both of us were now feeling a bit lost and not too sure about this adventure. We had smelled bakeries, Italian sandwich shops, grilled onions and hamburgers on almost every block.

"There, Curt, up there, see the Rinso box? That's our goal. We made it, we have really made it! Just like Lewis and Clark, this is history!"

The ride back seemed easier but much longer. Neither of us had peddled this much all year. All of these years later, I still marvel at Luke's gutsy idea. My estimate, and it's only an estimate, would be ten miles each way. It was almost dark as we opened the yard gate. We were exhausted! All that I can remember about that evening was the worry about Mom or Dad finding out where we had been. I'm sure that we both had no problem sleeping that night! Funny thing, some considered Luke a bit of a sissy because he was never in any fights. Well, they were so wrong about Luke. He would climb to the highest point of any tree. He would jump off of roofs and places that I wouldn't dare to go! He would hold a firecracker as the wick burned toward the business end, just to test his young masculinity. He was simply not a combative kid.

"School's out, school's out, teacher let the monkeys out!" That's the cry as we race down the school stairs. All of those hot, sticky, miserable days of tests are over. We're all seventh graders now. At least I think so— there are a couple of kids that weren't too sure this morning. Hope they made it, I really do! It's a day of pure bliss for the kids at the Catholic schools on Chicago's Southside. Summer vacation is finally here. The publics still have a week or so to go. Tough break!"

Baseball on My Mind ©

WORKIN' KID

"This is going to be a great summer vacation, Mom! Dad is going to give me the job on the print dryer for about two months. He says that this way, I'll still have plenty of time for baseball and other fun after the Fourth of July! I can hardly believe that I will be making twelve bucks a week, plus my bonus money. My math tells me that I'll knock down about a hundred bucks by the Fourth of July. Plus, I'll get some money from Dad for painting the outside of the fence. One thing is for sure, Mom. I'm going to get one of those BBQ Grills from Sears. I'll be the chef at our Fourth of July bash. I may even buy a real baseball uniform from *Baseball Digest*."

"One thing is for sure, I'm going to buy myself a resin bag at Morey Mages sports store. I've always wanted to have one so that I can get a good grip on the ball, like Bob Rush and those guys. It keeps your hands from getting too sweaty. Wow, what a great summer. Yeah, it'll be a real great summer. The first thing in the morning, Dad's gonna show me how to run the print dryer. He said that it would be a good idea to eat a good breakfast every morning because this was grown-up work and the days are going to be long."

Dad said that I could play my Emerson radio while I work. It was fun being at work with Dad. He had one helluva sense of humor and many time-worn clichés. When something really cracked Dad up, he'd say, "That's funnier than the Pope in pink tights!" No matter how many times we heard that, we would bust up every time. It was certainly an image that was hard for anyone to conjure up. I don't think that one would have gone over very well with Fr. Walsh; but then again, you just never know!

First Week on the Job ©

My first payday had arrived. I was squeezing twelve dollars and an extra few bucks in my fist. Dad said that this was an exceptionally busy week. The big guys received their overtime salary, so Dad thought that I deserved a bit more too! Percy drove me to Sears because he knew that I'd never be able to carry my purchase home. I bought that red enameled BBQ Grill that I had been admiring for some time. During the upcoming weeks I embellished my BBQ supplies with a set of wood-handled, stainless steel utensils and a big bag of hickory chips. The family was still using this red grill when I left for the Army many years later. I still have those "made in the USA" utensils.

As the summer rolled on, I got pretty quick at the dryer. I was always staying ahead of the printers, and that allowed for some fun time. I had my glove and a pink Hi-Flyer ball on the shelf behind me. I would take the timer out to the yard with me. There was usually about fifteen minutes before the next batch. Heck, that's enough time to throw a couple of quick innings off the wall. "I'm determined to learn some new pitches this summer, but I can't do that with this pink rubber ball. Gotta get to the park."

I can now go to Grand Crossing Park on my bike. Last year Dad said, "No, that's too far for an eleven-year-old." This year, I'm twelve and I have my new Schwinn, and the park is only about a mile away. Dad said, "Okay, but only on Saturdays, Curt!"

After the Fourth of July, I'll be able to go any day and get there real early so that I can be there for a whole game. I already know some of the guys that might be there. There's Vinnie, Chink, Banana-Nose, Vich and a lot more of the Italian guys. A lot of the guys show up rain or shine. The Italian guys are usually real good players. I know that Vinnie sure as hell is. He's about three years older than I am. He's not real big, but he's a muscular little guy. He can pitch, play the infield and man, can he hit! He can also run like the wind!

Chief Don Eagle Dad's Favorite Wrestler

The photo job turned out to have a feature that I hadn't thought about. I am seeing a lot of pictures of kids from the neighborhood and school, and some famous faces. Last week, some pictures of Babe Ruth came through. They had been taken a couple of years ago, right before he died. I'm not supposed to tell, but Dad printed some extras for me. I've seen pictures of Jack Dempsey, Luke Appling, Pinky Lee and Tony Zale too. Yesterday, I saw a set of pictures that were taken at The International Amphitheatre on Halsted Street. The famous wrestler Chief Don Eagle was in several of them. Now, you know that Dad printed a few extras of those prints. Dad just loves wrestling. He says that he knows that it's fake, but he still loves to watch it on TV. We all do! Just before Todd went into the Corps, he and Dad were fortunate enough to meet Chief Don Eagle at the Palm Grove Inn. I guess that he chatted with them a bit and signed Todd's napkin. Todd probably stashed it somewhere around the house. Poor Chief—he ended up committing suicide in 1966.

Unfortunately, Peggy Sue's parents never come in, so there are no pictures of that little sweetie to be seen. Most of the girls from school go to the photo shop in South Chicago because it's owned by one of the girls' folks. Too bad, 'cause most of the vacation shots that I do see are of kids that I don't care much about.

Wow, having my radio next to me is just great. I hear the top ten and all of the new songs all day long. Johnnie Ray has been beltin' out "The Little White Cloud That Cried" and "Cry." One of the well known disc jockeys on WIND is saying that Johnnie is blind. That's a bunch of bull! Actually, he sees just fine. The guy happens to wear a hearing aid. Blind? That dumb DJ should do his homework like us kids do. Teresa Brewer, Patti Page, Perry Como, Eddie Fisher, I have my own concert everyday, right here at work!

As close as I was to the sales counter, I had the opportunity to see a lot of the characters that came into Dad's store. There were the newspaper reporters, the real estate guys and the insurance agents with their gross-looking photos that I never wanted to look at as I worked. The Coke driver and I became good buddies. He always looked so neat in his uniform. It was a soft tan with thin red stripes. He was a veteran of WWII, and that qualified him as a hero in my book. He taught me how to load the Coke machine. It had this large, spring-loaded wheel inside. It held eighty-six bottles of pop. I was warned about the strength of that wheel and the damage that it could do if I were to make a wrong move. "It'll take your arm off, Curt! You need to do it just as I do. Watch me!" This extra duty netted me free Cokes for the summer. All I had to do was keep score, and he'd credit Dad for those that I drank.

There was one guy that had a face that was made of Silly Putty. At least that's how it appeared to Junior and me. He had this strange ability to contort his face like a rubber mask. He could look like four or five masks within a few moments. One day, as this man was leaving, Junior asked Dad who he was. Dad, busy as usual, simply said, "Oh, just some clown!"

Lo and behold, the next time Junior spotted him in the store, he asked, "Are you really a clown?" From that time on, we referred to him as "Mr. McClown"!

Before the summer came to an end, I had a bit of an accident. We were hanging around in the new home that was under construction just across from 1540. Julie's had been selling these neat little clay pipes for a dime. Each one had a different facial figure on its bowl. Some were dogs, and there were bears and tigers. Mine was a dog. An idea had struck a few of us. Luke, Sean and I were going to smoke our pipes. "Let's try to borrow a couple of cigarettes from home, and we'll smoke the tobacco in our pipes tonight."

We had our smoke in the privacy of this construction site and were all feeling a little bit woozy. As I darted across 83rd, there was a black '37 Chevy coming from the west with no headlights on. I was hit and thrown several feet. My head landed just inches from the curb. I wasn't even crying, just scared stiff that I'd be in trouble. "Luke, I hope that Dad or Mom don't smell the cigarette smoke on my breath." Two young guys jumped out of their Chevy and came to my aid. Fortunately for me, the extent of my injuries was a big fat swollen and sprained ankle. Neither Mom nor Dad ever detected the smell of smoke on my breath. At least, I don't think that they did.

Christmas is very special in another way for Junior and me this year. Mom and Dad are letting us have our own little Christmas tree in our bedroom. It's almost Christmas day and the tree lot on Stony has plenty of little ones left. Between the two of us, we talk the guy out of a four-foot beauty for just two bucks. We haul our Alpine treasure up the back stairs. An old stand in the basement is plenty strong enough for our little pine tree. With only the leftover ornaments and lights, we put together quite a nice tree. We each manufactured a few homemade gems too! Now, we don't mind going to bed a little early. We lie there and tell Christmas stories of past years. "Luke got this and Sis got that," and so on. As we jump into bed on Sunday evening, we both say, simultaneously, **"I can hardly believe that tomorrow is Christmas Eve!"**

Spring has brought some nice, warm weather to our Southside. Buck and I decided to clean the basement. This was a chance to really give the ol' basement a do-over. Dad installed a new oil heating system as well as a gas water heater this winter. There is no longer any need for the coal bin or the old hot water furnace. Buck knew that I loved to do sweaty jobs. I always referred to this as "changing my oil." I'd say, a little sweating is good for anybody!

"The first project is the toughest one, Curt. We're gonna knock the coal bin apart and haul the lumber up to the prairie." Buck was advising me of today's goals as we went through all of the tools, Dad's and mine. "Here, Curt, hang on to this crowbar. I'm tryin' to find a small sledgehammer. Don't you guys have a damn sledgehammer anywhere around here? We need to knock these railroad ties off with something heavy!"

"Buck, relax and let me go up to the back room. There's a big one up there. Be right back!"

Soon, we were ripping this piece of history to bits. I kept thinking of Luther. This was his bench, or somethin'! Maybe, just maybe, he'd never return if we removed his seat. I hated this little concrete room out here in the back. It was always dark and damp, and it had too many nooks and crannies to suit me. I remember when I was little; I would hardly ever come out here. I knew better than to tell Buck or Todd that I was afraid of anything! Nevertheless, I still hated this damn dark hole. It was spooky and I wasn't the only Erler kid that thought so, I know!

We worked our tails off 'til noon, or so. "Break time. I need a smoke!" Buck was reaching for his pack of Chesterfields. That's all that he ever smoked. He pulled some change from his gray chinos. "Here, why don't you run up to the store and grab us a couple of bottles of Coke? I'll be out back. Here, grab a couple of those two-by-fours on your way up!"

When we returned from our break, I went to my bench and tuned my Emerson to WIND. I needed some top tunes to keep me motivated. Joni James was singing her big hit, "Why Don't You Believe Me?" I was beginning to think that I might, just might, be in love with her. I told Buck this and he just gave me his little snicker. "Heck," I said, "she's from right here on our Southside. (Joni was actually born Giovanna Carmella Babbo.) I think that she's a Bowen High chick. Maybe I'll get to see her someday."

By late afternoon the basement was lookin' mighty empty. I'm quite sure that Luther thought so too! As we were hauling the old cast iron water heater out to the gangway, Buck said, "Leave that here. It'll get you a few bucks from the Rags and Old Iron Man."

Finally, I had figured it out: "Rags-O-Lyon" really does make sense—rags and old iron. Yeah, that makes a lotta sense!

We hosed the basement down with hot water from Mom's utilty sink. Buck walked around throwin' handfuls of Spic 'n' Span all over the floor. He handed me an old broom. He was also armed, with the big push broom. "You start over there, in the front corner, and I'll start back here. Let's scrub 'er down!" Had I said something about sweaty jobs? This was one heck of a workout!

I was thinking, "In a way, it's a good thing that Todd isn't here, because I couldn't pitch an inning today!" The finished product, however, was the sweetest smelling basement anywhere! As Kay Starr finished up her number one song, "Wheel of Fortune," Buck had this kid finished up too! "I'm whipped, big brother. Let's go upstairs 'n' see what Mom's cookin' up for supper!"

As the next few weeks of spring rolled on, I managed to get all of those six-by-six support pillars painted with battleship gray paint. "A new roller rink has been born!" I thought to myself. This basement was great for skating and Band-Aid hockey. I would use a new roll of Johnson & Johnson adhesive tape for a puck. I placed a chair at either end of my rink as a goal. I'd have my own one-man game while listening to the Blackhawks on my Emerson. Bob Elson, the Sox announcer, would call the last half of the Hawk home games on WCFL. This made my games much more realistic as one of the Bentley Brothers would shoot 'n' score!

Junior - Luke - Mom - Buck - Curt ©

Just for the record, Buck's idea of saving that cast iron water heater netted me five bucks from the Rags and Old Iron Man!

"With my basement all squeaky clean, I think I'll go down and putter around at my bench, Mom. I'll be back up before nine." Down the stairs I go, anxious to see the new basement at night. The radio is still tuned to WIND as I pull the light switch. My first thoughts are, "Wow, this is great. This place is so clean. It smells like Mom's laundry hanging out in the yard! I'm ready for some good music while I putter around. I'm going to rearrange my whole workbench. I sure can't leave it all messy anymore."

The DJ mentions the time. Geez, its 8:45, I better head upstairs. I turn to the open stairway behind me. These steps have no backs on them. You can see right through them. "Oh, no, I don't believe this. He's found a new haunting place—under the staircase!" Luther is in a standing position for the first time. Actually, he's kind of hunched over and peering through the steps at me. He's peering, but I can't see the color of his eyes. I'm not really convinced that there are any eyes there! I wasn't in the habit of using swear words, at least not out loud. "Damn it, damn it!" All I could think is, "How in the hell am I gonna get out of here? He'll grab my ankles if I go up those stairs!" I don't know what makes me think that this will work, but it does! I grab a cut-off piece of two-by-four and prepare for my move. With my hand on the light string, all in one motion I pitch the wood toward the rear of the basement and run like hell!

Without any doubt, this is the loudest that I've ever heard my heart pounding! Now, I know that my new basement is still not just mine! As I arrive upstairs still scared out of my wits, it's the same old scene. Mom is brewing an evening pot of coffee, and everyone else is oblivious to my trials. I wash my hands and face and hurry through the dining room, thinking, "Good night, you lucky people!"

Curt & Junior Playin' Guns ©

Did someone say "summer vacation"? Well yes, but this summer would be hampered somewhat. Sister Leonard felt it necessary to send a few of us boys to summer school. We would be attending St. Alibe's for about five weeks. The classroom hours were short, but just long enough to mess with a kid's agenda. There were two cool nuns there to teach us. They were from down South, and they talked kinda' funny. Everything seemed to start with, "Y'all." They taught us just two subjects, English and math—y'know arithmetic! Why me? Those were my two strongest subjects. This just made no sense at all. I would have thought that Sister

Leonard would have said something like, "What those boys need is to get some religion!"

All in all, it wasn't a bad experience at all. There were more laughs in those classrooms in a few weeks than in all of seventh grade! We loved those nuns a lot. Riding home on the Schwinn on our last day, I said to Dave, "Too bad that St. Felicitas can't recruit them." Dave would ride on my handlebars each day. Each day, on the way home, he bought me a cold pop at Liebner's candy store.

I'm really counting on a lot of baseball at Grand Crossing, or anywhere else that I can play. I also have to paint Percy's garage. I promised that I would, and there's sure to be a reward!

It seems that wherever a project would take me, I'd bring my Emerson portable radio. When I could, I'd just hook up an extension cord. This way, I saved on those great big expensive batteries. Music was always my fuel.

As Jo Stafford warbles "You Belong to Me" and Buddy Morrow wails away with "Night Train," I begin my painting. Percy has let me pick the colors. It's been a nasty lookin' green since it was built. It's time for a new look. It's going to be a chocolate brown with a cream trim. It seems that most of the garages up and down our alley just sit there and look ugly. I want ours to knock 'em out! As I apply the final strokes to the window frames, Al Martino is crooning one for the girls out there, "Here in My Heart."

I believe that it went all the way to number one on the charts. I met Al many years later and gave him a copy of this 45rpm. It was a disc jockey copy on red vinyl. He was most appreciative as he responded, "Gee, it's been a long time since the Chicago days, thanks Curt!"

Percy walks out with a Coke for me as I am cleaning the brushes and my cream-colored hands. He's very surprised that I'm finishing it up today. "That's quite a nice job for thirteen-year-old boy, damn nice. I like the way you did the trim. Wow, you even shined all of the windows! Hang on—I'll be right back, Curt."

When he returns, he hands me a crisp twenty dollar bill. "Okay, the painting season is over," I declare to myself. "This will be great. I think that my baseball season will begin tomorrow!

For some guys it's the thought of hitting one out in the ninth. Yeah, that's cool, but I have always loved the challenge of that batter just sixty feet, six inches away. They come in all shapes and sizes. Some have a lot of ability, others just a lot of attitude. From the time that I knew how to hold, throw, catch and hit that little sphere, I was hooked on pitching. I've often heard that hitting that ball with a round stick is the toughest feat in sports. With the ball approaching at various speeds and from different directions, this seems like a logical assumption. I try to keep that thought alive!

Todd had worked with me for a long time before he became a Marine. He taught me the basics, like hitting the strike zone, throwing hard and not giving up when things get kind of tough. He was always patient while he created his pretend games, which gave me a feel for actual competition. Todd could sure frustrate me at times, though. He'd have me in the ninth inning with some nobody pinch hitter coming up. The game depended on this batter. *Crack,* my best pitch sails on to Waveland Avenue. The game is suddenly over. I lost!

Todd would usually know the lineups of the Cubs opponent that day. When the Dodgers were in town, I'd be facing Snyder, Hodges, Robinson, Campy, Reese and the rest. He'd have a pre-game meeting with me. "Okay, kid, Snyder's in a bad slump. Just keep the ball down and away. Campy's hittin' everything in sight. Stay up and in his face." Believe me, if I didn't follow the game plan, I got hammered!

There is a guy on the Phillies that was to be my nemesis. Todd had predetermined this fact. Dick Whitman, who in the hell has ever heard of a Dick Whitman? He was about a .225 hitter with some power. Todd instructed me to throw him my best fastball, but never shoulder high to this "swing for the fences" guy. If it's too slow, he'll rip one past my ribcage. If it's up a little bit, Todd will be announcing, "Gone, outta here!" I can hear it now! The toughest part about Todd's little scenario was that he always saved this guy for me to face in the ninth. Todd would always announce what the Cubs did in their half of the inning.

It's the eighth, and the Cubs finally got a couple of runs. Sauer hit a two-run homer onto Waveland. I feel pretty good as I enter the ninth with a 2 to 0 lead. My arm by this time is about to fall off. Balls and strikes become much more defined. First guy up drills my first pitch out on Sheffield. Now it's 2 to 1, and I'm pretty rattled. The next guy goes easily on my first pitch. It's a slow-rolling ground out to Smalley. Now I'm losing arm strength and control. Todd knows it. It's his way with "the kid."

One out, two to go, and still holding a one-run lead. With all that I can muster up, I throw three as hard as I can. Frankly, I don't give a damn where they go. I get the benefit of the doubt on a couple and strike the guy out. Two out and the arm feels like lead. I walk Andy Seminick, their catcher, on four pitches. Up comes my nemesis, Dick Whitman. I always have to hear about the sneer on his face, the kicking and digging in the box and the flexing of his muscles. Sometimes I'd get a couple of strikes on him. In this case, I just throw as hard as I can and wait for Todd to announce my fate. Sometimes I lost, but as a rule Todd would have my hero, Andy Pafko, making a sensational running catch in the ivy. I ran across a Mr. Whitman's bubble gum card several years later. I wore it for weeks inside of my baseball spikes just for spite!

With a well-earned victory under my belt, I'm ready for a bottle of Coke. But this is not to be. Instead, I hear this: "Kid, I'm in trouble in the nightcap. I sure could use an inning from you." Here I am dreaming about signing autographs at the Waveland Avenue gate, and I've got to pitch even more.

An inning my fanny, it was often two or three. At dinner I could hardly get the spoon to my mouth. Dad would notice my struggles with my eating utensils. While everyone else was enjoying Mom's pork chops, I couldn't get my right hand to my mouth. "Curt, what's wrong with you?"

I would just look sheepishly at Todd and say, "Oh, nothin' Dad. My arm's just a little sore today, that's all." I knew that he knew, but nothing more would be said. In today's world, this would be unacceptable, but that's how it was back then, on the Southside!

"Todd's not here to work with me anymore, so I'll need to learn more on my own. I need to start learning to throw some of the harder pitches."

My New Baseball Grips ©

Todd in Korea – 1952 ©

"Hey, Mom, I'm going to ride over to Grand Crossing to play some ball. Without Todd around, I need to find someone that loves baseball as much as he and I do. I can sorta throw a curveball, but it doesn't always work. I do know how to fool 'em with my let-up pitch. I'll be real happy to play against real live guys again this summer."

I head for Grand Crossing to see who is at the park. Everyone seems to have their own little neck of the woods. This is certainly one of mine. This place always has enough guys around to have some kind of a game, even when we have to close one of the outfields. When we don't have enough guys to fill all of the positions, we close either right or left at the batter's choice. If you hit one to the closed field, you're automatically out! Vinnie from 82nd and a bunch of his "dago" buddies are there. There are quite a few guys that are much older than me. Hey, as long as you have the attitude that you can play, they don't care how big or old you are. They just don't want any crybabies!

It turns out to be more of a practice session, just a lot of fun! Most of my time is spent shaggin' fly balls, but that's okay with me. The beauty of our kind of baseball was that back then, baseball wasn't some psychological learning experience, it was a kid's game, played by kids and controlled by kids.

After a good workout, I'm headin' home and thinking, "Hey, I've got a little summer cash in my jeans. I'll just stop at Kladis' on 82nd Street on my way home. I'll grab my favorite summer treat, a nice thick coffee soda. Maybe that little redhead from Avalon Park School will be there. I wish I could think of her name—Carol, I think."

One cool, clear March evening, Percy and I took a ride to the East Side. He had to drop off some photos for a customer over that way. He always enjoyed having one of us kids to keep him company. "Curt, do you want to take a little spin with me in about half an hour?"

"Yeah, I'm almost done with this dumb homework. Don't go without me."

We pulled away in his new '53 Pontiac Catalina. It had a two-tone paint job, a laurel green top and soft, creamy green on the bottom. I loved the smell of the leather interior. He had installed wire wheels. This was one cool lookin' ride! The *Dragnet* theme was playing as we began our little journey. Dad used to tell us that a lot of Slavs lived on the east side. I was never too sure what a Slav was, but who cared anyway? I did like going to that area because there were a lot of tracks and trains over that way. Like so many boys, I loved trains of all kinds. There were steel mills, factories, little shops and cool old wooden houses in this area of the Southside. I said to Percy, "I like it over here. If the Slavs live here, they're really lucky."

As soon as he had accomplished his mission, he pulled up at a neighborhood candy store. He pulled out a buck and said, "Would you run in and grab a *Sun-Times* for me? Why don't you pick up a couple of candy bars for us too?"

I jumped out and ran into the store. As soon as I hit the door, I could smell someone's dinner cooking. "Cabbage and ... what? Cabbage and somethin', not sure what it was. Yuk!" I heard the lady screaming back to someone in their humble little abode behind the store. It sounded like Polish, but I wasn't sure.

"What d' ya' want, boy?"

I dropped the paper on the gray and pink linoleum-covered counter. "I got the paper, and do you have any Old Nick bars?"

"Yeah, that's sixteen cents."

With my big transaction completed, I raced back to the Pontiac. Percy immediately noticed the picture on the front page. **STALIN IS DEAD** the headlines read. There was a very large picture of this man lying in a coffin. I took a quick peek and then turned away. I had never seen a dead person. Sure, I had seen the war pictures of dead bodies, but nothing so close, nothing so defined as this close-up shot. This image stayed with me for many years. I did not like seeing that at all!

Getting Old! ©

FRIDAY NIGHT DANCES

Friday night dances were held quite often during our final year at St. Felicitas. Most of the kids in our parish had pretty cool basements that allowed us party goers a bit of privacy. These little socials were usually hosted by the girls in our class. I'm quite sure that their moms were to be credited with a large amount of the preparations. I know, for a fact, they were aware of most of our activities while in their homes.

Most parents, however, were not likely aware of the kissing games that were often on the agenda at these little social events. Most of the guys were less inclined to get excited about this than the girls were. Guys can be big chickens at times like this! There was one girl that we used to kid about when we were away from the girls. She was known to virtually pick a guy up and give him a big kiss. I was fortunate enough to escape this little exercise. On the other hand, there were some girls that would not play these games.

The main activity was girls dancing with girls. We guys were usually hanging around the utilty tubs that were full of ice and bottles of Coca-Cola and 7-Up. The phonograph was a big attraction too. Dave, Jack and I were mesmerized when we first heard Bill Haley and The Comets singing "Rock the Joint" and "Crazy Man, Crazy." This was a brand new sound on a record label that we had never seen before. This bright orange-labeled 78 rpm disc read "Essex Records, Phila, Pa."

Having a big sis as my party planner, I was fortunate enough to pull off three neat get-togethers during our final year. A Halloween party was held in the back room of Dad's store. Sis and I worked for days to convert this old darkroom into a dance hall. I'm sure that this was the most unusual venue of the year. The floors were as bumpy as a washboard from years of numerous photo chemicals that coated the once-hardwood floor. Along one wall there were these six-foot-deep ceramic developing tanks. Everywhere you would look, there was something that said "Kodak."

Nevertheless, it was one large room with plenty of room for rockin' and rollin'!

Being the host and having this inside information, I had the opportunity to ask Peggy Sue long before the other guys could have. By the time I arrived home on the day that the invitations had been hand-delivered, she had agreed to go with me. "Peggy Sue has confirmed," I yelled to Sis as I entered the kitchen. "Fantastic, just fantastic! Peggy Sue will be my date on Halloween!"

Mom and Sis were happy for me, but not half as happy as I was. This girl drew boys like an open bottle of 7-Up draws wasps! "Happy Halloween, Mom, Happy Halloween, Sis, Happy Halloween, world!" Halloween was still two weeks away, but it was time to celebrate.

The Halloween Party was actually held on Friday the 30th, which was our typical dance night. I proudly walked to Peggy Sue's house to pick her up. We talked quite a bit as we slowly walked back to 83rd Street. This was pure bliss for me. I was with Peggy Sue, alone in the evening, for the first time ever! As we wandered east down 83rd Street, we could see a couple of cars dropping off some kids. That was okay; Sis was there to greet them.

"That looks like Kathy," Peggy Sue said as she spotted her best friend heading for the door. Once at the scene, the girls gravitated to one side of the room and the boys to the other side. So, what's new? "Til I Waltz Again with You" by little Tessy Brewer was the hit of the night. "You, you, you, there's no one but you," by the Ames Brothers, caught my attention all evening. This, of course, was due to my special guest. We may have broken the world's record for Coke consumption that night.

When the bewitching hour arrived, it was time to end this wonderful night of fun and friends. Several of the kids were picked up by their parents. Sis was at the door to greet each car or parent on foot. A bunch of us guys decided that we'd walk some of the girls home. This, of course, wasn't going to give me a chance for that very unlikely good night kiss. We all laughed, and some of the chicks were singing, *"Don't let the stars get in your eyes, don't let the moon break your heart."* The guys were checkin' out all of the new Fords 'n' Chevys. It was one great Halloween for this fourteen-year-old Southsider! On the weekend, some flowers were left for "someone" by "someone" on a porch on Dorchester Avenue.

Monday was a free day because All Saints Day fell on Sunday this year. As soon as my feet hit the playground on Tuesday morning, I could hear Dave as he ran toward me. "Damn, did you hear that Mother Audrey has heard about the kissing games?"

"Oh yeah? Who told, do ya' know?"

Dave replied with something like this. Nope, it was probably some of the girls that weren't asked. That's their way of gettin' even.

Sure enough, soon after Sister Alfreda began her classes, Mother Audrey came stomping in. The theme of our big lecture was, "Shop-worn Girls." She was actually shaking as she spoke. The party goers were singled out and given some kind of penance. Y'know, write, "I will not kiss until I'm forty-five years old" a million times or something like that. Dave and I were chuckling after school. "Can you dig it, shop-worn girls?"

Goodbye to St. Felicitas ©

Junior is now "Pepsi," and he loves his new nickname! One of the mechanics at the Gulf station has dubbed him this because he has this habit of consuming several ten-ounce bottles of Pepsi most every day. There is a vending machine in the waiting room that dispenses this unusual size of Pepsi. Junior—oops, I mean Pepsi—is known to hang around this little device at very opportune moments. The big guys are suckers for his fun-loving and friendly personality. So Pepsi it is, from now on!

One more big party day to go, and then it's over, all over! It was June 14th, 1953, and we were finally graduating. Such bliss! It was now approaching 4:00 PM and the nuns were giving us our last warnings about behavior and what they expected from us that afternoon. We wore powder-blue caps and gowns, ribbons, the whole deal. It was time to see what else Chi-Town had to offer. It would be on to Mt. Carmel, Mendel, and Leo. For Curt, it would be Homer High--ugh! The girls went on to St. Aquinas, Loretta, Mercy and other local high schools. It was "Goodbye" to that big red brick school and the wee little brown brick church. These two buildings taught us so much more than we had realized.

Many of the kids held an open house at their respective homes. Mom and Dad let me throw a little bash in the yard. Sis once again did most of the planning and serving. I was able to do some DJ work and still revel with my friends. Needless to say, the phonograph was blasting at full volume. I'm sure that it could be heard all the way to the convent, and maybe the rectory. We sure hoped so! There was plenty of Bill Haley played this night.

We served fruit punch in a great big punch bowl. Sis concocted this brew from the brand new juice of the day, Hawaiian fruit punch, which was mixed with seltzer, fruit juices and 7-Up. There were snacks of all kinds to go with it. Sis had also stashed some of my favorite Canfield's pop, the new raspberry. Eddie Hubbard had been pitching this and the new strawberry flavor every night on his Top Ten radio show, *The ABC Club*. There was a quart bottle in the old clubhouse for me. I was wearing my box toe blue suede shoes from Flagg Brothers at 63rd and Halsted. Most of the guys were wearing box toes of some kind. Pegged pants and turned-up collars were happenin' too. Heck, we were rock and roll cats.

A special event for me this summer evening was my fist pack of Lucky Strikes! Dad had caught me smoking in the basement earlier that year. We were boxing in our makeshift ring down there. Dad detected the smell and had a talk with me about sports and cigarettes. Unfortunately, Dad didn't make too much of an impression on me with this pitch. Considering that five of my brothers, Mom and Dad himself were smokers, I wasn't going to go down easily. One day a few weeks later, a conversation turned to smoking. Dad had changed the rules a bit. He said, "At least wait until you graduate."

Todd had just returned from seventeen months in Korea. He was home on a thirty-day leave. His presence was great on its own, but he also knew of Dad's rules. Todd, being Todd, and always my buddy, had left a nice fresh pack of Luckies on the picnic table for his "kid brother." Now, you know what a hot commodity they became that evening! I shared them with my buddies as we wandered from open house to open house.

When morning came, Mom saw the pack on the kitchen table. There were only a couple left in the pack. "Curt, did you smoke all of these cigarettes?"

"No, Mom, I only smoked a few. I shared them with the guys."

I had learned so much more than the academics during the past eight years. My education at St. Felicitas was embellished with discipline, respect, reverence, integrity, a deep faith and love! I owe so much to the nuns that endured me during those eight years, each of them making her impression(s) on me in her own way. In some cases, that meant, "Ouch!" I thank Sister Nila for being so special during my third and fourth grades. I was very shy during classes, but she had some special effect on me. I often refer to Sister Nila as my Saint Nila! Thanks to Sister Alfreda for her patience as I grew a bit less shy and somewhat testy. Father Cusack was always my quiet mentor. He allowed this non-Catholic kid the opportunity to be somewhat subjective on matters of religion. The fact still remains, as helpful and kind as the nuns were, I still liked lunchtime, final bell, recess and summer vacation much more than the books. The school carnivals weren't bad either.

St. Felicitas carnival time was time to check out the new rides and games. This was also a good time to follow the girls. What would a carnival be without girls? I knew that there'd be a Tilt-A-Whirl, my favorite. I've never been big on heights so I was not a ferris wheel fan. To be on that top car when the guy stops the wheel was not my idea of fun. If I was with someone that considered it funny to "rock the boat," I'd threaten them with their life. Of all of the games there, I loved knockin' over the bottles with those "made in Japan" baseballs. They weren't real baseballs. They were cheaply made baseballs without the horsehide cover.

This was the first night of the annual event. It was the also the first night that there would be no nuns or priests that could tell me what to do. All I could think was, "Freedom, oh this feels good. No silly rules, no rulers, just fun. I hope that I do see Father Cusack, though. Father has always let me speak my mind and cast my non-Catholic questions his way. I'm not Catholic and that is, for sure, a handicap around here. I've lived with that for eight years at this school, and still seemed to survive. At least now, I'm on my own. Heck I'm a customer. Yeah, a customer, how 'bout that?"

It was getting close to getting home time when I spotted Ron. Ron had been in my class for all eight years at Felicitas. His nickname was "Ronnie the Cat" because he always wore the latest styles. He sometimes wore stuff that we hadn't even seen yet. He was the first guy that I ever saw wearing draped pants. These were cut so that the pant legs around the thighs were big and baggy. The secret is to buy them with a longer inseam than you normally wear. Then have them fitted and cut to your length. Voila, you got yourself a pair of cool-lookin' drapes! Ron was not shy about wearing unusual colors. During our eight years at Felicitas, Ron and I had never really hung around together. That was about to change. During the last hour or so before heading home, we really hit it off! Ron loved music, hot rods and cool threads, and he also smoked.

We each purchased a one dollar chance on the cool '53 Ford Victoria that the church was raffling off as a fund raiser. It was Flamingo Red with a continental kit. We also played the cigarette game for awhile and Ron won several packs. This game was played with either, quarters or full packs of smokes as your wager. The counter around the booth's perimeter had images of different brands of cigarettes painted on it. You would place your wager on the brand that you were betting on. The man at the booth would spin this big roulette-type wheel. If the needle landed on your brand, the wheel would dictate your prize. If you bet on Lucky Strikes, you might win two packs, three packs, whatever it said. You could also just break even with "One Pack" being displayed on the wheel. Ron got hot and won a ton of Chesterfields. As I had already run out of money, he traded some in for my Luckies. He always was a real buddy.

Mr. Fanning was manning the pitching booth one evening and needed some assistance. This was a perfect chance for me, so I offered my services. "Is it okay if I throw some while there are no customers?"

"Sure, Curt, that's fine. You go right ahead. Your activity might draw some attention to the booth ... Not bad, Mr. Erler, not bad at all!"

I had a bit of luck and the bottles seemed to be going down easily. Before very long, the carnival was jam-packed with parishioners and neighbors There were folks from nearby parishes, kids from God knows where. So much for my freebies. It was back to work for me.

Jim Rivera of the White Sox stopped by to say "Hi." Actually, he kind of implied to Ron and me that he liked seeing all of the girls. "Jungle Jim," as he was called, was already drawing a crowd of females. Yeah, maybe this cat was good lookin', but damn, he was 30-plus years old! We don't need him around stealin' our chicks. He had just come over from the St. Louis Browns at the end of the '52 season. He was hitting a whopping .240 or so. Ron was more interested in talking to him than I was. Ron was the Sox fan, not me!

Ron made reference to his old team. "Where do you think the Browns will end up this year?"

He replied quickly: "The cellar, they usually do, don't they?" He was prophetic with his prediction, 'the cellar' it was as they ended up in last place. It was also their last year ever! The 1954 season opened with the new Baltimore Orioles. The Browns were gone forever.

At the end of the evening, Mr. Fanning gave me several of the balls that were showing a bit of wear. These were just fine for our little grounder games. He was always very gracious to everyone, an ever-giving man! My Dad and Percy knew him well from his many visits to Cash Erler's Photo Shop.

The day after Ron and I had met at the carnival, we were back together early in the morning. "What do you want to do?" Ron inquired politely.

"I don't know. What do you wanna do?"

We went back and forth until we decided that it was time for a bottle of Kayo chocolate down at Julie's. That day flew by as we discussed all of the cool things that we'd be doing this summer. We played ball, built model cars, listened to a ton of music, enjoyed the stock car races at 87th Street Speedway, chased a few girls. We both enjoyed our newfound friendship. Summer, in fact, did fly by.

"**Todd has been in an accident!**" Percy was sticking his head out of the front door as Ron and I were sippin' a Coke out in front. It was October 3rd,1953, a day that I'll never forget. "Todd's in the Naval Hospital at Camp Lajeune. He was hit by a car last night. Come on in, Dad will tell you more. Ron, you can come on in too!"

Dad went on to explain what he was told on the phone. It seems that Todd and his buddy, Mc Sweeney, were returning to base after a weekend pass. As they were approaching the main gate, a drunken sergeant and his girlfriend hit them at a pretty high speed. Todd and his friend were thrown some thirty feet or so. Unfortunately, his buddy was killed. Todd was in a coma with serious injuries to his head and leg. I can still recall what my first action was. I walked down the stairs and out the front door. Within minutes, I was lighting a candle at the altar at St. Felicitas Church. I just knew that this would help Todd!

In the morning Dad was talking to Mom: "Todd needs family with him when he becomes conscious again. Winona, you and Sis should go there to support him." Dad, with Sis's assistance, arranged for Mom and her to go to North Carolina and be with Todd. Sis was in her senior year at Homer High. Some kind of plan was worked out for her to continue her studies while she was away.

Todd remained in this coma for many weeks. As soon as it was deemed safe, he was transferred to the Great Lakes Naval Hospital. This was a big relief to all involved. Mom could return to her home and the responsibilities of a Mom. Todd was now able to see more of the family as he recovered. Sis and I would take the North Shore line up to Great Lakes for our Saturday visits. On those long train rides to Great Lakes, we were fueled by the anticipation of seeing Todd. The return ride was always rewarding because we had seen his improvement and got him to laugh a little. This was the case, each and every trip. Sis always made sure that I got my Denver Sandwich candy bar at the little store in the train station in Waukegan. She would sometimes nod off, with her head against the train window on the trip back home.

What a relief, being able to sit at his side. Todd, as expected, was making the best of his injuries. With no further details here, I'll just say this: Todd's motto has always been, "Ya gotta wanna!" Well, he applied this attitude of self-discipline and fortitude for many, many months. For the record, Todd recovered beyond the limits that were handed to him that October evening. He married his one and only love, Betty Lou. He had a very successful career in the insurance business. He and Betty Lou have raised four wonderful kids. They recently celebrated their fiftieth wedding anniversary. God bless them both!

BIG BOY BASEBALL

Baseball, Baseball, Baseball! ©

Summer brings more guys from distant neighborhoods to Grand Crossing Park. Some of them come from as far away as 22nd Street. Many of their dads and moms work at Superior Match Company on 76th Street. Chicago has so many cultures and so many characters! Not unlike our family and neighbors, we are always using ethnic descriptions for our baseball buddies. In our own terminology, we called our friends "dagos," "micks," "Polacks," "krauts," "Slavs," "Serbs,", "cros," "frogs," "wops," "bo-hunks," and one kid had the nickname of "Chink'! He is the first Asian kid that I've known to play baseball. I have the privilege of having two ethnic nicknames. A "kraut" might call me a "frog" and a "frog" might call me a "kraut." You see, it's really all very harmless. Someone at the park dubbed us the "Ethnic All-Stars."

While the main thrust here is playing baseball, it seems that someone is always fighting. I know that I was! Actually, I love quiet times and I enjoy quiet, thoughtful people. Somewhere along the way, I have become very competitive, and this isn't always good. I have too damn much pride and never want to lose, at anything! Nevertheless, I still love people and want them to love me. A punch in the mouth goes away; not being loved does not!

Simmons and his big ass returns to taunt us again. This big kid with the arm of a big leaguer seems to just toy with us some days. He is a lefty and has what I guess is the proverbial natural curve ball. It has been said that a baseball doesn't really curve. "It's just an optical illusion," they say. Well, let me say this: "They're wrong, very wrong!" Simmons' ball is almost unhitable. It curves. Believe me, it *really* curves! Ron and I first ran into him on the diamond in the far southwest corner of Avalon Park. Two teams were playing with eight to a team. As we approached to watch, one of them called out, "Hey, you guys wanna play?" Ron played right field for one team and I did the same for the other group. This was my first look at Simmons. By the way, that's all I did, look at Simmons—not even a foul tip!

"Damn, there's old horse-butt over there!" as I spot Simmons throwing to some guy out in left.

Vinnie is looking at me as he's reaching for his perpetual snack. He always carries a few cloves of garlic in his pocket. With a little pinch, he removes the dry paper like skin and pops it in his mouth. "What's this 'horse butt' stuff?"

"Simmons, ... he's got a butt like a damn pony."

He laughs while emitting his signature breath. "Curt, that's because he has a strong lower body. That's where he gets his leg strength from. It gives him more power to push off. Take a look at a major league pitcher, and you'll see that most of them are built that way."

"Who the hell wants to look at some major leaguer's butt? I guess that I'll have to get by without leg strength and push-off, 'cause I can hardly keep my pants up! I'll just fox 'em. I'll keep pitchin' with my head. I believe that I can think better than most guys can hit. That's my theory!"

At this young age, I began to realize how much an arm could hurt. I had taught myself how to throw a curve ball and some other pitches that were known to be abnormal to the human anatomy. For a young boy, I was suffering far too much. I kept thinking, "This is supposed to be fun." I began to read books and manuals on pitching. I learned some new grips and releases over the winter.

All of this training was important to me for another very special reason. I was continually telling Mom that someday I would be a major leaguer and buy her a ranch house. I must have told her this a hundred times. At times, I felt that she really did believe me.

I figure that maybe Vinnie will work with me. I admire his craftsman approach to baseball. When he plays at shortstop, he seems to be floating. When he plays a hot grounder, he has this little way of giving in a bit as he gloves it. I've seen him on the mound where you'd swear he was talkin' to the ball. He is never happy with his last performance.

"Vinnie, can you catch me for awhile? I'm workin' on a couple of new pitches."

"Sure, man, we ain't gonna have many guys comin' in this rain anyway!"

"I've come up with one that I'm able to throw with some accuracy. It's a variation on some things that I've read. I place my index and middle fingers with the seams on top. The first knuckle of my thumb goes across the bottom seam closest to my body. I throw this one right over the top with a release point a little later, or lower than normal. As I release the ball, I pinch that bottom seam. Y'know how you squeeze the skin off of your damn garlic? Well, that's what I do. I kinda' pinch the ball as I release it. Picture having a lemon or watermelon seed between your thumb and index finger. Squish, and that seed goes flyin'! The result, when executed properly, is a fast ball that appears to be coming fat and juicy in the batter's eyes. At the last moment, the ball will, or should, rise. It's simply a matter of physics; it now has a backspin! I can take this same grip and tuck it back a little in my hand, thus slowing the ball down. This pitch shows the same motion, but the slower speed can be fairly deceptive."

"Okay, let's see how it works, Curt!"

After a few trial and error throws, it's doing something alright. I am pretty damn proud!

"Ya' got somethin' there, Erler. Not bad. Ya' should work on it today, if we ever get anybody out here!"

We start up a twelve-man revolving game. With just that many guys, most of us will rotate from position to position as everybody takes their at-bats. Sometimes, the pitcher remains the pitcher except while he takes his "raps." With Simmons here, I lose any chance to pitch today. He is simply the best around, and it's his choice. "Who cares? I'm just glad to be here and not some stuffy classroom with all of those rules and regulations." Pitch, hit, catch, shag fly balls, I don't care. Now, with Simmons pitching, I'm in no hurry to hit. I don't remember ever getting more than a foul tip off of him.

Another arm saver for me was a submarine delivery. It was a nasty-looking pitch to a right-handed hitter and so much easier on the arm. This was just the pitch for those tough guys with that bad-ass sneer. The ball would appear destined to plunk him somewhere on his overrated anatomy. Of course, it would normally end up on the outer half, leaving "slugger" spinning in vain. This was the real fruit of my efforts, a batter screwing himself into the ground!

I also read about "soft hands" in Lou Boudreau's little handbook. The idea was to give a little as the ball reached your glove. Vinnie would throw me grounders with a steel ball. It was a bit smaller than a nine-inch baseball. It was made of some kind of shiny steel, almost like a big ball bearing, but it was hollow! I guess that his dad had done this with him when he was younger. You learn to move back with the ball, thus taking the sting out of it and ensuring less rebound action. Once you learned this technique, you were no longer afraid of that hardball. You were now a much better fielder. Vinnie and I were not close at all outside of playing ball together, but we both lived for baseball. He was a few years older, and we had little else in common.

As you look around this park, you'll see that it is right in the center of one of our typical Southside blue-collar neighborhoods. Down the right field line, and across the street, you see a big yellow stone parochial grammar school, Saint Francis De Paula. Across the street and down the left field line there's a large sprawling red brick high school. If you were capable of hitting one a block and a half, you might hit a Southside factory. The street that runs along the farthest east portion of the park is lined with humble bungalows and two-flats. The quality of life, in our eyes, is perfect. There's hard work, simple pleasures, family and ethnic traditions, morals and patriotism. There's also some damn good pizza pie over at Mama Mia's on 76th Street! This Southside is truly a big hunk of heaven!

Let's talk a bit about Vich. His dad has moved the family here from St. Louis. This is so that he can work over at Superior Match on 76th. His mom also works there, in the receiving department. The word is, her arms are as big as Vich's. His dad is quite renowned as a bowler. He doesn't use the holes in the ball. He just palms the ball and lets it rip with amazing accuracy. It's this type of industry that makes Chicago what it is. Right down 76th Street, Solo Cup also employs several hundred folks.

Vich is a guy that's hard to figure out. He's a rather large guy for his age, whatever that may be. He's every bit of six feet tall and well over two hundred pounds. If someone asks him if his name is "Vic," he replies, "Vich, rhymes with 'son of a bitch'!" He always seems to have this insidious little laugh. He's not laughing at me, or anybody. This is just part of his persona. It appears that he has only one type of shirt. He always wears an old Army-issue olive drab undershirt. I hope that he owns more than one! It could be that he just wants to show off his large biceps, but I doubt it.

He is a monster to pitch to! As he stands in the batter's box, he never has a stance. He just stands there with the bat in any one of his various positions. Sometimes the bat will be just resting on his shoulder. He often has the bat held with just his left hand, dangling to his side, and other times he'll spin it like a baton. If the pitch arrives in his zone, all hell breaks loose. *Thud*—the sound is totally different than that of any other hitter that I've ever faced. The speed and trajectory of his line drives are damn scary, often not more than two feet off the ground! I don't dare throw one between the letters and the belt. He may just drive it through my navel and out L-3 on my spine! His very high pop-ups have come to be known as "rainmakers."

He can crunch a nine-inch baseball harder than anyone that I've ever seen. His dad has made this bat for him. It looks more like a caveman's club. It appears to be one big fat doll rod with just a bit of a tapered handle! I don't know what it is made of, but it sure is one helluva weapon. Vich normally plays in right field, where he seems most suited. One might say that his instincts are not that hot. He seldom makes a clean catch. I've actually seen balls bounce off of him! However, once the ball is in his hands, a runner is dead meat. If he wanders too far, Vich will nail him! Speaking of ball bearings, his relay feels like a nine-inch ball bearing! His arm is like a big-ass rubber band with a sling-shot action. You'd think that it's Vinnie's steel ball. Vich throws his "shot put" about ninety miles an hour. At times like this, I'm glad that I'm not a second baseman. He doesn't even realize it's just something that he does!

A few days later, we are able to field two full teams. Great—Vinnie picks me 'cause he knows that I want to pitch. Their first guy up is this scrawny guy that I've never seen before. He gets my test pitch, over his head and off of the backstop. All I can hear is, "Ah shit!" When he returns to the box, he is eight to ten inches off the plate. Three pitches later, he is repeating his first statement!

Simmons is pitching for the other guys. His catcher, as always, is one of my least favorite guys out here, Chink! He and I have a thing about pitches in close. When he's catching, I get brushed back. When he's batting, I love to tuck 'em under his chin. My first at bat, and Simmons comes too far inside and I don't move. I figure, this is one way to beat him. At least I'm on base against big butt! Vinnie starts singing, "It only hurts for a little while" as I get plunked. As our game goes on, Simmons has his way with me—swing, miss, swing, miss! A base on balls is my big contribution off of Simmons today. So what's new?

It's getting very wet and pretty damn dark. The game is tied, and the other guys have a guy on second with nobody out. I doubt that anybody else really cares who wins today, but Chink is trying to bunt this guy to third. I call down to home plate, "How chicken can ya' get? It's rainy and wet, you clown!" I miss, way outside with my first pitch. My second pitch goes up and in, real close to Chink's chin! He drops his bat and moves quickly toward the mound. All at once, he just stops and goes back to the box. He lines a screamer right past me on the next pitch. Vinnie snags it, flips to second, double play! The next guy takes some futile swings and walks away wiping the rain off of his bat as though the rain had struck him out. I knew better! The game ends with a downpour of summer rain. Game tied, nobody wins today!

As we all begin to leave, Vinnie says, "You're right, Curt, he is a horse's ass!"

"That's not what I said, Vinnie!"

"I know, but look at him. I guess Simmons will always be Simmons," as he walks away with his strut and his best friend, his gym bag! "Wanna go for a sausage sandwich at Mama Mia's? I'm buyin'."

This was a very rare social invitation from Vinnie, but I thought that I'd better get peddling home with all of the rain. "Nah. Thanks, though. Maybe next week?"

As I reach our neighborhood, I stop at Julie's for a bottle of pop. "Let me think. Do I want a nice cold Old Colony lime or an Old Dutch cream soda?" I opt for the lime and grab a Powerhouse candy bar.

Ron had a special way of looking at me when he knew that I was being ridiculous. "Hey, Ron, I have an idea. Watch this! My latest brainstorm is this little status symbol. This is something that I have never seen done before. I have here a nice new Gem razor blade. With the touch of a fine artist, I'll carve 'A C E' on my left bicep. It'll bleed a little and it will hardly hurt. See? Now I have my nickname where the whole world can see it. As the scab appears, it'll look even cooler. Rainbow Beach, here I come!" He gave me the "ridiculous" look!

"My bike, where in the hell is my Schwinn?" It was nearing Thanksgiving Day as Percy and Todd spotted us kids and our sweet treats from Julie's. Something new had been added to that magnificent candy case. Marshmallow turkeys were somewhat like the Easter peeps that are so common today. A golden-brown sugar coated these little marshmallow-shaped turkeys, drumsticks and all! These pre-holiday birds were two cents apiece. Todd and Percy decided that they were going to buy 'em all! They handed me five bucks and said, "Buy all that Julie has. This is more than enough." I jumped on my "Cadillac" and shot down the alley. I was going to be quite the celebrity with this transaction.

Julie removed the display box from the counter. "Here, Curt. I have another two boxes back here. Ninety-one all together. Let's make it a dollar seventy-five for all of them." As I walked out and down the concrete stoop, no Schwinn in sight!

There had been nobody out front when I pulled up earlier. In my haste and excitement, I had forgotten to turn the key on the fork lock. "Okay, where's my bike? C'mon, you guys are hiding it. Where is it?"

"No, Curt, there was no bike here when we got here, honest!"

My heart was in my throat. There was simply no value that I could have placed on that bike. The bunch of us looked around the corners, all up and down the alleys. It was gone!

My walk home, down the alley, seemed to last forever. I was in a fog. "My bike was stolen down at Julie's. Nobody knows who it could have been."

I could see Todd's fist clinch up. "Curt, are you sure that somebody down there isn't kidding with you? Or is someone tryin' to get even for something?"

"No, Todd. Probably some guy just noticed that it was not locked and grabbed it. Let's face it, it's a darn nice-lookin' Schwinn! Or at least it was, anyway."

Cary walked in the store and heard our conversation. "I'll be damned. I saw a kid riding south on Stony. I thought that the bike looked like Curt's."

Todd and I just gave Cary our meanest look. "Thanks, Cary. Thanks for your help. Yeah, all of your help. Thanks for turning around and checkin' for me. I hate you!" I threw the change down next to the turkey boxes and ran upstairs. Well, so much for Curt owning the coolest bike in the neighborhood. So much for owning any bike. Those days were over, forever! Dad was not too pleased when he heard about Cary letting the suspect get away unchallenged.

The radio is blaring out, *"Sh-Boom, Sh-Boom, Life Could Be A Dream"* by the Crew Cuts. Ron and I have just chalked our strike zone on the brick wall. It's time for nine innings of one-on-one with our ten-cent rubber ball. Pepsi comes running in from the alley. "Curt, Nitwitz and another guy were pushin' me around down at Julie's."

Nothing more had to be said. Down the alley we run. There was Nitwitz with the other guy still having their little chuckle. "Hey, I hear you're pickin' on my kid brother, Nitwitz." *Whack*! I pop him on the side of his face. I just shove the other guy because he is a couple of years younger than me. "You, get the hell outta here, now!"

A few years later, I'd pay for this incident.

"Fairy tales can come true, it can happen to you. If you're young at heart." Believe it or not, that's what was spinning on my turntable when the phone down in the store began ringing. "Curt, it's the store phone, wanna get it?" Percy was having his evening cup of coffee with Mom in the living room. I ran down those nineteen stairs so as not to miss the call.

"Hi, is Curt there? Is this Curt?"

"Yeah, it's Curt. Is this Peggy Sue?" There is no way that I could miss that heavenly voice.

"Yes, Curt, it is! Would you like to go to the Carmel Social with me on December 3rd?"

I'm stunned. It's been well over a year since I've heard this sweet voice. "Sure, yeah, I'd love to go. Tell me more about it." I was thinking, "Yes, Peggy Sue. Fairy tales can come true!"

We discussed our arrangements over the next few days. "It looks like there'll be four of us going together. Red Top is going with Jack. Does that sound okay to you?"

To be honest, it could have been Bushman dating Olive Oil. I didn't care. I was goin' with Peggy Sue! It took me all of a half second to reply. "Yeah, that sounds great to me."

Our two school buddies were both great companions. Jack was a cool, good-lookin' kid, and Red Top was always a neat kid! Her Dad was a neighborhood hero. He was responsible for those chocolate chip doughnuts and, of course, my all time favorites, those meringue-filled cream horns.

December 3rd, and it's the day of the Snow Ball dance at Mount Carmel High School. Jack and I tried to act like grown-ups. He and I met in front of my Dad's store. After we walked to Peggy Sue's house, we called a cab. We picked up Red Top and off we went to 63rd Street. We had a good time at the dance, although it has often been noted by many that I dance somewhat like a middle linebacker! After the dance, we went to The Patio on 71st Street. We had a table right at the front window. Shrimp cocktails were the choices of Peggy Sue and Curt. We thought that this sounded classy, never realizing that this was simply an appetizer! Who cared? We were just kids havin' fun, and besides, I love shrimp!

After walking Peggy Sue to her front door, I held her by the waist. As I leaned forward seeking my special good night, Peggy Sue said, "On the cheek." I can still smell her powder!

Dad surprised me with a complete set of AMT dealer cars on Christmas morning. He had witnessed Ron and me buying, building and customizing model cars all year.

"Man, are we gonna have a ball customizing all of these '55s, Ron! Can you come over for awhile later, or I'll come over?" It's after dinner and at this age, I don't mind going out on Christmas night. In years past,

Pepsi and I had never dreamed of leaving our stash behind on the big day!

It's a cool, blue evening, with the light of the full moon exemplifying the mood of this wonderful day. I decide to bring the two-tone blue '55 Dodge with me to show off at the Laffey residence. As I walk down Stony to the north, I think to myself, "Dad is trying to make up for the loss of my Schwinn, I just know it." Ron and I take a little walk after a nice visit with his folks and the festivities have finally wound down. Christmas presents are discussed. Next year is also talked about with new hope.

For the most part, we just enjoy the peace of this special day. As we pass the newsstand at 79th, there is that familiar smell of a kerosene lantern. It almost seems as though you can hear your own breath, it's that quiet tonight. This is the first Christmas evening that I have ever been out, with the exception of driving Gramma and Aunt Selma home in one of Percy's carriages!

Christmas has been extended by an extra day this year as we all gather with my big brothers on Sunday. Todd and Percy are now sharing a neat apartment on 82nd. Betty Lou and Todd gave me a cool leather-sleeved letter jacket. Something I'll never have a chance to earn in high school. High school didn't last that long for me!

Betty Lou and Todd – Christmas of '54 ©

SCHOOL'S OUT – FOREVER!

It's January of '55 and I'm now sixteen years old. "Now, I can leave Homer High!" I explained to Ron and Mom as we sat in the kitchen having a cup. "I can go to Wescott Continuation School over at 80th and Normal. I know a girl that has just enrolled there, and she says that it's okay. Homer High is just not for me, Mom. Two of my P.E. teachers kinda' like boys, and I don't like that! The wrestling coach yells at me every time I seem to have the upper hand in a match. He yells, "Erler, you can't do this, you can't do that. He just plain doesn't like the name 'Erler'. I know that! The saddest part of all of this is that he's also the baseball coach. Wouldn't it be just peachy for this Erler to have this character telling me that I can't throw this, I can't throw that? Frankly, I'm tired of looking at him in his pink and charcoal bowling shirts!"

Todd could never get along with him, either. Mrs. Hernia, the vice-principal, is constantly yelling at me. 'Pull those Levis up, Mr. Erler. What's that book that you're reading, Mr. Erler? Give me that pocketbook, Mr. Erler! When are you going to get a haircut, Mr. Erler? Now, where are you going, Mr. Erler?' Gee, it's just great being called 'Mr. Erler,' but this lady might catch more bees with a little honey rather than her damn vinegar! I'm not her prisoner. I'm a young boy and a student at a public school. She should be forced to sit in on some classes at St. Felicitas. Maybe then she'd get it! Anyway, Mom, that's what I'll do. I'll go to Wescott. Maybe they'll offer some good shop classes. This way, I can get something useful out of school and still keep a job.

Within a week, I was working at the welding shop down at 81st and Stony. Bob and Vern treated me like a son. Within a month, I had dropped out of Wescott. Here at the welding shop, I was taught how to arc weld, braze and use the cutting torch. "Hell, this is more than I had learned at Homer, and it's a lot more applicable to my lifestyle. I'm much more at home with blue-collar guys, Mom. And the paychecks are mighty nice too."

Vinnie calls from Lou's Drug Store: "Hey, Erler, come here a minute." I walk across 82nd from Julie's, where I was enjoying an evening bottle of pop. "Does your sister put out?"

Without a word, I throw the hardest right hook that I have ever thrown at anybody. It catches him high on the left side of his forehead. He falls back against the mailbox, but not down to the sidewalk. He looks at me, shocked at what has just happened. At that moment, I'm sure that this thing has only just begun. I realize that he is two or three years older than me. If someone would have asked me, "Hey, Vinnie's down at the corner, wanna' fight him?" I wouldn't have even considered it. This was different. I had no time to make that decision.

He doesn't say another word and doesn't make any counter moves. It's over. I believe that he knew that, as young as I was, I loved my sister, and nobody was going to talk that way about her. He also realized that there were seven Erler boys! Little was said by anybody that evening, or ever. However, his big chubby brother knew what had happened and always treated me like dirt after that. That was just fine with me, 'cause he ate more damn garlic than Vinnie, and he smelled like day-old pizza. Now, at least I was assured that I would never be close enough to smell his damn breath again. The next time Vinnie and I were together at Grand Crossing, we went about our baseball business. I was happy with this outcome. I doubt that Sis ever knew anything about the incident.

Ron and I have just returned from our favorite record store down at 67th and Stony. We had heard this new R&B 45 called "Speedo" by The Cadillacs. It's on a label that we have never seen before—JOZ/Josie. On about the third play, we hear big bro' Cary out in the kitchen as he is sucking up all of Mom's coffee again.

He has this to say about our new music find: "Why does Curt listen to that crappy music?" With that, I walk into the kitchen and stand right in front of his chair. Now, let's remember, this is a very similar scene to the one back when the newspaper was reporting that this little five-year-old was "lost"!

"Hey, Cary, doncha' think that maybe your getting a little too old to be bad-mouthing your not-so-little brother? Why are you still wearing that crappy shirt? It seems that you've been wearing it for years. Weren't you wearing that thing when we picked up my Schwinn about a hundred years ago? I also know that you messed up my chances of buying that '37 Willy's last month! It was going to be purchased with my money, and Mom was all for it until you interfered. Thirty-five bucks, yeah, just thirty-five bucks, and you screwed it up for me! I had plans to repair it and make a few bucks so that I could buy a '40 Ford coupe. Thanks for nothin'! I suggest that you stop messing with my life and do a little patchin' up with your own affairs! Just get back to your 'big people talk'."

No response from Cary.

"Love ya', Mom!" was all I said as I returned to my bedroom and my "crappy" music, which I loved. Now, I played the flip side, even louder! Funny thing, the other side's title was, "Let Me Explain"! Ron seemed to enjoy my actions this time. He usually preferred it when I let things slide rather than cause any unnecessary commotion.

It's Monday, May 30th, Memorial Day. Ron, Pepsi and I are having a game off the garage. We're listening to the Indy 500 on my trusty Emerson as we play. This is a game that was invented by a buddy of mine's brother. The pitcher stands in front of the garage door and arches his pitch across the alley to the batter. The object is to hit a raggedy old softball onto the roof softly enough that it will roll back down in fair territory—"fair territory" being defined by the dimensions of the garage doors. The doors are also the game board for this event. Anything that hits below the halfway mark on the door is a single. Anything that hits the top half is a double. The trim counts as a triple. The batter, however, is restricted from slamming the ball. He must just sort of pop it back toward the pitcher. This is a judgment call and is hardly ever disputed. The pitcher, in effect, becomes somewhat of a goalie. As the Indy coverage continues, we hear the call: Bill Vukovich is killed as his car is broadsided by Johnny Boyd. Vukovich's car went airborne and over the wall. Bill's car landed on its nose and bounced as it exploded into flames. Our Indy 500 hero is dead.

Like so many summer days, this morning started out overcast and rainy. The first thing that I do on these mornings is head for the yard to check the ground conditions. "Is it playable?" I think to myself, "Hell yes, by the time we are all at the park, the sun will have dried things out, and there'll be plenty of guys there. We're going to play today!"

As predicted, it's an excellent turnout at Grand Crossing today. There are several guys here that I've never seen before. I see that tall black kid that used to be in one of my P.E. classes. He's is in the outfield loosening up. "Hey, Basket, who's that guy out there in left? I remember that he was an all-sports type guy, but I can't think of his name. I know that he's a lefty and he doesn't smile much."

Basket replies with this guy's name posthaste! "Carter, you mean Carter. Yeah, he's all jock, but zero personality."

If you're wondering about this "Basket" thing, here's the scoop. We call him that 'cause he catches everything in sight, and effortlessly too!

"Hey, Vinnie, I see that my dearest, warmest buddy, Mr. Simmons, is gonna be pitching against us today. I wouldn't have it any other way, because if he's pitching for them, he can't be pitchin' for us! That leads me to believe that I'll be pitching this morning."

My first at-bat, and I'm ready to try anything against this monster. "I'm chokin' up, Vinnie. I'm gonna get some kind of a hit off this clown today."

Just two pitches into my experiment, I get hit hard right where a guy doesn't want to get hit. I'm down in a heap writhing in agony. Vinnie and this Greek kid, Tommy, come to see how I'm doin'.

"Vinnie, get someone to run for me. I just ain't able to run right now!" We have no substitution rules, so I can go back in once I regain my composure. As I get to my feet and walk, hunched over, to the sidelines, two jerks on the other team are laughing. I immediately think, "I'll remember those ugly bastards. I'll get 'em!"

I'm back on the mound in the top of the inning. The second guy up is one of the laughing boys. "Hey, Smiley, watch your ass, I got somethin' for ya'!" I throw one right into his front knee and drop him.

Up quickly, he now comes flying at me while making comments about my facial features, namely my nose! He's throwing punches like a wild man. To his discredit, it's nothing very significant. I use the old "Buck" treatment. I just continue to pound his ribs with short rights. I never even throw a left and never go to his head. He went down whining like a baby.

Buck had taught me this strategy when I was still pretty short. He said that this was the best offense for a short guy. Buck is the only Erler boy that's not six feet, or even close to it. He is, however, one tough cat! I'm now six foot somethin', but this still worked very well for me today.

There was quite a bit of tension after this incident. We never did finish the game.

It's to be my last game at Grand Crossing, ever! Of course, none of us ever knew these things. Our lives were all going in different directions as we grew a bit older. There are some more new names out here today. There's a "Bony," a "Ski" and some cat named "Dog"—can you believe it? "Banana Nose" is always here! He seems way too shy to have to cope with a nickname like that. Vinnie always tells me the same thing: "This guy's not really very athletic, but he always shows up." Slip, a guy that I hadn't seen in quite awhile, was there with a new catcher's mitt. It was a big palomino tan Wilson. This was a major league glove. I wanted to pitch to this great target. There are several new Italian guys, some with names that I can't pronounce. Others with names that I won't repeat!

It's about eleven, and it's time to choose up. Vinnie and Cap, another new guy that I don't know, are the captains. Vinnie picks Bony. I guess the guy can really hit. Cap picks me because a couple of guys told him that I throw a lot of high, tight stuff. This adds to my value, as I won't be throwin' at him!

"I hear that you like to throw at heads and knees, man!"

"Nah, I just like to think while I pitch. I'm not always lookin' to blow 'em past the other guys. Just like to have fun and win! To me, losing is like watchin' someone else eating your ice cream cone!"

Slip is going to be my catcher. It couldn't have worked out any better. We decide on just a few signs. They are the fastball, the curveball and the at-him pitch. The at-him is a simple point of his thumb to the targeted area of the batter's anatomy. Not a target, like hit him, just "at him"! I let him know about my new "pinch" pitch. "It's just a fastball that rises, if it's workin'! I'll bring my glove to my mouth when I'm gonna throw it!"

Vinnie is pitching for his team. We play about five innings before attrition begins to set in. A lot of guys say that they have jobs to go to and other excuses. We have hit Vinnie pretty good and we're leading eight to two.

Spaghetti is sounding pretty damn good about now. Seven or eight of us decide on pasta over at Mama Mia's, our pizza pie queen. Julius La

Rosa is doing his "Eh Cumpari" on the juke when we arrive. The smell of oregano, sausage and cheese are permeating the air. Cooled down after our icy Cokes, most of us order the Pasta Feast. This is one helluva bargain. It's a heaping bowl of Mama's spaghetti, or mostaccioli, and a big hunk of sausage or a couple of meatballs. All of this and a basket of her crispy garlic bread for a buck and a quarter! Some of the guys can't afford this "fancy" dining. There's always someone kind enough to share. In other cases, we'll pop for a guy's lunch if he's really broke. This is usually a judgment call because some guys will play you for a fool. I sit next to Slip as we laugh at the crazy dance steps that some cats made while avoiding our "errant pitches." I ask Slip if his last name was "Cover." He says, "No, man, my real name is Hank. It's Hank Slipkowski."

That's the way it was on those wonderful days of summer and baseball! On other days, most of us went our separate ways. Vinnie lived down on 82nd, but we seldom had more to say than "Hey," and a "Hey back atcha'!"

I now have a regular girlfriend. No more chasin' skirts, at least for now! Last year, I met this pretty Swedish blonde while strollin' down 79th Street. She is a very cute little chick with a great Swedish accent, "Yah shuuur"! By now, Ingrid and I are together several days each week. There's also a pretty good sized group of kids that we spend most of our time with. The beach is one venue that seems to have our attention. It's convenient, sunny and free! Ron, as always, is with me almost every day.

Smoked pork; I was working with one of my favorite commodities— smokey cuts of pork! I worked for this little smoked meat company over on 95th. The owner was an extremely quiet little man. He spoke only when he was directing me in my duties. One of my jobs was pulling the pig parts from barrels of ice-cold brine and laying them on smoke racks. The most challenging parts were the tails. You grab 'em too hard and *squirt*! they fly across the room. He kind of frowned on that. My biggest treat was rolling the big racks of pork in and out of this big brick smokehouse. It was enough to make one salivate, and it was warm in there.

Then, a few days each week, we had to deliver this now very pink meat to the black areas of the Southside. Our delivery vehicle was an old blue Dodge panel truck. Our route began around 63rd and Stony where the El tracks begin, or end, depending on your travel plans. First stop was normally at 63rd and Dante Avenue. From there, we continued on driving, primarily to the west, until the truck was empty. That became rather exciting on cold, dark December evenings. I was always amused as we would throw a wooden barrel over our shoulders and a pig hock would fall out and into the dirty snow on the street or sidewalk. He'd simply pick it up and either blow on it or wipe it on his puffy old blue jacket. For weeks he didn't speak more than a half dozen words a day. On delivery nights, I'd try to ascertain just when we might be done for the day. I never received a straight answer. He'd just shrug and grunt a bit!

One December day, I was working my fanny off and freezing my hands red in that damn ice water. Pigs feet were squirting across the sawdust-covered floor when I suddenly heard a new song by The Three Chuckles. I loved this group led by Teddy Randazzo. While I was faking work for a few moments, he saw me actually standing still for more than a second as I listened to "Times Two, I Love You."

This little man was a task master. He started to get on me, so I just took off my apron, threw it on my stainless steel workbench and uttered those famous words, "I quit!" While trying to keep me as his slave, he asked if I felt overworked and if this work really bothered me. My response was short and sweet; "I'm just not used to playing with dead pigs!" I walked home from 95th while trying to remember the lyrics to my newest favorite song. *"Take everyone who's been in love times two, plus every star that shines above times two, when you're through, you'll have the answer darling, how much times two, I love you."*

By the way, the end of the year came and no W-2 form. When I inquired, he said, "Oh, you didn't make that much money."

Time for Dad Cash to step up. "Seems to me that Curt made enough money for you to withhold federal deductions. I'll have one of my older sons drive Curt over there tomorrow for his W-2 form." I got my W-2 with no further conversation!

As the year of 1955 was coming to a close, the Cubs released or traded several of our favorites within a two week period. We no longer had Hal Jeffcoat, Frankie Baumholtz, Randy Jackson, Walker Cooper or the fine relief pitcher Don Elston. I guess that all a good Cubs fan can do is, *"Wait 'til next year."*

ROCKIN', FIGHTIN' AND RACIN'

Who's this guy that's 'down at the end of Lonely Street', Ron? We gotta head down to 67th and pick up that 45." Ron and I went down to see our friend at the record store next to the Jackson Park Theatre. She was half black and half something else, and a real buddy to us. She kept us aware of the newest rock 'n' roll and R&B 45s. We were there for hours again as Marie played every 45 that we pulled from the rack. It turned out that this Elvis cat was on two different labels. Some were on RCA and the others on the Sun label out of Memphis. We each bought one of the RCA 45s. I grabbed "Heartbreak Hotel" with "I Was the One" on the flip. Ron bought a copy of "Money Honey" with "One Sided Love Affair" on the other side.

Ron learned the lyrics and the Elvis style on "Money Honey." Many nights were spent rehearsing before he went downtown to participate in an Elvis contest. He didn't win, but those that were there said that he was just great! I was busy fixin' cars and couldn't make that scene. As most record collectors now know, those Sun 45s would have been much better, investment wise. But who was investing?

I'm managing the Texaco station at 82nd and Stony. They're easy guys to work for, primarily because they are absentee owners. They are seldom around and have entrusted me with their little investment. I work my rear off to keep this place clean and profitable. It offers me the chance to keep my '50 Merc' running as quick as most, and quicker than many! There are two different night-shift guys. They're both pretty cool guys. One is from St. Felicitas, and Dave is from the Westside. He's toolin' around in a brand new '56 Ford Vicky. It's the same color scheme as my old Schwinn, so y'know that I gotta like it!

Clyde McPhatter, Ivory Joe Hunter, Elvis and Gene Vincent are all regulars here. Regulars, that is, on the radio that I have playing out in front. I have a lot of new customers since taking over in January. The back room is becoming busier each week. Some days, I can't get away at my normal quitting time due to repairs, etc. I'm always telling Mom, "As long as it's going to make that place more profitable, I don't mind working late. I receive little bonus checks ever few weeks from the older partner. He seems to have a lot of respect for my allegiance." When I leave on these late nights, I have a favorite destination. Calmar's over on Ashland Avenue makes the greatest beef and Italian sausage sandwiches for seventy-five cents.

"Hi, Rose, can I get a sausage sandwich and a big Coke ta go?" This was a little side door off of the alley. You could be out of there in two minutes and enjoy a late dinner while diggin' some great tunes on WBEE out of Gary, Indiana.

Ron is at Mendel High studying on this Wednesday in June. He is preparing for his semester finals, which are about to begin. Soon, he'll be out for the summer. He will be spending a lot of time at Texaco with me. I roll on down to Kladis' at lunch time. I'm salivating for a cheeseburger and a coffee soda. I will be receiving much more! I'm sitting in the plywood booth with a couple of kids that hang out here. There is a lot of laughing and wiggling around in the booth behind me. This piece of plywood is very thin and not much to buffer this action. I pull my arm forward and then pound my elbow into the plywood. "Hey, I don't need a damn back massage over here!"

"Drop dead!" is the response from my neighbor.

In a split second, I'm up and in front of this foursome. "Who's the big mouth?"

A rather large farmer-lookin' kid jumps to his feet. "I guess that would be me! What ya' gonna do about it?"

With nothing more to be said, we all head for the little concrete area out back. This guy is a walking John Deere commercial! Both "tough guys" have their dukes up and ready for action. Splat, I'm down to my knees! This big guy is takin' no prisoners as he repeats the action. Back on my feet, I'm able to land a few glancing blows as he whips my butt!

As it becomes obvious that the argument is over, he reaches out with his big paw to help me up. In his Roebuck jeans and goofy lookin' shirt, he pats me on the back and says, "Hey, let's go in and finish up our lunch, man. I'm Jerry's cousin Abel. And you're Curt, right? I'm just visiting my aunt and uncle over in Burnside."

This cat was more than Abel—he was very able! With one sore head, I drive back to Texaco, a much humbler cat! All I can think is, "Man, am I glad that Ingrid and Ron didn't witness that slaughter!"

As a rule, Saturday nights were reserved for Ingrid and the Double Drive-in Theatre over on Southwest Highway. At this point, it seemed that we were to be partners for life. Or at least it seemed that way to this young Southside kid! We always had a lot of fun together. We had quite a ring of friends to have fun with. Bowling alleys, beaches, local drugstores, pizza joints, soda shops and just hangin' around kept us busy. There were also a few fights to keep the guys loose! Any time that Ron would walk through the front at Avalon Pizza, someone would play J-7 on the Seeburg—"Night Train" by Ernie Englund. That was his theme song!

Dancin' and Draggin' on the East Side – On nights that I didn't spend with Ingrid, we cats had several choices. If the guys were feeling brave, we'd go to the Westside. We'd cruise the Canaryville area as the guys looked for chicks. During the Back of the Yards Fair, we could almost be assured of a little action.

Forty-third and Damen was like another country to most of us. Yeah, it's on the Southside, but it's the Westside, and therein lies the difference. They were "them" and we were "us"! For the most part, they were Irish, German, Italian and Polish just like most of us. How all of these kids knew that we were from seven or eight miles away, I'll never know. They knew all right, and the reception was virtually nonexistent. A little girl hunting would likely end up in a fight or two. A friendly two-block drag race would sometimes warm the chill in the air. There were several neighborhoods that were somewhat clannish, but this particular area was always a potential war zone! Other areas that would usually provide excitement were Burnside and Hegwisch. There was a parish in Hegwisch that was heavily stocked with pretty Polish girls. This was over around 103rd and the Avenues. I think it may have been Avenue L. We called them "the Avenues" just as a reference point. A big dance hall on east 83rd around Baltimore was also a hot spot.

"There you go, man, they're playin' the right tunes!" Ron yelled out over the drone of this large hall. *"Earth angel, earth angel, will you be mine? My darling dear, love you all the time. I'm just a fool, a fool in love with you."* He knew that "Earth Angel" was my all-time favorite!

"Hey, Vince, I thought that we were lookin' for chicks. All I see are ugly guys plastered against those two mustard-colored walls."

"Turn around, Curt. There are two more walls!"

Sure enough, this place was absolutely wall-to-wall chicks! There was that same aura in there as the Back of the Yards scene. Just after Vince got hooked up with some pretty little Slavic chick, some local guy yelled out, "Hey, cats, I hate to interrupt your dancin', but there's a drag race about to happen on 83rd Street."

The parking lot and streets were almost as populated as the hall. There was no smoking allowed inside. At any one time, there may have been fifty kids out front and in the back puffin' their Luckies, Chesterfields, Camels and Marlboros.

Once outside, we witness the action. A big '51 Merc' rag top is revvin' it up as this little cat jumps in and slams the door of his buddy's red '40 Ford coupe. "Hey, Ron, dig it. That little coupe has a set of steel packs that could punch a hole in your eardrums!"

After the ground rules are laid down, both cars slowly roll past Commercial Avenue as many of us run the distance on foot. At Burley Avenue, one guy drops his arm, and they're off! From Burley Avenue to Green Bay Avenue it's nothin' but smoke and rubber! Someone tells us, "It was the coupe, by two car lengths!" Just another Friday night on the Southside!

The great blues singer Joe Turner moved into a large, yellow-brick, twelve flat around the corner from Ingrid on Maryland Avenue. This building was considered to be very luxurious, with expensive apartments. I can't remember how many times I'd take Ingrid home and then go around the corner hoping to see "Big Joe." Some nights, I'd wait there as late as one in the morning. I finally came to the conclusion that Big Joe kept much different hours than I did.

Little dust rings were rising from each drop of rain that splashed on my dry windowsill. They looked like little smoke rings puffing up from the concrete slab outside of my bedroom window. I was in one of those moods where I didn't know whether I wanted to go out or just stay in and dig some music. I opted for some Sinatra and Roy Hamilton records. After about an hour of this nonproductive loafing, I decided to get something done. For days now, I'd been sanding and grinding. I was preparing the Mercury for a good coat of primer. My trusty Craftsman quarter-inch drill was beginning to squeal quite loudly. I picked up a new pair of brushes for the motor at Sears yesterday. So, down to the workbench I went. "Slow Walk" by Sil Austin was playin' softly as I worked. The old brushes were removed and I was ready to finish up.

Stronger than ever, that wet sod smell was suddenly present. To understand this scene, I must explain the water tanks. Dad had a water filtration system for the photo finishing operation upstairs. It consisted of three six-foot tall tanks. These tanks seemed to be clad in galvanized steel. In the heat of the summer, they would become ice cold and sweaty with condensation. These three tanks stood just in front of the utility sinks under the rear window. As the sod smell struck me, I turned, rather slowly this time. As I looked toward the rear of the basement and those tanks, there appeared to be a fourth tank. A tall, dark silhouette stood, motionless. I did stare longer than I normally would. I wanted to be sure that it was actually there. I dropped my tools, pulled the string and took off once again!

Ron & Curt ~ My '50 Merc' @ Texaco – 1956 ©

The school carnival somehow seems much smaller. Ron and I decide to check out the old stomping grounds. We make a visit to the St. Felicitas carnival. Most of the rides are the same as back in '53 and '54. The girls seem much younger, 'cause they are! The music is much better: "Heartbreak Hotel," "My Prayer" and a lot of Bill Haley and his Comets.

After a couple of spins on the Tilt-a-Whirl and a Coke, we are about ready to pack it in. As we walk south to the parking lot, I spot Teresa, aka Bambino, from our Harper Avenue gang. She is sitting in the front seat of a car while this guy Mort is screaming obscenities at her and yanking on her arm. This is a girl that I've known since the early days on Harper. "Damn it, Ron. I taught her how to hold a baseball bat when she was just a little 'squirt! Pepsi, Sean, Casey, the Kentucky Boys, we were a gang of friends for many years. Bullshit, this guy's not gonna get away with this!"

Now Mort is not a stranger to me. He is a year, year-and-a-half older than me and is known to be pretty tough. "Leave her alone, damn it! Get the hell away from her. Teresa, ya' all right?"

With this, Mort comes at me, swearing and threatening me. It isn't too long before I land some real serious shots to his mug. I am having one helluva adrenalin rush. I couldn't stop if I tried! It doesn't stop, not in the least. I have him in a headlock and continue to pound away. I know that if I let him go, he could make a serious comeback, and I don't wish to risk anything like that. Besides that, he was picking on a young lady, and that's just not cool! This young lady was near and dear to all of us guys on Harper.

The next night, we felt compelled to return. Pepsi spotted me as he nursed a bottle of his namesake at the refreshment stand. "Curt, did you see Mort? His face is a mess, his eyes are all swollen and ..." He had not heard the story yet and had no idea that it was his big bro' who had inflicted the damage.

"Yeah, I know, Pepsi. I did it, last night! He was pickin' on Teresa, and we got into it!"

"Geez, man, he looks terrible!" Pepsi was a bit aghast, but proud, I know!

Father Cusack is over visiting one of the booths along the Stony Island side. Father is smokin' a cigarette and having one of his non-alcoholic, Kingsbury beers. "Curt, come here!" he calls as Ron and I are roaming around looking for familiar faces. "Curt, there are a bunch of guys that want to see you across Stony. Curt, there's quite a few of them, and they're mostly the Irish and Italian guys, y'know what I mean? I guess that Mort wants to get some revenge for last night."

"Thanks, Father, I'll go see!"

Ron looks at Father as if to say, "He's goin', no matter what!"

Pepsi, Ron and I walk across Stony and there they are, a bunch of them just salivating for my blood. As I approach the alley between Stony Island and East End, I begin to hear, "Hey, Erler, Mort was drunk last night. You were lucky, man."

"Come on, Erler, try it again!" is coming from last night's victim.

"I'm not gonna start hittin' you again. If you want some, just take your best shot, come on!"

This bs goes on for a few minutes, and before I know what hit me, I'm down on my face. Mort jumps on his prey and gets a scissors lock on my neck. Now, before I go any further, I need to state my feelings on what constitutes a real fight. It's simple—the last man standing is the winner. Nothing is more meaningless to me than two guys rolling on the ground, grunting and swearing at each other until one says, "uncle" or "I give." This is not the way men fight! In any case, I am barely able to breathe, so Mort gets his wish. He thinks that he has squared things and saved face with his buddies. This is about all that Mort could muster up, it seems. If you've ever played football and received a block or a tackle in the middle of your back, you know what I was up against when I went down. The wind had been knocked out of me, and I was easy pickin's for my two foes. Sour grapes? Maybe, but it sure as hell was not a real fight!

It was many, many years later before I heard what had actually happened. Frankly, I had never given it much thought. A neighbor of mine who can only be described as the typical no-brains jock was the idiot that delivered the two-handed blow to my back causing me to go down. He had a case against me from the time he moved into the neighborhood. It was simple: I was neither Catholic nor Irish, something that he just couldn't handle, I guess. His little brother always liked me, and that didn't help.

Just to close this little saga, one sunny day that same summer, I spotted Mort in front of St. Felicitas. I pulled the ol' Merc' over, got out and approached him. "How'd you like to have the rubber match?" He just continued on and said, "Nah!"

The old '50 Merc' now has a new heart! I have purchased a 1941 Ford Coupe with a newly rebuilt flathead. My good friend Dean is a buddy of stock car driver Bunny Emery at the 87th Street Speedway. Bunny has finally gone to the overheads and is now driving a big bad blue Mercury. Dean swung the deal, and I have this little coupe for small change. It already purrs like a kitten, but Ron and I envision more than a purr! With little more to do, we slip in a three-quarter-inch Isky cam and some new hotter ignition parts. Installed in its new home, it now seems to roar! One little problem is the carb linkage. My Mercury was rigged with a push linkage and the new carb setup calls for a pull. "We'll just have to replace that intake manifold and pop a couple of Holleys on this thing." For the time being, we rig our own "pull" carburetion system. We devise a cable that we have run to the left side coming up from under the dashboard. Now, I simply have to learn to pull that cable for acceleration. This is fine for the time being. We take the Merc' out to the old road near the speedway for a little test run. This little Ford "flatty" is hot, real hot! With a couple of extra bucks in hand, it's time to hit the old "boneyard" on 71st as Ron and I shop for some carburetion help. A new intake manifold and a set of Holley carbs have the Merc' ROARING this time!

My alarm clock was ol' Sol on these hot summer mornings. My bedroom had an eastern exposure. As the sun lifted, it was kissing the Cash Erler Photos sign on the brick wall outside. I was lying there with no shirt, just pouring sweat. I loved it! I guess this qualifies me as some kind of a masochist. I just can't help it. I love hot weather, real hot weather, anytime! This morning, it'll be a cool shower and off to pick up my friends. We're going to the Sand Dunes to celebrate the Fourth of July. This time, there'll be no Rhoda and Cary. Just a bunch of fun-loving friends! I can still hear Mitch Miller's orchestra playing "Song for a Summer's Night." A rather odd favorite for a Rock 'n' Roller, but I loved that tune. Still do!

"Soft winds, blow, blow..." This is the sound coming from the old Seeburg jukebox as I enter Rib Pit Number 2 on South Park Avenue. It's Dinah Washington and the Delta Rhythm Boys doing there current hit tune. A couple of Dee's buddies have introduced me to this juke joint! I grab a stool at the counter and order my small order of rib tips. The couple that run this place are real cool folks. They get a kick out of us white cats coming in to dig their cookin' and cool sounds. It's just a weekday afternoon, so all is quiet. On Friday and Saturday nights, the Seeburg gets rolled out back where there's a hardwood dance floor. The essence of smoking hickory wood envelopes the neighborhood.

It took me a few visits to receive an official invitation to "Come by some weekend and see what really goes on here." It didn't take much nudging for me to give it a whirl. Ron and I were used to being the only "gray boys" in a crowd. Argia B., the guy that invented the famous Mumbo Sauce, was the owner of this place and another. Thus Rib Pit Number 1 really does exist! Ron and I enjoyed our Friday night visit, but it was pretty evident that we were not getting the same red carpet treatment that we had enjoyed at other black establishments. We pretty much settled for our afternoon lunches the rest of the summer. As I look back, the ribs were some of the best ever, anywhere!

Ingrid is having a bit of a problem with a guy at Homer High. So I've been told, though not by her—she knows my temperament too well! I guess this jerk was taking some liberties touching her as she passed him in the hall. He is a black kid and this makes it kinda tough. The majority of the students here are white, and there is already plenty of racial tension. For me, it's not a matter of what he is, just a matter of addressing the situation with him, whatever that entails. He messed with my girl!

I take a break from work and drive over to my old hangout, the diamond across from Homer High. Dressed in my Texaco uniform, I stick out like a sore thumb. As I sit behind home plate, up against the backstop watching for this guy, the security guard approaches me. "Hey, I remember you. What are you doin' here?"

"I just stole home, how 'bout you?" was my wise-ass answer.

"Well, I don't want to see you on the school grounds, understand?"

"Sure, yeah, sure. Bye now!" It's been a few years since I've seen this man and I've never had any problems with him. I guess that he's just doing his job.

Perry, a guy that I know through Dee, walks over and asks, "Ya' lookin' for that colored kid? He's gone man, gone!" The guy that I'm waiting for apparently has slipped out the gym door with a bunch of other guys.

Now, you may ask, "colored kid"? "Yeah, "colored kid"—because back then, we were not all hung up on political correctness. We were a much more honest society. Hey, I'm a kraut and it doesn't even hurt! I grew up with that old theory, "*Sticks 'n' stones will break your bones, but names will never hurt you."* Trust me, we never played cowboys and Native Americans—never! You'll find no deliberate political correctness in these writings, just true facts and feelings. It's already quite evident that I have a lot of different brands in my group of acquaintances! As it turned out, this guy never bothered Ingrid again.

Woody was with me on the day that we met Ingrid. Woody and I had met while at Homer High. He was from New York and a very hip and mature cat. Fact was, he had kissed Ingrid soon after our meeting her. A day or so later, I had determined that this was my little girlfriend, not his! He had made a couple of derogatory remarks about her on the day that we met her. I had not forgotten his comments. In spite of this, Woody and I were pretty tight, with a lot of common interests.

One evening we were walking west on 82nd looking for something to do. Woody came up with a lame idea for something to do! It involved Ingrid, and it didn't set very well with me. I gave him the opportunity to rescind. He didn't. I gave him another chance, this time with my right fist clinched and at my side. We were standing at the alley between Ellis and Ingleside Avenues.

Once more: "Woody, you don't mean that, do you?"

With his patented smirk and menacing eyes, he responded, "Hey, cat, why not?"

I popped him! One right hand to his chops resulted in three loosened teeth and a broken jaw! He had his chance, and yet he persisted. The results of his tormenting were rather devastating. Before I go any further, I must tell you that his approach to these situations was always this - and I quote. *"Don't just stand there, off him, off his ass!"* While in reform school, he had learned not to take any prisoners, but just get it on! While I had regrets about the results of my action, I had no regrets about my motivation.

As it turned out, one of our buddies took him to the hospital. Neither Woody nor our buddy wanted me to be implicated in any battery charges. They fabricated a story about some guys assaulting him while he was walking home.

We had coffee in Mom's kitchen the next afternoon. Mom and Sis had no clue as to what had really transpired last night. His jaw was wired for several weeks. As a bit of humor, I bought him a glass straw from the drugstore for sippin' his hot coffee and other beverages! He giggled through his new look! We remained good friends for many years after this incident. In fact, his mother always made sure that I was with him when he stayed out late. She always said, "Curt will always take care of Woody"!

Christmas Eve and the soft, fluffy snow is falling. Mom and I are up late as Mom finishes up her holiday baking and as we work in the kitchen preparing for tomorrow's great feast. There is that typical wintry chill outside. However, with the heat of the oven to warm our kitchen, we're able leave the window open. Now we can listen to the little concert coming from the St. Felicitas belfry. As long as I live, I will never forget this wonderful night. I have never heard nor seen anything quite so beautiful. As the church bells ring and the soft snowflakes fall, we are transported to the pages of a child's storybook! Our backyard looks as though it has been spread with vanilla ice cream and little mounds of whipped cream here and there. Suddenly, the chimes are quiet and the vocal sounds of Christmas hymns come floating through the night air. The beautiful voices are soft and gentle. The earth's snowy blanket is providing the acoustics of a concert hall. This is such a poignant scene that I later make a written note of it for posterity.

"Mom, don't you wish that everyone could experience this evening, just as we are tonight? All people, everywhere, deserve to share the special Spirit of Christmas in such a wonderful way."

As I attempt to sing, *"May your days be merry and bright. And may all your Christmases be white,"* I wisely interrupt myself with, "Merry Christmas, Mom!"

This Christmas has seemed so special to me in so many ways. I have purchased a diamond ring for Ingrid. While neither of us had talked seriously about marriage, it seems almost imminent to me! Christmas evening, I drive over to pick up Ingrid. Her Mom and Dad are very cordial considering the fact that I am stealing their daughter for the remainder of this special day. I have a glass of warm Glogg with her dad.

Mom, as always, has the coffee pot perkin'. Her graham cracker pudding has yet to be served. We opt to sit around in the kitchen for our dessert. Mom and Sis are glad to be my witness to this big surprise. Ingrid has no clue what I am up to. She is wearing a bright red Christmassy sweater, and she looks stunning to me. I consider this ring as a commitment, at least on my part. Someone once told me that a diamond ring given as a gift doesn't necessarily hold a young lady to the normal commitment of marriage. We'll wait and see!

"Curt, is that you?" There was no sneakin' in at our house. I had been out quite late and was attempting to navigate those squeaky stairs. There were nineteen steps, and each of the Erler boys thought that they knew just which ones would give them away. There was no fooling Mom! She was in bed, but never sleeping until all of her loved ones were home.

"Yeah, Mom, it's just me!" I called back. She jumped up and headed for the kitchen to put the teapot on. She enjoyed talking to me after I had been out late. This was not an interrogation, simply a keen interest in what we all did. She was a loving Mom who had a special relationship with each of her eight children. I think that there was a little bit of Cupid in her too!

Having seven sons, she seemed to enjoy hearing about all of our girlfriends. No matter what shift I worked, or what event I may have attended, Mom was always there willing to offer food and/or refreshments, at any hour. These late-night gab sessions were good for both of us.

Mom asked, "Curt, do you have that new record, 'The Twelfth of Never'?"

"Sure, Mom, that's Johnny Mathis. They're playing the other side a lot on WMAQ. It's cool, too. That one is 'Chances Are'. It seems to be the hit side. I'll play it for you in the morning when everyone is awake."

Mom has a keen ear for music because she used to sing when she was younger. We often catch her in the kitchen singing with the tunes on the radio. One of her favorites of recent times, believe it or not, is "Don't Be Cruel," by Elvis. Even Mom's canary goes nuts when I crank up the volume on that one! No, Mom hasn't attempted to sing that one! For a sixty-one-year-old mother with a pack of crazy kids, she remains incredibly hip.

Without any doubt, 1957 was one of the most memorable years of my life. So many of life's unexpected events seemed to gang up on me this year. There will be heartbreak, employment struggles and death. This was a big load for an eighteen-year-old.

As the year begins, my employment suddenly ends. The Standard gas station where I had been working changes hands. It seems that there are enough family members to staff this facility. "Okay, that makes sense," I think. "I'll get hooked up somewhere soon, I'm sure."

The garage across the street from the Standard station offered me a job as a mechanic within that first week. However, that was short-lived too due to the sale of the property to a local manufacturer. End of new job! Being an eternal optimist, I thought, "That's alright, Chicago's Southside will not let this kid down. It never has. There's something out there for me."

Knowing that I had to grab some kind of a job to hold me over, I began scouring the classifieds. "Hey, Ron, here's one that I can probably land. They need a gas station attendant at the Shamrock gas station on 87th Street. It ain't a lot of bread, but it's a paycheck."

The next morning, I went there and talked to the owner. He advised me that the opening was for nights only. He told me to think it over for a couple of days. The night guy wasn't leaving until next week. He said, "If you're interested, I'd like to have you join us."

I thought, "Hmm, I'll have to toss this around. Do I really want to work the graveyard?" I walked across 87th to a little diner there. I dropped a quarter into the Wurlitzer and began picking my tunes. "Too Much" was Elvis's current hit, but I was always looking at the flip sides for more surprises. The flip on this one was "Playing for Keeps," and I played it three times.

"This is great, isn't it?" the blonde beauty behind the counter kinda whispered.

"Yeah, anything Elvis does is great, but this is one helluva ballad." I told her that I might be working across the street soon.

She said, "Well, now you know where the best juke box is."

Before I left, she gave me her phone number. I decided against the job due to the shift, and I wasn't going to see Blondie anyway, because I did have a fiancé. The following week, I read in the *Trib* that two guys had held up that gas station and brutally murdered the attendant; it was the graveyard guy!

As I sat at the counter at The Hot Dog Pit on Stony Island, I watched this very pretty young lady pull into the Texaco station next door. She was driving a racing-green Triumph TR-3. It was great lookin', and so was she! The Texaco attendant was more than a little helpful to this girl. He was bobbin' and weavin', trying to get different perspectives on her frame—not the car's, hers! He did everything but wash 'n' wax the damn thing for her. Seeing that car on a beautiful spring day, the ol' spring fever was kickin' in. I realized that I had to get it in gear. I needed to land a good paying job if I wanted to have the things that I wanted.

Unbelievably, when I got home, Mom says, "A Mr. Leonard called and said that he may have a good job for you. I guess that you have done a lot of work on his Oldsmobile over at Dobson Automotive. He seems to like you a lot."

"Yep, I know that man, he's a real cool guy. I'll call him right now."

Mr. Leonard had a good friend at the Pennsylvania Railroad, and he knew that I was looking for work. He told me that this man wanted to meet me as soon as possible. I arranged a meeting for the next afternoon. He told me that if I passed the physical and the written test, I would likely get the job. Mom was almost as excited as I was. Buck was now a switchman for the "J" (Elgin, Joliet and Eastern Railroad), and she knew that he made heavy bread there. Well, actually, Mom only knew that he was well paid; "heavy bread" never entered her mind. Buck just called it "The J" because that sounded tougher to him.

Mom told me to go to the basement and bring up the damp laundry. "I'll iron that nice blue denim shirt that you like so much. You can wear that because this is a working man's job."

Yeah, that seemed right—blue collar, that seemed just right. I ran to the basement the back way. As big and tough as I thought I was, I was thinking, "Luther, don't be there, please don't be there. I don't need any of that today." No problem, Luther wasn't there. As I ran back up the stairs, I was singing, "I've *been workin' on the railroad*." The next day, I passed both the physical and the written tests.

I'm about to become a trainman/brakeman/switchman for the P-Company. Fantastic, I can do that!

I call Ron that afternoon to announce the news. As always, his unwavering faith in me is evident. He was just telling his folks that I'd probably land the job. Ron is getting close to graduating from Mendel Catholic High School. From there he will likely join his father at the Rock Island Line. Now, we will both be railroad guys. The big difference will be that Ron will also enroll in the Midwestern Broadcasting School. He really wants to become a DJ or radio personality, as they sometimes call them.

Railroad Days! ©

I had just one week of orientation and was now going to be working with real trains. My first job assignment was the second shift at the 12th Street coach yards. As I rode the I.C. train from 83rd to 12th Street, all I could think was, "What in the hell am I going to be doing today?" I had no clue as to what this job entailed. After the first couple of hours my thoughts were, "Damn, this is nothing like I had expected. I'm working with an old engineer with absolutely no personality. The fireman could only fall into one category. He is a real jerk! How ridiculous is this anyway? There is no longer a need for a fireman. There's no damn furnace, thus no fire!" This is so typical of a Teamster's Union job. The unions drive these large companies; they are the real boss.

"Hey, what am I bitchin' about? I have my new position in life." This was not the chummiest group of guys that you've ever met. It was much like working in the Land of Misfit Toys! In any case, I could survive these clowns until the next job bidding came up later in the month.

As I arrived for my second day of work with these two "glowing personality" guys, I immediately headed for the engine. I figured that I'd drop my lunch off there and see what was up today. Neither of the guys said a word. Frick and Frack just looked at me and continued their little ol' lady jabber, totally ignoring me. I didn't even know their names; they never even introduced themselves. I'm sure that they just considered me the rookie, or a kid. "Kid, my ass. I'm a welder, a mechanic. I have a good-lookin' blonde fiancé, and I'm a pretty damn good ball player. I'm also six feet, two inches tall. That's something neither of them will ever be. Screw 'em!" I grabbed my lunch and left them in their little world. "What the hell do I care? I'm getting paid an enormous salary to play with big-ass, oversized, Lionel Trains."

I walked back to say "Hi" to another switchman, Big Bob! "Those jerks in the engine sure are friendly guys, aren't they?"

Big Bob kinda grinned and said, "About all those guys are good at is hiding the engine." That didn't mean much to me until he explained. "The guys in the tower can observe most of the action in the yard. A lot of the engineers are very adept at seeking out little hiding places. This guy's one of the best. He is a lazy son-of-a-bitch!" He then began to brief me on what we'd be doing today. He also showed me a good place to stash my lunch. I had written "Rat Poison" in black crayon on my lunch bag. Hey, I don't want anybody messin' with my peanut butter 'n' lettuce sandwich!

A few weeks have gone by, and I'm getting a bit more confident. In the yardhouse, it seems that I'm always bumping heads with this Russian guy. He works on some other crew. This guy doesn't seem to care for the Southside Kid. He is always making comments about my rookie status. He's one very big and stupid SOB, so I haven't really let him get to me too much. I figure that he's awfully damn big and obviously shows no respect for anyone here. His comments about the good ol' USA are disturbing some of the older guys, but none of them have spoken up yet.

One night, after making some ethnic comments about him, I have my encounter. I was used to taking care of myself and not really afraid of him, just wary of him. There's something that three people have instilled in me. Dad, Todd and Buck always told me, "Don't ever be looking to throw the second punch, because there may only be one punch thrown." There is nothing more devastating than being sucker punched, I know! This guy could probably crush my face with one blow. So, I'll just keep my guard up, and if it comes to a faceoff, I'm just goin' for it.

As I leave the yards that night at midnight, I'm crossing the bridge on 12th Street. The Shedd Aquarium is in full view as I near the station. I'm going to catch my Illinois Central ride home. There was this brotherhood thing between the different railroads that netted me a free pass on the IC Railroad. About halfway across the bridge, I hear footsteps. I'm pretty sure that it's my "Commie" enemy. The steps become quicker and more obvious. He wants to get me before I reach that IC station. Buck has taught me how to use my switch lantern as a weapon in such a situation. It has this six-inch cage on the bottom to protect the bulb inside. Buck always said, "Just hold that handle with all ya' got and cram that cage in your enemy's face!" This was not something that I had ever intended on doing, but hey, it's that time now! As I spin around, sure enough it's my Russian nemesis mumbling something in a kind of muffled voice. I'm sure he is about to cold-cock me. Not a chance. I let go with a roundhouse right, the lantern being my new fist. *Splat*! I nail him on the left side of his face. He falls against the concrete railing and moans something in his guttural language. I move quickly away from him. I walk backwards for several steps. I then turn and continue my walk to my IC ride. I move a bit quicker than before, but I don't run, because my mentors would not approve of this style of an exit.

As my train pulls away, I take a couple of deep breathes. I'm headin' home for my evening coffee, and meathead must be hurtin' a wee bit. I notice that my lantern has gotten a bit bent up. I chuckle to myself because now I know that this is a definite victory!

The next day, old Russkie is a no-show. Ward, the yardmaster, tells us that Russkie had an accident the evening before. No shit. I saw it happen! One of my younger buddies notices that my lantern is bent a bit around that cage. I reply, "Probably hit something very hard, don't ya' think?"

It was almost a week before Russkie returned to the job, and nothing was said when he returned. There was still some evidence of his "accident" on that ugly face. Within a week, we were both working other assignments. Goodbye, Mr. Russkie!

A bit later in the summer, Mom was hinting about how neat my switch lantern would be for her garden trips in the evening. She was forever changing the sprinklers out there. Some nights Mom would be up and down those stairs until midnight and even later. As we know the back stairway and gangway were kind of dark. One of these lanterns would be great for Mom. I toyed with ordering a new one for work and giving her my old, now bent-up lantern. I couldn't do it. Just didn't seem right, knowing its history. I bought Mom a nice shiny new one, and she used it every night.

Mom Adorning T-Bird 116 ©

In all of my ecstasy over my new job and the great union salary, I decided to buy some new wheels. My '50 Merc' is still undergoing some work since its engine transplant. I can't seem to dedicate the necessary time to complete the job because I am working these different shifts. Ron and I go shopping up and down Stony Island, from 83rd to 75th. There are tons of car dealers, new and used.

"Whoa, Ron, look here. Three T-Birds lookin' for a daddy!" We check them all out.

The yellow '55: "No way," Ron laughingly proclaims. "No damn way Curt's drivin' that."

"Ron, this '57 looks cool, but take a peek at the mileage—47,000, way too used for me. I think that this '56 black beauty is for me. A neat-looking white nylon top, continental kit and 1,100 miles. Could that be for real, only 1,100 miles?"

The next morning the dealer tells me, "Drive it down to your Dad's shop. If he's willing to cosign, you'll be drivin' it today!" Dad cosigns for me, and the '56 black beauty is mine. Yep, the 1,100 miles on the odometer is the correct mileage. I know the dealer and he explains its history. The original owner bought a Crown Vicky and the Bird and then decided that he couldn't afford both cars. That's my good fortune, because this little Bird is a winner.

Now I'll call Ingrid and see what time I should pick her up. She has no idea what a cool ride we'll have this evening!

Ingrid & Curt ©

Before long, this car came to be known as T-Bird 116. I'll let you figure out why! That weekend, Ron, Ingrid and I added several miles to the 1,100 already on the odometer. We cruised, with the top down, of course. Out to Beverly Hills and Evergreen Park we rode, smilin' all the while. We had the radio blaring as Elvis wailed, "Jailhouse Rock!" I can still see the gleeful looks in their eyes. While the ol' Merc' was a cool ride, it couldn't compare to this feeling. A warm summer day on our Southside of Chi-Town. In fact, it was an incredible day! As we returned to one of our stomping grounds around 79th and Cottage Grove, Sam Cooke was serenading us with "You Send Me." Later, Ron lamented about all of the chicks that we couldn't even attempt to pick up due to our third rider, my fiancé.

I bid on the job that seemed to be the most exciting—working "the hump" at 71st and Hamilton. I thought, "How lucky—a guy with no whiskers (seniority) nailing down this prime assignment." What I didn't realize was that it was summertime now, and the old-timers looked for jobs with less sun exposure and physical activity. They loved the cushy graveyard shifts where most of the activity involved pinochle and rummy games in the yardhouse. Yep, a lot of these railroad cats really loved to loaf much more than they loved their choo-choo trains!

Driving to work in my new ride is cool, but bittersweet. It's tough to ride through the neighborhoods with the top down listening to "Come Go with Me" and knowing that it will be ten tonight before I can ride again. Hey, a hundred and fourteen bucks is a pretty heavy car payment. I have to work today.

One day I pulled up to the hump while Keely Smith was singing "Whippoorwill," a great record. I just had to sit long enough to hear it all. As I climbed the hill, the yardmaster was watching me. He kinda grinned and shook his head. I'm sure that his teenage son was not drivin' in this kinda style. That Keely song will always take me back to that moment.

The main thrust of our job at the hump was putting trains together. A train would arrive at this steep downgrade, thus "the hump." It would be "shoving," or going in reverse. Each rail car was assigned its own spur in order to form an outgoing train. For instance, two cars for track five would be cut loose and sent down the hump with the switch opened to a particular spur, or track.

Now is where the "brakeman" title comes into play. I jump aboard the car, or cars, that are cut loose from the mother train. My job is to ride the car(s) down the grade while applying the needed braking to ensure a safe connection to the existing cars on that spur. There are several different types of brakes depending on what make, or how old the car is. A lot of these brakes are rusty and some just plain defective. Most of these rides are slow and sure, usually culminating in a nice quiet coupling. Other rides are a bit hairier due to the weight of the cargo or the condition and type of brake. It's a neat feeling, riding way up there while the boxcar goes, "clickity-clack, clickity-clack" as the rail bed below gives in a bit with each foot traveled. The faster rides are not always the safest. The one thing that you learn is that there is no escaping once these cars get rolling. Sometimes, you get a car with a bad, or temperamental brake. You just can't slow the thing down in time for the coupling process. No matter how hard this meeting of the cars is going to be, you have to ride it out. You can't jump off of the top of a boxcar without risking injury or death.

I've had to use plenty of Ben Gay on my chest since my new career began. When you come in hard, all you can do is hang on tight and support yourself against the brake wheel. Considering that this chest on my one-hundred-and-fifty pound body is far from iron or steel, it's the loser every time!

After awhile, I gained a reputation for handling these cars as though they were carrying plutonium. I really enjoyed the unpredictable challenge of the rides. The sensation that struck me every time that I heard those coupling knuckles closing quietly was my therapy.

I heard the call, "Hey, Queenie, here's a load of Ford-O-Matics for Detroit. Let's give 'em a soft landing." This particular commodity usually came three cars at a time. I loved it, I really loved it! These cars were usually newer and a much better ride, and they sported nice new brakes. After your cars reached their assigned track, you made the trek back up the hump, where the yardmaster would call your name again. And down the hill you'd ride once more. To me, it seemed like a carnival, so I'd hustle back to the top.

Where the nickname "Queenie" ever came from, I'll never know. It may have had something to do with my eagerness. It wasn't a negative, I know. One thing that I was sure of was that I had gained a lot of respect from those cranky old-timers. The proof of the puddin' was when Swede, a little mite of a Swedish man, and I were making our way up the hill. He never hurried; in fact, he often hid. He scratched his silver hair, laughed a bit and pulled his half pint of Seagram's from his back pocket. "Hey, Queenie, have a sip. Ya' earned it."

"No thanks, Swede. Can't drink and ride at the same time. But thanks, thanks a lot."

With that, he took the last slug and just pitched the empty bottle down the hill on the east side of the yard where T-Bird 116 was so carefully parked. Fortunately, his arm wasn't so hot. His empty didn't reach my car.

Y'know, some of these switchmen were kinda' strange, but I never tired of the train stories that they often told.

"T-Bird 116" – 1957 ©

Bye Bye Love! Just as things were looking great, my world began to cave in around me. Ingrid's parents had decided to return to Sweden. She was still a minor and, I guess, that was their privilege. This was obviously fueled by the diamond ring that I had given Ingrid last Christmas.

Ron and I were sitting in the yard. He was proclaiming, "What a great summer we're having Curt. We both have good-paying jobs. You've got the T-Bird. I'm enrolled in broadcasting school. Things are gettin' better every day."

Then I broke the news to him. "They're taking Ingrid away from me. They're all going back to Sweden in a few weeks. I'm sure that this Southside kid is their main incentive. Yeah, I'm sure. I guess I don't meet their standards. Just don't know. What in the hell can I do, Ron? Sis has already hinted at taking us over to Crown Point, Indiana, where we could get married. We're just not ready for that. It wouldn't work out. Y'know, Ron—not enough money and the friction that it would cause with her folks. Just not a good idea. Don't you agree?"

Ron responded with a rather timid nod of the head. He didn't want either one of us to be sorry later.

The date had been set. Ingrid would be leaving the USA on Sunday, July 7th. This was now cut in stone. They really were leaving. On Friday, June 29th, we went to the Double Drive-in for the last time. *Heaven Knows, Mr. Allison* was the featured movie that night. I didn't give damn about Mr. Allison. Who in the hell was he, anyway? The next day I took Ingrid to some relatives' or friends' home over in Burnside. I guess it was a bon voyage party. This was to be our last goodbye. On the trip over there, The Moonglows were singing, "We Go Together." What a tough tune for us to hear at that moment. Ron and I just dropped her off, and that was that. Her parents were already there, I think. We were not part of that scene, so we spilt. My gut told me, "It's over. I'll never see her again." Bye-bye Love!!!!

The following Wednesday, July 3rd, I was about to park on Harper Avenue after work. I could hear Ingrid's voice. She had come by to wish Sis a happy birthday. I could see them through the kitchen window, across the yard. Mom, Sis and my little Svenska Flicka were all in plain sight. My guess was that she also figured that we could say goodbye again. I couldn't take that roller coaster ride again. Sweden was a helluva long way from Avalon Park, and I didn't want to talk about it anymore. I slipped the Bird into first gear and quietly pulled away. I drove to The Hot Dog Pit and choked down a steak sandwich and a cup of java. I just didn't want to be alone. Mrs. G asked, "Rare, Curt?" I just nodded, yes. She was too damn smart not to know. Something was wrong, but she kept her cool and let it go. There were several other friendly, familiar faces there, and that helped me maintain my composure.

Before that week ended I was in a deep funk. I didn't know what I wanted to do from one moment to the next. I was lost in thoughts of "what if?" This was very perplexing to Ron. He summed it up with a quick and impromptu statement. He simply looked me straight in the eyes and said, "Curt, you can't tell the wind which way to blow!" This little bit of philosophy has changed my outlook so many times since that moment. "Thanks, Ron!"

It's another bright sunny day on the Southside. Baseball weather, for sure, don't you guys think so? What else can you do at the end of a love affair? At least that's what Sinatra or Damone would say. Let's go!"

Pepsi, Ron and I grab a few gloves, bats and balls. We all jump in T-Bird 116 and head for Avalon Park. As usual, the good diamond in the back is busy. Pepsi suggests, "Let's just go up front, near the hill. We'll hit some out!"

My response is positive. "Hey, guys, I may love to pitch, but I also love to shag 'em too! This is my kind of outfield. With all of this clover growing wild, it's like running on velvet."

My shoes and shirt go flying as Ron and I head for the outfield. "This is one cool way to get an even tan, man." I'm having a ball, diving, leaping and trying to make shoestring catches with no shoes on! After awhile, Ron retires to the hill over on the side, but Pepsi keeps sockin' 'em out to me.

When I finally run out of gas, I just hit the grass and lie there staring up at the sky. My mind is far away—likely, somewhere in Sweden. I'm trying real hard to adapt, but it's tough. Some young girls have been watching our efforts during the past half hour or so. Pepsi is pointing out to me as he talks to them. A couple of minutes later, two of these girls come up to me and ask for my autograph.

"Lee, would you sign this?" comes from one of them. She asks me, "What number do you wear, Lee?"

The Cubs had made a trade early in the season for Lee Walls. He was a tall, younger guy, so Pepsi thought that he'd have some fun. He has told these kids that I am Lee Walls. Pepsi's back there laughin' his ass off as I write, "Love to ya' – Al Wells'"

They never even look at my deliberately, misspelled name. "Hey, if that makes 'em happy, that's cool."

Pepsi is still laughing as we drive down Stony to Richard's Drive-in for a cold strawberry shake. It's a great place to sit with the top down, and besides that, Susie works here. She's kind of a tall, strawberry blonde. Since I have switched from the Merc' to the Bird, she's paying more attention.

"Fickle chicks, where are their standards anyway?" I whisper to Ron as Susie places her number 16 card on my windshield, smiling her lipstick off!

"Wake up little Susie." No, it's not playing on the juke box—I'm just having some fun with those lyrics as she walks away.

A quick spin forward. One morning last summer (2005), I drove to a diamond in Rancho Bernardo. This is a rather affluent area, and the parks are great. As I was about to open the trunk, this pretty little silver-haired lady approached. "Are you going for a run?"

"No, Ma'am, I can't do that anymore. I'm going to try to hit some of these over that fence over there." Even at my age, I still carry a couple of Louisville Sluggers and some baseballs in the trunk.

She continued talking, attempting to tell me her life story as we walked. I went down on the field. She found a seat in the grandstands. I've never had the privilege of playing in front of thousands of fans. Now, this one little eighty-four-year-old lady had me all stressed out with her attendance at this informal batting practice!

I popped some up, hit some weak grounders and did hit a few fairly solid shots. I never did hit any over that fence. When I ran out of gas, I rounded up the balls and headed for the car. As we walked back to the car, she asked me about myself. I told her that I was writing this book. She wrote my name down and said, "I'm going to be watching for your book."

Well, little lady, if you're watching, you're in it!

"Erler, last time I saw ya', you whacked me pretty good. I've been in prison for awhile and I've learned a few things. Wanna try that again?"

We were shooting some eight ball at Stevenson's Bowling Alley on 79th. Table number nine, our favorite, was over in the corner next to the Seeburg, which was playing "Day by Day" by the Four Freshmen. Ron and I, along with Patrick, a casual acquaintance, were having a relaxing time at one of our favorite haunts.

It was Nitwitz and three large jailbird buddies who were right in my face! With little or no choice, I simply set my cue stick down and replied, "Let's go!" Following these four intruders, we began heading for the stairs that would lead us up to 79th Street. As soon as I reached the door and took a step forward, *Splat*! Nitwitz had turned and thrown his new weapon, a sucker punch! I went down with the blow. As I began to rise, I could feel the warm blood running over my lips. My nose was gushing pretty good. This was nothing new to me; my nose had been known to erupt with as little as a storm warning! The black and white tile in the entryway way was suddenly taking on a new pattern. Another blast to the top of my head had me reeling. As I finally reached my feet, and seeing double, I almost went down again, but now I was throwing some counter shots at my enemy. If anyone was betting, I was already the loser.

We fought, diagonally, across 79th and all the way down to Evans Avenue. I could see saliva slipping out of both corners of his mouth. This cat seemed to be possessed, truly possessed! I was receiving a thorough pounding. It seemed as though I should have had Everlast stamped on my face, like the punching bags down at the gym. I can still see Ron's sad-puppy look as I was being smacked. There was nothing that he could do with these other guys on guard. Someone called out, "Cops!" There was a squad car coming from the west. The jailbirds disappeared faster than an ice cube on a hot August sidewalk! The cop car just rolled by. They had no clue that there was any such activity.

If there is one experience that is almost as rewarding as winning, it's the pampering by your friends after a rousing defeat. Strangers and friends alike were treating me as though I had just returned from a war. Actually, it was just a battle; maybe the war was not over! Ron and a few guys walked down to Walgreen's with me. They chipped in and popped for a thick 'n' creamy chocolate malt for their fallen warrior.

As the summer rolls on, I meet many new friends, both chicks 'n' cats. I have made up my mind to just carry on with life. Technically, I'm still engaged, I guess. Now all I have is a laminated picture on my dashboard to remind me. It also seems to serve as a deterrent anytime that I meet a female. I am, however, beginning to detect a little less emotion in those letters from Sweden, and they're less frequent. What the hell, Ingrid's got to be hangin' out with both old and new friends too.

One sunny afternoon, Ron and I spotted three girls walking west on 82nd. Ron was somewhat enamored with the one in the middle. As we approached them, Ron called out, "Hey, Blondie, come here. I wanna see if you're for real!"

The reply was, "Why don't you come here?"

Well, that was easy enough. As we got to the alley between Blackstone and Dante, I maneuvered the Bird onto the sidewalk. Ron's little beauty began to giggle a bit.

"Curt, look who's comin'!" I looked up and to my surprise, Pepsi was coming in the opposite direction, and also on the sidewalk. He was in his White '48 Ford Coupe with a couple of buddies, heading right toward us. The girls all seemed to enjoy our antics. We left Pepsi and his buddies with the girls.

My good buddy Casey and I were just pulling out of George's, the Greek diner at 87th and Dante. "Geez, Casey, look who's comin' our way. It's Peaches, ya' know, Peggy Sue. I haven't seen her since she asked me to that Mt. Carmel social. She's gorgeous! Yeah, come to think of it, she only lives about a block away."

Casey was already going to Loyola, and Peggy Sue had some questions to ask him. As they chatted about college through Casey's window, she gave me one of the sweetest smiles that I had ever received from anybody. I nodded for her to come over to my side. As she stuck her pretty head inside, I whispered, "You're more beautiful than ever!"

As she checked out my car, she asked, "Yours?" At that moment, she saw my laminated picture of Ingrid. "Who's that?"

I kind of mumbled, "Uh, oh that's my fiancé." That was the end of that and, unfortunately, I never saw Peggy Sue again. Finis!

I had met one cool character this year. He worked at the Gulf gas station next door to 1540. He rode a big-ass Harley and wore those mirrored shades. When I called him "Marlon," he always gave out with his toothy grin. Fact is, I always called him "Marlon." It just fit. He normally wore a black motorcycle jacket, the kind with the zippers and snaps everywhere. As any cool '50s biker would, he always had a pair of leather gloves hanging from one pocket or another. Once in awhile as he pushed his shades up with his index finger, he'd say, "Who's this guy Brando anyway?" and once again, the toothy grin.

When work was over, we'd begin our nightly task lookin' around the area, checkin' out the local scenery. There were a couple of younger girls out in the Oak Lawn area that we kinda dug. One of their families owned horses and seemed to be "in the chips." We'd hang out on the outskirts of their white-fenced little ranchito. We figured that their folks were not too receptive to these cats on the motorcycle. After a couple of trips, we agreed that there were other fish to fry. When you're that age, it's easy to fall out of love, too!

Marlon also had a '55 Studebaker that he called his "Golden Hawk." It wasn't really a Golden Hawk. It just had some added glitz that he borrowed from a real Golden Hawk. We were headin' out to his Mom's in Dolton one rainy afternoon. As we crossed the wet and slippery steel-grated bridge on the Calumet Expressway, he lost it! We went into a spin, three full revolutions. I grabbed the dashboard. "Hail Mary" was all that I could think of at that moment. As we completed the third spin, he hit the gas, and damned if we weren't headin' straight south again.

"You never hit a damn thing and we're still goin' south. Too cool!" We just looked at each other and cracked up. We laughed our asses off all the way to Dolton. I still miss this guy today. He was one of a kind!

Marlon introduced Ron and me to Senior Blues—that's what we called this jazzy cat. Senior managed the record store at 86th and Cottage Grove. Marlon knew that we loved jazz, and Senior was truly a jazz aficionado. He was very receptive to Ron and me. He had a thing about nicknames and asked us what we liked to be called. "Curt, what would be a good nickname for you?

"'Rod.' I've always dug that name. Yeah, 'Rod' will be fine." You see, Senior was a lot older than us, so we felt somewhat obligated to play his little name game.

Ron, not being easily swayed, and very articulate, said, "I kind of like 'Ron.' Will that do?"

Our new friend just loved Ron's integrity and attitude. "Hey, tell you what—each of you guys pick any LP that you want, anywhere in the store. It's on me."

It didn't take either of us very long to make our choices. Ron grabbed a stereo copy of Miles Davis's newest release. I had no problem, either—Joe Williams's first album ever. It was on the Regent label and very bluesy.

"This is one helluva way to start a friendship," I said to Marlon. The big toothy grin appeared once more!

I became Senior Blues's private mechanic—another side job during my slow days at the P-Company, which were hampering my pocket money a bit. I maintained his stupid-looking pea-green Dodge and a company delivery vehicle. As time went on, I also worked nights. Senior was amazed at our (Ron's and mine) knowledge of music. Hell, we were mighty eclectic guys. We knew our stuff: jazz, rock 'n' roll, rhythm and blues, pop. But absolutely no clue on that easy listening garbage.

My railroading has been slow lately. I'm on the extra board. According to the manual this means, *"Unassigned engineers or trainmen used to protect vacancies or make up extra crews as needed,"* or, simply, they call you when they need you. I don't mind that too much, 'cause the weather is great.

When they did call me in, I always enjoyed the new venue. Seldom did I get a call to the same job during this time. The one exception was the Broadway Limited job. This was a daytime shift and usually netted me an "early quit." If the job was completed before your shift was over, you still got your eight hours pay. There's that Teamsters thing again; we were always well covered! Some days, you could slip away right away. Others, you had to fake it for awhile first.

Well, let me tell you, I was never in a hurry to leave this job. We assembled the Broadway Limited each day. It left Chicago, bound for New York, at 4:00 PM every weekday. Once the train was assembled, I'd head for the last car, the club car. I may have been all grown up in many ways, but I still knew how to pretend. "This damn car is right out of the movies. I'll just find a nice comfy seat for the ride today. I'll pretend that I'm Mr. Somebody," I'd say to myself. There were a few times when I actually dozed off during these little daydreams!

Speaking of dozing off, I did just that one evening while standing on the bottom step of a caboose. The extra board guy had called with an assignment. Pepsi took the call. When the guy was told that I wasn't home, he asked if Pepsi would take the message. By accepting that message on my end, I was obligated to report to the rail yard at 55th and Stewart at 2:00 PM. He broke the news to me about noon as I arrived home. "Damn, man, why in the hell did you do that?"

Hey. Pepsi didn't know how it worked. He was tryin' to be helpful. He knew that I was taking anything that they offered. He wasn't keeping score of my hours slept. We never got mad at each other—almost never! I had worked a long shift the previous day and then proceeded to go on a date until very late that night. Oh yeah, I was dating again. I figured that I owed it to myself. What the hell, I'm only gonna be young once, right? There was not much sleep for this switchman the previous night.

There are typically three switchmen to a train. We had a front man, a middle man and a rear man. I had the rear on this particular night. As the train shoved back toward the 12th Street yard, the caboose became the lead car. Now, I was actually the front man, and responsible for seeing that all the switches were open as we shoved north. Standing on the bottom step of the caboose, I began watching the switches as we proceeded north.

"Erler, bad switch, Erler!" The middle man was tapping me on the shoulder. I looked up and there was The Loop right in front of me!

"Is that the Wrigley Building?" I blurted out. "Damn, I've been sleeping for miles while standing on this bottom step."

Fortunately, this was one cool cat. He said, "Get your ass into that caboose and get some sleep, kid."

I caught a break in more ways than one that day. I could have been fired, or maybe much worse. As Cahn and VanHeusen wrote, *"This is my kind of town, Chicago is. My kind of town, Chicago is. My kind of people too, people who smile at you."*

One hot August night, Ron and I were sitting in front of this chick Barb's house in Marynook. She had been my railroad eve date of the previous RR story. If you know Avalon Park, you know that this little Marynook burb was built right on top of our old Swamp. This was one of greatest prairies known to man. It had been dubbed simply "The Swamp." This was where we wanna-be cowboys and Indians had our frontier. I'd bring my bow 'n' arrows and spend the better part of the day there. Some guys came armed with their Red Rider BB guns. There were pheasants, mallard ducks, frogs, toads and, of course, guppies and tadpoles. Never did kill anything, didn't want to! Those pheasants and ducks probably would have laughed at my marksmanship anyway. I'd find some rusty cans for my targets. Man, those arrows were expensive! If I left home with three (that's a lot), I usually returned home with one at best! I spent many days there when I played hooky from school. We had it all there!

This little burb in the city was the typical postwar suburban community, tucked in right here on the Southside. As we shot the bull, it turned out that Barb was born in the same town as Ron—Mokena, Illinois. It's just forty miles or so southwest of our world. Being the spontaneous sort, I said, "Well, let's go see what this Mokena looks like. Jump in, Barb!" Ron was cool enough to exit while Barb slid in next to me. He hit the radio switch and tuned in on some tough sounds—"Tear Drops," by Lee Andrews and the Hearts, Buddy Knox's "Party Doll" and many more. My mood was great. I love goin' places that I've never been. I was even singing, and that's not something that I'm very good at: *"Love, love is strange..."* I was slaughtering Mickey and Sylvia's neat song.

Now mind you, I had nothing serious going on with Barb. I had recently taken on a very casual attitude when meeting new females. My favorite casual girl was Trudy. She worked down in The Loop at Maling Shoes. I would often pick up Ron after his broadcasting classes. I had met Trudy at a downtown coffee shop one evening as I waited for Ron. I began seeing her after she got off of work. Ron thought that she was kind of cute too! Trudy was a classy little lady.

There were a couple of cute chicks in the area that I liked being with, but I had been hurt recently, and I wasn't too receptive to this love thing. One of the Aquinas girls that knew of my Ingrid woes seemed a bit to threatening for me. I was told of this statement: "He's under my wing now." That was the end of that!

Another Aquinas chick that was having some problems at home suggested the following as we pulled up at her home one evening. "Let's just take off!" I think that she liked T-Bird 116 every bit as much as she cared for me.

Well, I'll tell what. Billie Holiday had the answer to this kind of talk. She once said, *"Don't threaten me with love, baby. Let's just go walking in the rain."*

We pulled into this vast metropolis of Mokena. I'd guess that it was about four blocks long! We pulled into the only drive-in joint in town. Before long, Ron was gassin' with some chick about some families that they both knew. On the other hand, Barb, my kinda' date for the night, hooked up with a bunch of guys. They wandered down the street a bit. I saw her sippin' some booze from a bottle that one guy had. No big deal, I hardly knew her. But we were in my car, and that ain't cool. I got talking to these twin brothers that were pretty cool guys. Their dad owned the local construction company. They didn't have anything real good to say about Barb. After awhile, this town was getting smaller and Ron and I were ready to head for Chicago Heights, where we knew some carhops.

"Come on, Barb, train's pullin' out," I said lightheartedly.

"Yeah, be right there!" she called back. Five minutes later, my twin buddies were giving me the thumbs down sign. They knew that she was getting pretty stiff.

"Last call!" I yelled this time. No response from the little lush. Ron and I looked at each other. I gave a wink and waved to the twins.

"We're outta' here," Ron said to them.

I smiled and said, "Well, at least Barb is back home!"

Dee with some last minute adjustments to T-Bird 116 ©

I had recently chalked up a decisive victory over another '56 Ford. It was a Vicky that was known to be pretty tough. I was feelin' my oats when the next challenge was thrown my way. Mike, an old classmate from St. Felicitas, had just bought a white '57 Chevy. It was a cool ride, for sure, but we constantly barbed each other about which car was the fastest. Hanging around the Gulf station at 83rd street one night, we decided on the ground rules.

"Okay, we'll each take one passenger as a witness. This way, the added weight will equal out. We'll go from a dead start for the quarter mile event. Then we'll go from a rolling sixty for the top-end winner."

We agreed and headed for the Calumet Expressway. Our riders would be watching for the state police and would witness both finishes. The quarter mile was based on a couple of markers.

The stage was now set. We both got off to great starts. The quarter mile wasn't long enough for that hot Chevy. I nipped him, but he was comin' on and flew by me after the fact! Now it was crunch time—top end was next. We would keep eye contact as we both watched our speedometers reach sixty mph. We'd even up while maintaining our sixty mph. It was decided that Ron would yell "Go!" as he dropped his hand out the window.

"Go!" was called and the race was on. It couldn't have been more even as we reached ninety-two mph. All of a sudden, Mike just let up and backed off the gas. I had hit ninety-five-plus before Ron said, "He's waving. I guess he quit."

We pulled off at 130th with Mike catching up. He yelled over to us, "I was suckin' up too much fuel, man!" I had nothing to say 'cause that's not how it should have ended, not at all! In my mind, nothing was really settled. Mike was always a pretty cool guy, but this was uncool in my mind. His rather close-budgeted ways were his "out."

We had a bit of a physical run-in just weeks later. He wouldn't stop picking on Pepsi, and Pepsi was my kid brother. Our family mentors had pretty much instilled "family first" in all of us guys. Mike and I knocked each other around in the Gulf station lobby until the owner came between us. As I remember, the candy machine got the worst of it. No big deal; just life on the Southside.

A few nights later, Pepsi, Ron and I decided to take a ride out to Chicago Heights. There were multiple reasons for this little trip. Number one, I really had a case on this big, tall kitten that carhopped at the A&W drive-in on Route 30. Another reason, we were determined to do the long-awaited top speed run with the T-Bird. I had installed some new Mallory ignition parts and some hotter plugs, and the carb was finely adjusted. As long as we never finished the big race with the Chevy, might as well try it solo. Oh, the other reason—we always liked to make the return trip from The Heights with the top down and the volume up!

We were psyched and ready to roll. Once again, the riders had their responsibilities—watch the speedo and watch for the state police.

"Just be sure to watch for cops, okay?"

"No sweat," Pepsi replied. We were off. Once into third gear, I began to accelerate. Ron and Pepsi were calling out the speed: "Eighty, eighty-five, ninety!" At this point, I was a little tense. We were close to the ground and I could see it flying by. "Ninety-five, ninety-eight, one hundred, one-ten, one-thirteen, one-sixteen, and headlights gaining on us!"

Pepsi had spotted what was sure to be the law. I took my foot off of the gas, turned off my headlights and geared down as the tach dropped a bit. Just ahead was 130th. I turned right and quickly sped up again. I knew that the A&W was up there on the left, just a couple of blocks away. I flew in and spotted my tall carhop. She was always a beautiful sight, but this was the greatest that she had ever looked! As we pulled into the rear area, I waved for her to hurry. She was returning to the front door with an empty tray. "Hurry, hang that tray right here and grab three of anything as fast as you can. Thanks!"

Posthaste, we all had our drinks. A wink from our savior server, and *poof*, she left the scene just as quickly as she had served us. She was one cool and hip girl. We tried to look kicked back as Fats was singing somethin' about, "*I'm walkin*"! Our pursuer cruised by slowly, trying his best to look important. Einstein drove right past us without a second look. Hence "T-Bird 116" was born!

Dad's health was not very good as 1957 was coming to a close. He had lost a lot of that special humor, and his quick thinking was not as evident. Dad very likely knew that all was not well; he just didn't discuss it. Frankly, I believe that Percy should have had a better feel for Dad's health. He spent every day with him.

Thanksgiving Day, November 28th, as we all sat at the dining room table anticipating The Feast, Dad stood up and made an announcement: "Curt's going to carve today!" As simple as that. No discussion with me or anyone else. He went on to say that for many years, I had spent these holidays helping with the turkey and all that went on in the kitchen. I was extremely proud. Not simply because I was granted this honor. I was proud because my Dad, my very special Dad, was so thoughtful. Was this gesture a coincidence? I don't think so!

The following Tuesday morning, December 2nd, Pepsi came rushing into my bedroom. "Dad has fallen out of bed. He's lying on the floor and he's not speaking!" We ran to Dad's bed and he was still there, motionless. I reached under his legs and shoulders and lifted him to his bed. He was barely whispering as he made a short statement to me.

He passed away that afternoon while on his way to the hospital with Todd at his side. I was grateful that Todd was with Dad when he "left us"! It was approximately 3:30 PM. The cause had been diagnosed as a cerebral hemorrhage.

Dad once made this statement to me: "Curt, be anything. But be a gentleman!" I have tried to follow your lead, Dad!

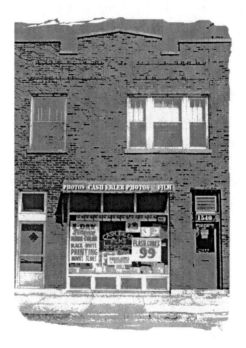

I Love You, Dad ©

I'm spending more time down in the store. Percy is somewhat out of sync'. In my heart, I feel that he had taken Dad for granted in recent times. Now, he misses him. We all do. Dad's health was slipping, and the photo finishing was not being done at this facility anymore. Therefore, Dad didn't have that heavy hand that he once had. He could and did run every facet of this enterprise. He built it with his sweat and blood. Dad's talent in the camera and photo business was exactly what put this place on the Southside map.

For years after Dad had gone, people would come in asking, "Where's Cash?" No matter whether Dad was as active or not, Dad was still the big draw. He was Cash Erler, and that's that!

On the other hand, I did have some compassion for Percy because he was suddenly alone all day, everyday. With the Pennsylvania Railroad's extra board slower than ever, I was going to be late with my T-Bird payment. I called the finance company seeking an extension for this month. I explained my work situation and also mentioned Dad's passing. The kind gentleman on the phone said, "Mr. Erler, your car is free and clear. Your insurance will cover the balance, as your Dad was the cosigner. You'll just need to get some documents to me. Don't worry about any more payments. I'll handle everything in the meantime."

Before saying a word to Percy, I told Mom what I had learned. Mom was very relieved for my sake. At that moment, I knew what I had to do. "Mom, I know how much equity, I have in the Bird, seven hundred bucks, I'm gonna sell it. This way you can realize the benefit of the insurance." I ran a couple of ads in the *Trib* and *Sun-Times.* Nothing doing, it was the middle of winter and it was a rag-top.

Percy's boyhood friend had opened a car lot on the site of my old Texaco station. I went down to 82nd and struck a consignment deal with John. I told him that I'd leave it on the lot and would settle for the first $1,800. Any amount over that was his commission. I don't think that Percy was too hot on the idea of me making this deal with his ol' buddy. By the way, this guy was nobody's buddy! Percy kinda' felt usurped, I guess.

He made his presence known at the lot during the next week. There happened to be a '57 Caddy Sedan De Ville that caught his eye. He came to me with this offer: Why don't I let John take your T-Bird as a trade-in. This way you'll be cashed out for your seven hundred and I'll pay Mom the other $1,100 in monthly payments.

"Okay, Percy. But first, I'm gonna take my T-Bird 116 on a little ride." Little did he or Mom know what that "116" stood for. "When I get back, you can do your deal, if Mom approves."

I called Ron that night after he got off of work. "Ron, can you take a few days off of work? You'll have to call your DJ friends downtown too, 'cause we may be gone for a week or so."

"Curt, what in the hell are you talking about? Where are we going?"

"I don't know. How about Kentucky and Tennessee? I'm sellin' the Bird, so we need to take it on one last little cruise."

Ron, I could tell, was eager. He had never been past Mokena to my knowledge. Ron optimistically replied, "I'll talk to my Mom and Dad and be over there about seven. We can talk more about it then."

THE SOUTHSIDE KIDS HIT THE ROAD

Ronnie the Cat on a windy hill in Kentucky – February 1958 ©

Ron and I know that even the most dedicated Southside kid has to do a little exploring! A couple of mornings later, Ron and I were packed and ready for our adventure. His folks had us over for breakfast the morning that we left. I think that they wanted to talk to me about a safe trip, etc. How else would loving parents respond with their only child taking his first trip away from home? Breakfast went well, and off we went.

We covered Ohio, Kentucky, Tennessee and just touched on West Virginia. The highlights for both of us were The Blue Angel night club in Cincinnati and Boone's Tavern, which was on a college campus in Brea, Kentucky. Great food, great service and good lookin' college girls as waitresses. We dined on southern fried chicken, corn spoon-bread, fried okra and pecan pie. This wonderful old white mansion is still a landmark. The students are, for the most part, the staff.

The winding, snowy mountain roads were a blast too! T-Bird 116 never had so much fun! We heard more rockabilly artists than we had ever dreamed existed. I discovered a country/folk tune that's still a favorite today, "The Long Black Veil," by Lefty Frizzel. I also brought back the new Jimmie Rodgers LP for Pepsi. It was Jimmie's first album. Oh, how I love to travel!

Percy got his Caddy. And Mom? Well, to the best of my knowledge, she never received a cent. I made a point of taking Mom anywhere that she wanted to go in "her" Caddy. There was no requesting permission, I just did it!

Wedding bells are ringing. "Hell no, not mine, no way!" Sean and Casey's big sister was wed earlier today. A fine reception is being held at a hotel in the South Shore area. Was I invited? Probably not. Oh, maybe a casual verbal overtone. As it is, Pepsi, Ron, Vince and I just happen to drop in. After testing the fare and sipping on a beverage or three, I feel the urge to dance. Now, remember, I have been told that I dance like a linebacker. Who cares? I'm doing a fair job of fooling this friend of the bride and groom. Don't know who she is, but this is our second dance. This is a rather short and attractive woman, probably in her thirties. After knowing her for the last ten minutes, I feel confident that I'm not upsetting her or anyone else. She has ascertained the fact that I've known the whole gang, Sean, Casey and their sister Meg, for most of our lives.

As we dance and talk about the families, the bride's and mine, I feel a tap on my shoulder. I'm about to experience a brief encounter with Bambino.

"May I?" is the short request from an old friend. My new and much older friend turns and excuses herself. My new dancing partner is none other than Teresa aka Bambino, my childhood buddy from Harper Avenue. "You shouldn't be dancing with older women." These are the first words that I've heard from this girl for eons.

"Sophia Loren" is my first thought. This little Italian tomboy has evolved into a walking statue. It wouldn't be fair not to describe this lovely young girl. She's wearing a low-cut, black and white polka-dot dress and looking much like an Italian princess. No doubt, this little girl is now a show stopper!

"Fever" was the song that was playing, and fever it was! For the first time since Ingrid went away, I felt something very special. This was someone that I had only known as a neighborhood buddy. Oh yeah, we shared a childhood kiss once or twice. Other than that, it was "Hey, Bambino, can I borrow your new bat?" or "Are ya' gonna play? We're pickin' sides in a minute."

As we danced, she commented on seeing me with my Jimmy Dean car, referring to the Merc' and T-Bird 116. She also commented about always seeing me with my blonde girlfriend, Ingrid. It was so nice holding her in some way other than a full nelson or hammer lock, as I did when we wrestled as kids. I didn't even think of the night in '56 at the St. Felicitas carnival when I came to her aid. Neither of us mentioned it. I'd like to think that she did remember simply from her warm approach to this old playmate from Harper.

We talked a bit after our two brief dances. I was very tempted to part with a soft kiss, but the audience was too large, and I wasn't sure what her reaction might be. We said goodbye and we each went our own way. It was time to move on. Pepsi stayed on and probably did a little dancing of his own.

With the IC lines right across the street, Ron and I took a train ride downtown. Woody Herman was playing at the Blue Note. While most would think of him as Big Band, we knew that he was sounding more and more like Basie and Heath lately. A couple of cold Manhattans and some hard-driving jazz took my mind off of Teresa for awhile. Woody did one helluva job with his sexy sax solo on "Love Is a Many-Splendored Thing"!

Teresa had moved a few blocks west since I had last seen her. She gave me her address and phone number. I called her within a couple of days and arranged to stop by and visit. I was looking forward to saying 'Hi' to her mom and dad and younger sister. Her mom came to the door and called Teresa. She seemed cordial enough, but she did not ask me in. Teresa and I chatted for a little bit. While we were at the reception, we had talked about going out for dinner or a show. As soon as I mentioned this she said, "Mom and Dad have told me that I can't date you." I asked why. She just shrugged and dropped her head in what I perceived to be disappointment. I have never seen her again.

An Angel on Euclid! It was springtime and we had no wheels! Walking east on 87th after leaving Seaway Deli, Vince, Ron and I were suffering from spring fever.

"Hey, who's that—the little stacked chick ahead?" Vince asked with a rather cocky and confident swagger.

"She looks kinda chunky to me," Ron replied very quickly.

Vince wasn't easily convinced. "Let's pick it up a bit and we'll find out."

As we picked it up, she slowed to a crawl. She was somewhat curious too. We approached and Vince started his pitch. Ron and I were not getting involved in this scene. Just before reaching Euclid Avenue, Vince was scribbling down her phone number. Ron and I had decided that she was a bit too top-heavy! Hey, a chick could be top-notch, but top-heavy was a definite demerit in our book. "Top-heavy" took a left at Euclid. Vince now had her at a standstill, both seeming to be enjoying their prey.

We already knew several girls on this street-o-plenty! There was a little idle gossip with a couple of the chicks that we already knew. One was still on my s-list for grabbing the keys to T-Bird 116 last summer. We were washing it in front of her house. Suddenly, she grabbed the keys and ran in the front door. Being a few years older than this squirt, I wasn't havin' any kiddie games. I simply wanted my damn keys and to hell with the silly games. A brief conversation, and I was convinced that she hadn't grown up much in a year.

Wandering down the street, I spotted a rather attractive and much more mature-looking young female. After an informal introduction, we sat on the stoop of her front porch. Just as I may have been falling into infatuation, I see this lovely lass pushing a stroller. She was wearing a white sleeveless cotton blouse and red plaid shorts. A lovely Colleen to be sure! With all due respect to my new acquaintance, I asked, "Who's that chick with the baby?"

"Oh, that's Kathy, and that's her little sister in the stroller." I was very relieved by the little-sister news.

I thanked Debby, my new friend, and said, "Heck, I was thinking that she was someone's young wife. What a relief. Mind if I stroll over?"

Debby had not yet felt that infatuation, I guess, as she replied, "No, I don't care. But she has a boyfriend, and she's only fifteen." Now, a husband would have scared me off, but a boyfriend is never a brick wall.

I approached Kathy and said, "Hi!"

In a rather indifferent and bored reply, I barely heard, "Hello."

"So, you've got a little sister. That's cool. All I have is a big sister."

I knew just how far this chatter was getting me—nowhere! Soon after Kathy's one-word conversation, her Mom popped out the door and requested that she "come in now." During the next year or so, I kept my foot in the door with phone calls and short visits. Most of my phone calls seemed to be a bit tardy. "Kathleen's gone to bed, it's after nine. I'll tell her that you called." Kathy's mom was not having any of Romeo's line. Kathy remained extremely aloof.

Finally, I was promoted to a big brother kind of a friend. I had now become someone to tell her woes to. As time went on, I believe that she was trying to gain some insight into my lifestyle. We were on opposite ends of the spectrum. I still felt no real shutdown, just a lot of pride and caution. I wrote letters from far away places, trying to impress her with my worldliness. This was one well-disciplined young Irish Catholic lady!

Up on the Roof ©

The roof, now that's as fine a place as any to spend time. Once up there, we can see the whole world. Well, we can see all that is necessary. We can see *our* whole world! You don't have to live in Brooklyn or da' Bronx to enjoy rooftop fun.

"Hey, Ron, it's about time for the chicks to start arriving home from work and school. Let's hit the roof for awhile."

Ron is quick to reply. "Yeah, it's 5:25. A lot of the good buses are about due."

We grab the heavy old steel ladder and go up through the trapdoor to our little heaven on earth. Ron gazes out, looking each way, from the south, then the west, to the north and then the east where the buses will be arriving soon. "What a view. You can see everything from up here. We can see the whole neighborhood."

From this lofty perch, we view five gas stations, two barber shops, a couple of the local candy stores, the bakery, supermarkets and St. Felicitas. As we walk to the north end, we can survey the new stock at the used car lot on Stony. There are a lot of cool views from up here, but most importantly, it's the chicks! As each bus stops and unloads, our prey exit. Ron begins to sing, *"Pretty girls everywhere!"*

Some we knew from school, the pizza joints or the camera store, and some we simply wanted to know. That's where the fun began. Like any other group of human beings, they came in all types and temperaments. Some would disdain our smiles and "hellos." Some were simply too shy to look up, and others would anticipate it. Every now and then, some little doll would throw a kiss. Oh, is that great for the ego!

I had this little trick where I'd be sitting with my legs hanging on the outside of the roof. As I spotted my predetermined prey, at just the right moment, one of my moccasins would "accidentally" fall off. "Oh darn it. Would ya' do me a favor and just flip my shoe into the yard?" Some girls would ignore my request; others would oblige. In those positive cases, I'd be down there to thank her the next day. There were a couple of regulars who would stop for a chat, albeit a brief one.

We were always armed with a cold Coke and sometimes a can of Old Style. The radio cord was dropped down and through my bedroom window. This way, we could discuss the top tunes with some of our passers-by. This was almost like chumming fish. The music, in some cases, would stop a girl in her tracks. "What's that song they're playing? Who's that singing?"

Paul Anka, Buddy Holly and The Diamonds are getting a lot of attention lately, and of course, Elvis always does! The more mature girls seem to be getting into Frank Sinatra stuff. There is a certain young lady, much older than us, who just loves hearing our music. I try to spot her in time so that we can switch to one of our jazz stations. Gee, if only we were older!!!

We know that this roof is our own private park. Many Indy races have been listened to from this perch. We drop a clothesline down to the yard as a dumb waiter. Lawn chairs, coolers, a radio, you name it—we have it all up here.

The roof was especially neat at night. It was cooler up there, and there seemed to be a special feeling of being out of reach when we were up there. It was a great place to go when the world didn't seem to be treating you right. I often threatened to sleep up there some summer night. The fear of sleepwalking always seemed to curb that urge!

"**I'm buying the ribs if you'll take a little ride with me!**" This was my friend Dean on the phone. Dean was a good bit older than me. I met him while working at Dobson Automotive. He drove for Amber Bakery at 82nd and Dobson. As a member of the American Fifth Army division, Dean was active in such battles as Anzio in 1944 and many more. "I'm going to St. Louis tomorrow to complete my divorce obligations." The only detail remaining was for him to drive his ex back home to St. Louie. "I'll be leaving right after I finish my route, about one o'clock tomorrow. Do you want to help me drive? I'll buy us some good BBQ when we get there." He knew that I loved hickory-smoked ribs. His temping bait worked. Not only the ribs, but he had one of the toughest cars that I had ever driven. It was a red and white '55 Mercury Monterey.

"It's a deal, pick me up when you're leavin'. I'll be ready." About two o'clock the next afternoon, that cool ride pulled up in front of Cash Erler Photos.

"Let's hit it," Dean said. "Tootsie" (because I can't remember her name) was in the back seat with her perpetual somber little pout.

"Looks like I got shotgun today!" I exclaimed. Off we went, taking an awfully long ride for ribs. That was cool with me, 'cause I've always had that wanderin' way! Why be here when you can be there? We hit King's Highway outside of St. Louis about 7:45 pm. Tootsie was almost home. Woe is me. Gee, I'm going to miss that pout.

We dumped (oops, dropped) her off around 8:00 PM. After wiping all of that luscious spicy BBQ sauce off of my face, we began the trip back north. I managed to eat a half slab of spareribs and two hot links and poured down a couple of Dr. Peppers. What the hell, I was a growing boy! Shortly after we left the St. Louis area, a big white Coupe De Ville came flying by.

"He must be hittin' ninety, Curt."

"Yeah, he's sure flyin'!" In a moment; they were out of sight. Dean was getting a bit weary and asked me to take the wheel. He jumped into the back seat. He was snoring like mad within five minutes. It began to rain—and rain harder, and harder. I tuned in KMOX and caught the end of a Cardinals road game. This was followed by some damn good rock 'n' roll and R&B. One tough tune after another: King Pleasure's "Red Top," Georgia Gibbs doin' "Dance with me Henry," Ricky, Elvis, Bobby Darin and more.

Through the pouring rain, I spotted that white Caddy ahead. The rain had slowed him down a bit. "Oh, yeah, now it's time to test this Merc'," I told myself as I approached them and began to pass. As we were alongside of them, they waved and smiled. It was two middle-aged black cats. Frankly, as dark as it was, all I could really see were shiny white teeth, eyes and the one guy's cigarette. I passed them and kicked that Merc' in the ass. Eighty, eighty-five, and here they come haulin' ass. They passed me, and again that big smile.

"Uh oh," I thought, "we're in this 'til the end!" Within a minute I was flyin' by them again. The rain had not let up at all. As they approached and attempted to pass again, my foot hit the floorboard.

Dean woke up, oblivious to the action, and said, "How we doin' Curt?"

I replied, "It's rainin' like hell and we're winnin' right now. The needle is almost at the century mark! Those cats in the Caddy were playin' with me, so I'm giving them something to play with. Man this thing holds the road like it was glued to it."

Dean, still half asleep, kind of half whispered, "Better slow down, man."

I explained that I didn't want us to lose. "Guess what, they're backing off. Checkered flag, baby, checkered flag. This race is over!" They tooted and waved as they pulled into a diner.

"Want me to drive for awhile?" said Dean.

"No, I'm fine. Grab some more sleep. I'll behave."

Another sunny, Southside morning. My buddy Dane called. "Hey, Curt, I'm home on leave. Ya' gonna be home this morning?" Dane had joined the Air Force in '56.

"Yeah, sure, what do ya' wanna do?"

"I picked up a neat old BMW cycle down in Texas. Thought we'd take a ride!"

"Cool. When ya' comin' by?"

"Gotta run to the store with my Mom, then I'll head over."

Dane is close to six feet tall and nothing but muscle. He's a rather handsome blond-haired Scandinavian cat. We never really stated it, but we seemed to have this mutual respect for each other. Neither of us ever avoided a good fight. It boiled down to one thing: he never really wanted to take me on, and the feeling was mutual. We were pretty damn tight, and when we were together, we seldom had much to worry about.

Dane showed up about noon on his red BMW motorcycle. As always, he had stopped long enough to pick up a coffee ice cream soda for me at Kladis's Ice Cream Parlor. For a big tough guy, he had a heart of gold.

"Let's take 'er out on Doty and see how it rides," I said. Anyone from our Southside knows that Doty Avenue is where Stony Island becomes a highway. Once you pass the stoplight at 95th Street, you're on Doty Avenue, actually US Rte. 30. The speed limit increases by 20 miles an hour. It was normally the testing grounds for anyone with a new vehicle, young and old alike. We caught the red light at 95th Street. As it turned green, Dane really hit it. We were across 95th in a split second, and as he shifted gears I felt the rear end getting loose. He had hit a big black oil slick, and we were goin' down.

He dumped it to the right and went with the bike to the curb. With this maneuver, I was thrown off to the left. I hit the road and the oil slick. I continued on at a pretty good speed with traffic behind me. I probably looked as though I was sliding into second base. It felt like forever, and as I looked up, there was an eighteen-wheeler bearing down. All I saw was one big-ass bumper, grill and the undercarriage. I knew that it wouldn't be long, so I threw my right elbow to the ground, throwing me to the right. I rolled to the curb and the truck flashed by. Dane was sitting on the curb, a bit shook up but virtually unscathed, thank God! I stayed down, hurtin' all over my left side. I looked down and saw that my blue pegger pants were ripped and bloody. From my knee to my hip, I was two-toned, bloody red and greasy black. My elbow was not looking much better! We made eye contact, still silent. He smiled and I laughed because we were both okay!

Before we left the curb, a big dump truck pulled up. A big black man and a boy came running over. "I thought fir sure, we wuz comin' back to pick up a dead boy, we wuz sure!" he said with a look of terror still on his face. He was returning from the city dump at 103rd Street. He was heading north in the opposite lane when we went down. He cut a U-turn at 95th and hurried back to us. The boy, his son, sat down next to us and simply said, "Hi!" with a big smile. Back then, men didn't hug like some do today, but we shared hearty handshakes. I never saw these two caring people again, but I'll never forget them, ever!

We checked out the bike, and all seemed well mechanically. The right side had some scratches, but not bad, not bad at all! Immediately Dane said, "We'll go to my house and have Mom check ya' out." My mom did not like motorcycles. Cary had an old Indian for awhile and she dreaded it.

As we walked into Dane's house, his mom said, "Are you boys okay?" as she got a peek at my rather ragged outfit.

"Yeah, Mom, we took a little spill. Can you check Curt's leg? I think it's okay, but ..."

She ripped the pant leg open. My leg looked like dirty hamburger. She washed and dressed my leg and brought me a bottle of ice cold 7-up. "Dane, there's a pair of your blue pants in the damp clothes. Get them and I'll press them for Curt."

As fate would have it, they looked just like mine. I thought to myself, "Great. Now Mom won't have to know anything about this."

Now, you need to understand, Dane's mom was, as a rule, very quiet and quite strict. As most moms will do, she came to the aid of these two "kids," tough Air Force son or not!

Go west, young men! That was the urge that Ron and I were feeling by midsummer of '58. My second cousin, Bill, was visiting from Los Angeles with his mom, my favorite cousin, Peg. Bill was having a lot of fun being back on the Southside and wanted to stay a bit longer. We stayed out in the yard real late that night and came up with a plot that was sure to please all involved. Bill could stay with us a bit longer, and Peg could fly home as planned. Ron and I would accompany Bill on his flight back to Los Angeles.

"Mom, would you help me to convince Peg that Bill will be fine here with us and on the plane?"

Bill was a couple of years younger than us but one large, good-lookin' cat. He told us all about the cool beaches in LA and all of the chicks that he knew. Ron and I began our lobbying immediately. Peg was one sweet chick and hadn't forgotten what it was like to be a teenager.

Mom helped with her views: "Actually, having Curt and Ron by his side might be a good idea because I know that Bill's not too fond of flying. In fact, he commented to me that he wished that his dad would come out and drive them home."

Bill's dad, Big Bill, had been at the battle of Iwo Jima during the war. He was also a big good-lookin' guy with black wavy hair. He and Mom were very close, so she chatted with him long distance.

As soon as the word was "Go!" I called Ron. "Hey, Ron, it worked. Peg's working on the tickets for us. Bill can still use his ticket on whatever flight that she books for all of us. We're goin' to the beach man, the big beach!"

Within a few days, we were winging our way west. "Hey, Mom, we're taking a TWA DC-8. Ron and I can hardly wait for our first flight. Ron has already spent a bunch of bread on clothes. I'm heading for Sears when we arrive to buy a pair of those beachcombers like Bill's. He says that they're only six bucks and their Sears looks just like ours. I'll see what else those Sunny Cal guys are wearin'. I don't want to be no square out there. Bill tells me that it's a whole different world compared to the Southside."

"Eight hours, man. Can you believe that they can keep all of this steel up here for eight hours, man? Geez, Bill. Look down there. The cars and houses are beginning to look like ants!" While Bill had just been on a similar flight with his mom, he still wasn't havin' any of this.

"C'mon Curt, stop talkin' about that. Let's just have a Coke and talk about the beaches."

Ron, as usual, is cracking up as I continue to work on Bill. I take out my pocket knife and begin to act as though I'm loosening the screws around the porthole window. He threatens to tell the stewardess if I don't stop. "Damn it, Curt, stop doin' that or I'll tell her. I'm not bull-shittin' you!"

"Go ahead Bill, tell her. I'd like to meet her anyway!"

I stopped and all went well for the remainder of our flight. During the flight, as you might expect, I fell in love with a couple of the very pretty stewardesses. I had never met a real live stewardess before. I requested every snack and drink, even a pillow and any other amenities that were available. They never seemed to stop smiling as they strutted up and down the aisle in their impeccably neat uniforms. As the miles flew by, it became very obvious to me that none of these princesses were too interested in this nineteen-year-old boy!

After downing a half dozen Cokes and snacking ourselves to the max, we began to descend. The sights, as we approached the runway, were absolutely great to these Chi-Town guys. I'll never forget seeing all of those pastel-colored homes. They were pink, yellow, aqua, baby blue and mint green. This whole area seemed to be frozen in time, a throwback to the days of WWII. There seemed to be aircraft plants everywhere. These little cookie-cutter homes were, I'm sure, starter homes for the young war couples and factory workers of that era.

"Let's just grab a taxi, 'cause I don't know if Mom is awake this early." Bill looked just like a seasoned businessman hailing the cab. "A hundred and third 'n' Normandy, please!" he said to the cabbie as we threw our bags in the trunk.

Peg was elated to see us as she beamed her perpetual smile. If ever there was a prototype of the WWII bride, she was it! It was obvious that she had primped for our arrival. She was wearing her jumper-style housedress. A poster girl for war bonds, that was how she appeared to me. She had the coffee brewin' in minutes.

"How did the flight go, guys?"

Bill just gave me a glare, but he smiled and said, "Just great, Mom, real fine. It was cool."

After a chatty morning; Peg decided that Ron and I were old enough to share the two quarts of ABC lager that were in her Coldspot refrigerator. Poor Cuz' Bill had to sit and sip ice water as we drank from our frosty mugs! Ron seemed enamored with the gossip of the old days. Peg just loved to embarrass me with her stories of giving me baths in Mom's old kitchen sink.

By the time Big Bill arrived home from work, the brew was all gone. So Ron and I took the trip down to the Mayfair store to gather some more refreshments and some cold cuts. After all, Bill had worked hard all day. We saw no sense in him thirsting too long. We made another trip later on. Ron and I were now walking zombies. We crashed on their living room floor for the night!

Sunrise brought everything into perspective; we were in sunny California. What a great day Ron and I were about to have. After saying our farewells on Normandy Avenue, we checked into a motel on Vermont Avenue. Ron had noted that we would have a little kitchen there which would save us some bread. We checked in and immediately got directions to Sach's Records downtown. Senior had moved back home to Los Angeles and was, once again, managing a record store. We grabbed a bus on Vermont and headed straight to Sach's Records on Broadway, downtown LA.

Now, it was time to surprise Senior Blues. He had no clue that Ron and I were there. Ron walked into the store first, then I slipped in and went in a different direction. As we would expect, Miles was blowin' over the store's hi-fi system. Senior spun his head right, then left, and then said, "Hey, cats, what in the hell are ya' doin' in LA?"

"We came to buy records, man, whadaya' think?" was Ron's quick response.

Senior responded with his famous, "You guys are too much!"

We hung out with Senior all day. He took us to Chinatown for lunch. Then it was off to his pad. Being his former mechanic, I said, "Wow, I dig your wheels, but who did the weird exhaust pipe?" It was a two-tone blue '53 Caddy Coupe De Ville. It had one big chrome exhaust pipe right in the middle of the rear bumper.

Senior, not knowing a damn thing about cars, said, "That's how they make 'em, isn't it?"

After a good laugh, Ron and I didn't mention this rather bastardized Caddy again. We sat at his pad that evening and drank a bunch of Lucky Lager. Hey, we'd drink anything that he had available. We were fried from the past few days' events. After diggin' some Mulligan and Baker, Sam "The Man" Taylor and some Chris Connor, Senior says, "Hey, you guys want to use the car tomorrow?"

"Are you kidding? Hell yeah, we do!"

We drove Senior to work in the morning and left armed with a local map. It really didn't matter, because we had no clue as to where we wanted to go. We dropped him off and headed south. At least we had been there and had some idea of what was there.

"I'm buying the coffee and rolls if you can find some decent joint," Ron said as he adjusted his cool new shades.

I spotted this sign—"Scrivner's." "This looks like our Richard's on Stony Island. This is one neat drive-in and they have carhops. This is cool!"

We pulled in in "our" Caddy coupe, figuring that we'd impress the carhops. On second thought, this was kinda like an old guy's car. Maybe that's why their "Suzie" said, "Good morning, Sir. What would you like?"

You talk about a blow to any cat's ego, this was it! Actually, it turns out that she greeted a couple of other cars within earshot that same way. Relieved of our "old" image, we began our sweet talkin' with our new Suzie. She was about seventeen and cuter than a button, as Gramma would say.

Ron ordered in his DJ voice: "How 'bout a couple of coffees and two sweet rolls?"

This chick looked at Ron and inquired, "What are sweet rolls?"

After Ron desperately tried to describe our Southside treat, she said, "Oh, you mean a Danish. Would you like those warmed?"

Ron stuttered back, "Uh, yeah, please. Yes, warmed please." What did this California chick know anyway? She had never been to the Southside and certainly never had a sweet roll at Steffens bakery.

"Poor little girl, maybe we should bring her home with us and get her hip to our Chi-Town ways."

Ron was in one helluva happy mood. I think that we felt like ourselves again and back in the groove. He began to laugh and then retorted with his statement, "California ain't gonna change these cats, never! A sweet roll is always gonna be a sweet roll, not some damn sissy-ass Danish!"

We spent the next couple of days getting acclimated to this new scene. Hermosa Beach, Redondo Beach, we hit 'em all! "Hey Ron, lets go find us an oil well like ol' Jimmy Dean did in *Giant*."

"Cool, let's just do that man, we'll just do that. Where in the hell are they?"

"Don't know. We'll just ask the next little chickadee that we see. That sounds like an idea, man."

We began driving south until we hit another drive-in. "Now, let's get one thing straight. When we order our Cokes, we ain't listenin' to any of this 'soda' crap. A Coke is 'pop' and we ain't never gonna drink their 'soda'."

With no drive-ins in sight, we pulled into the lot of some dumpy joint in Manhattan Beach. No chickadee in there, just some old hen. She directed us to Palos Verdes, just south of Redondo Beach. "You'll see plenty of oil wells there, boys." Ron gave granny a big smile and his best Elvis voice: "Thank ya' maam. Thanks a lot, beautiful."

We did find a ton of oil, but none of it ours like Mr. Dean in *Giant*.

Palos Verdes Oil Derrick – Curt & Ron / July 1958 ©

On the trip back to Sach's Records, some guy used the back end of the Caddy for a battering ram. As we sat at a red light, the guy must have been dreamin', because he rammed us pretty good in the rear. Senior's black and blue mirror dice were shakin' like a man on a fuzzy tree, to borrow a line from Mr. Presley!

I looked in the rearview mirror. This jerk was laughing. Ron very nonchalantly stepped out and walked to the rear of our car. He came back quickly and said, "Nothin' man, no damage, nothin'. But that cat is laughin' like a lunatic!"

"Cool, watch this," I said to Ron. When the light turned green, I pulled forward a couple of feet, threw the ol' hydromatic into "R" for respond, or, more appropriately, retaliate, and then I floored it. *Crunch, poof* and a bunch of steam was now rushing from this dummy's wreck. I slipped it back into "D" for drive and silently pulled away. As I looked back in the mirror, the guy's old Dodge was lookin' like those oil wells that we had visited.

"I think he must have struck somethin', but it wasn't oil!" was Ron's closing comment.

We finished off our visit to Southern California with a return visit to Hermosa Beach on Friday afternoon. "Maybe we'll run into those little cuties again, Ron."

No luck, so we began to toss our sixteen-inch Clincher softball. When one got away, this couple brought it back with the most puzzled look on their chops. They examined it, looking as though we had just beheaded some Martian!

"What is this, some kind of a football?"

Ron, with his dry wit, replied, "Yeah, it's a Chicago-style football. Much easier to throw passes with. Thanks!"

We had decided to hitchhike our way back home. This would give us a chance to see what we hadn't seen on the plane ride here. Senior offered to drive us as far as the desert that evening when he got off of work. We were packed by five and waiting for Senior to get off at six. As was his custom when we visited the shop, he said, "Pick an album, guys, any one that you want." Ron, true to form, grabbed a jazz trumpet side. His choice was Clifford Brown on Emarcy. I opted for Julie London's "London by Night" on Liberty.

"I'm taking you cats to a cool little French café for your going-away dinner. It's called "Yves." It's on the Rose Parade route on Colorado Boulevard in Pasadena. Order anything that you want. It's my treat." Ron and I both ordered some French version of filet mignon. His was medium rare. Mine was just right—bloody rare!

As we began our journey east and toward Barstow, Ron and I decided that bon voyage drinks were in order. Senior, who was always willing to oblige, pulled into some Indian liquor store. "What are you guys going to drink?"

"Hell, we don't know."

"Be right back!"

Ron and I jumped out and went in with him. We had never seen Thunderbird wine before, but we had a strong affection for that name. "We'll each have one of those T-Bird wines, okay?"

"Cool. Whatever you cats want, that's fine."

Ron and I sipped and rambled on while Senior drove us to the wonderful berg of Daggett, California—population, none! At least that was the way it appeared to these two city slickers. We said our goodbyes as Senior pulled away, leaving the two little winos in his rearview mirror!

We noticed two young guys were already standing there, up the road a bit. There was a tall blond guy and a shorter Italian-looking guy. I walked up to the biggest guy and asked, "Are you guys hitchin' a ride?"

"Yeah, we are. Why?" he replied quickly.

"Just tryin' to be polite, man. We are too! We'll go in the truck stop and grab some coffee 'til you guys catch a lift."

"Oh, thanks man, thanks a lot," he replied.

Ron and I hauled our three suitcases across the parking lot of Kelly's Truck Stop. A couple of young guys, about our age, were behind the counter. It was late and probably not too cool for chicks to be workin' out here at this time of night. We played the juke and shot the bull with these guys for about an hour. As we listened to "Rebel Rouser" by Duane Eddy and, appropriately enough, "Who's Sorry Now" by Connie, Ron noticed that the other guys were gone. We quickly finished our coffee.

The one guy said, "Here, take a to-go cup of this black java. I think that you need it."

This had to be the worst cup of coffee that I had ever tasted. Our T-Bird vino had taken it's toll on these boys. We staked out our positions on the side of the road. Ron was a bit west of me, about a hundred feet. Our theory was that a driver might be more likely to stop for one guy. If one did, I'd hustle over and join in. It was now past midnight, and nobody even slowed down all night.

It was now Saturday morning, and that desert sun was already frying us. The festive drinks from Friday had now zapped us of our normal silly humor. As the day wore on, I kept seeing these Santa Fe freight trains going by, heading east. The tracks were right across the highway, Route 66. Some were slow enough to grab a ride. Unfortunately, Ron did not have the same feeling that I did for these big Lionels! I said, "Ron, take a look over there. What do ya' see?"

"Sand, damn sand. What in the hell do you think that I see?" He was having no hobo rides in the mood that he was in.

We tried drinking the water in the truck stop. It was a brownish-green and beyond swallowing. I asked one of our friends at the counter, "What in the hell is in this water?" He said, "It's artesian well water." My research tells us the following:

"… a well that taps an aquifer that is "confined." This aquifer is water-bearing rock below ground that is surrounded by other rock or material that does not allow water to pass through. So, the water in this aquifer is squeezed by the other rocks, creating pressure in the water-bearing aquifer. When an artesian aquifer is tapped by a well the pressure pushes the water up the well, sometimes all the way to

the surface, creating a flowing well. Imagine it as a very wet sponge
contained in a closed plastic bag. Put a straw through the bag into the
sponge, hold the bag tightly around the straw, and **Squeeze**—*that*
would be artesian water squirting you in the face."

We each grabbed a bottle of orange pop, some local brand. There
was still no action on the side of this road to hell. Sometime around 3:00
AM Sunday morning, and about a half dozen orange pops later, I headed
to the rear of the now infamous Kelly's Truck Stop to use the little
boy's room. As I returned, Ron announced, "Hey, Curt, the California
Highway Patrol has been by twice. They're makin' a U-turn down there
right now."

"Grab your bags, Ron, let's get inside!"

As soon as we got inside, those same young guys said, "Hey, give
us your bags." They immediately put them behind the counter and out
of sight.

With our bags safely hidden, we ordered pie 'n' milk and played
some more tunes on the Seeburg. "You Cheated, You Lied" were the lyrics
coming from that jukebox. "Damn, who played that?" Ron whispered to
me. The CHP guys came in and sat at a booth towards the rear of the
diner. We paid little or no attention to them. We figured that all was
cool!

After stuffing their faces, these would-be cowboy sheriffs slowly
walked toward our seats at the counter. "Git up, git your bags!" the
fat(est) one groaned to us. "Give 'em their bags!" he told the kid behind
the counter.

They ordered us out front and proceeded to tear our suitcases apart.
As fate would have it, I had been given a bowie knife as a souvenir. You
talk about bad timing—I just couldn't believe that this was happening.
Now, we just had to be bad guys! We seemed doomed and had no idea
what in the hell was coming next. "I'll take that," Fatty said to Not-as-
Fatty! Both of them with the seat of their pants as shiny as a mirror from

sittin' on their asses. Well, there goes my newest gift, but who cares? I have about as much use for a bowie knife as I do for a root canal! I'll bet ya' that one of those cops ended up with my souvenir for his collection.

The Souvenir Knife ©

After stuffing our property back in our bags, we were escorted to their patrol car. I muttered to myself, "'Patrol car? What in the hell are they talking about? It's a damn squad car!" I asked Fatty what they thought that we had done. He retorted, "You know damn well what ya' done, now shut up and git in!"

Silence was all that I could hear from poor Ron. He wasn't as talkative with these clowns as I was. His usual humorous demeanor was not one that matched this situation, not at all! We were going west again, not a pleasant trip. As we drove through this devil's outpost, we passed several hitchhikers. I guessed that fact ruled out that terrible offense. They pulled in to a CHP station in Victorville. Here, we were going to be separated into two patrol cars. Now they began to handcuff us. I blurted out, "Hey, listen. I've cooperated so far, but we haven't done a damn thing wrong. I've never been handcuffed before and I don't like it. They're cold and you're wrong. Get these damn things off of us!"

"Shut up and get in," was the only response.

"When you guys find out that we're innocent of whatever the hell you think we've done, these cuffs are mine. You're not getting them back!"

In the meantime, Ron was even less fortunate. They had him cuffed with his hands behind his back. They shoved him into the back seat. "Bastards, rotten bastards!" was all that I could think.

Off we went. We were now told that we were going to the San Berdo' slammer. Ain't this just ducky? Ron had our only pack of smokes, but he couldn't use them anyway with his hands behind his back. I asked my chauffer if I could bum a smoke. I had caught a break; this guy was from the Southside of Chicago. He offered me one of his Winstons. Hell, an English Oval would have tasted great at this point. With my new-look grip, my hands bound by two shiny handcuffs, I puffed slowly while he lit it for me. As I composed myself, I asked him, "Really, what is it that you guys think we've done? It can't be hitchhiking—we've passed many doin' that."

He said, "Car theft, armed robbery and kidnapping, among other things."

"Oh, is that all?" was my rather shocked reply. I kept thinking, "We must be driving on some other planet. I've never seen so many weird plants and trees anywhere!" As we approached the CHP station in San Berdo' aka San Bernardino, my Chicago friend told me that they had the victim there. "Hot damn!" that was all I needed to hear. "We're outta here soon, real soon!"

As poor Ron unfolded himself from the back seat of his limo ride, he looked so sad. I could have cried just seeing his spirits so damaged by those jerks. He had been pushed into the rear seat back at Victorville and was not as fortunate as I had been. I had my Chicago guy to chat with as I rode up front with him. As we were marched up a makeshift plywood walkway, we had a fairly large audience of nosy folks. This facility was in the process of being remodeled. Here we were, handcuffed like common felons, and all we ever did is laugh and enjoy life and people. It just seemed so unfair. I can still see those gawking faces looking at Ron and me. This vision has remained with me for 48 years, and obviously will never go away.

We walked inside, and within one minute we heard, "That's not them!" It was the victim, a Mr. Duchelle, a rather short, gray-haired gent. True to my commitment, I pointed toward Ron's hands and shouted, "Get these goddamn cuffs off of us--*now*!" An officer stepped toward me to unlock mine. I pointed to Ron. He moved toward Ron, who was as close to crying as I had been earlier that day. They removed them from both of us. I made overtones of keeping my pair, but this was no time to push my hand. We were about to be free again! We were extremely relieved and ready to get the hell out of the building. Instead of releasing us, they marched us into another room. Here, they made us stand in front of a desk while some guy pored over mug shots. I truly believe that they were so damn proud that were not yet ready to admit their mistake. This mug-shot guy actually stopped and stared at a mug with a big bald head. This was strictly an exercise in harassment.

A friendly and decent-mannered sergeant came in to talk with us. He explained that two guys had been picked up by the victim. They robbed him and stole his '56 Chevy. One was tall and light haired, the other shorter with dark hair. They, like us, were carrying three suitcases. It didn't take us long to conclude that it was the two guys hitchhiking in Daggett on Friday night. The sergeant asked us where we were going.

I replied with my thumb in the hitchhiking pose: "Chicago, and in the same way, hitchhiking. So, if that's against your laws, you might as well book us on that right now."

He smiled as he typed this little index card. "Here, son, you can hitchhike anywhere in the country with this. Any problems, have 'em call me. Hang on. I'll get you a ride back to Daggett. They drove us the ninety miles back to Daggett at about ninety mph in a new Mercury turnpike cruiser.

Maybe I knew that someday I'd write a book. I have kept this little pass all these years.

```
TO WHOM IT MAY CONCERN
   R.J.Laffey and L.C.Erler have been checked
 by the california Highway Patrol and the
 San Bernardino Sheriff's Office and have
 been cleared of any connection with theft of
 1956 Chevy & Kidnapping of Duchelle.

 Glen Smart, Sgt Calif Highway Patrol.
 Dated at San Bernardino, Calif. 7-20-1958.
 7-50AM.
```

CHP USA Hitchhiker's Pass!

Dust flying everywhere, our driver was roaring into the lot in front of Kelly's. "Goodbye, CHP, hope we never see another!" Ron chirped as that turnpike cruiser screeched back onto Route 66.

We went inside to greet our buddies. They fried up some bacon and eggs for us. "On the house, guys," the taller kid announced.

We told them the whole story. We quickly devoured our first real food since Yves, way back in Pasadena. The guys wished us good luck as we wandered back to our post. Good luck it was to be. An hour later, a '50 Olds pulled over, the driver asked where we were headed.

"Chicago, we're tryin' to get to Chicago."

"Jump in. I'll take you as far as I can. I'm heading for New Orleans. Just got out of the Navy and I'm headin' home."

We drove in silence for the rest of the day. No matter how we tried, this cat had little more to say. I guess he was thinkin' of some chick back home. He was definitely on a mission. As the day grew hotter, so did the floorboards of his Olds. This was one little oven with the desert roasting at about a hundred degrees.

The sun had finally disappeared, and our Navy friend was getting tired. He said, "I'm gonna pull over and get some sleep. If you prefer to catch another ride, take care and good luck."

Neither Ron nor I felt like rolling the dice again. "But if you guys want to catch some shuteye too, that's fine." He stretched out on the front seat.

"Ron, go ahead and grab some sleep in the back. I'll just lie on the roof and dig all of these stars. I've never seen so many!" I just stared at the sky while attempting to recount the experiences of the past few days. Simply by virtue of the sun being down and our bodies being zapped, we all fell asleep for a few hours. No doubt that we needed it. It had been awhile for Ron and me.

That damn sun sure wasn't sleepin' very long—it was suddenly sunrise. Within an hour, we were in Holbrook, Arizona. "Time for breakfast, don't ya' think?" our nameless driver asked.

"Sure. Curt and I are buying, okay?"

He accepted, and we strolled into another place that, no doubt, had the famous artesian well water. "This joint makes me think of an old Richard Widmark movie," was Ron's quote of the day! Ron and I avoided any chance of drinking that stuff again. We both ordered milk with our flapjacks and ham. While we ate, "nameless" was discussing his route with a local. As fate would have it, the guy grabbed the map and showed him the southern route. Goodbye, Navy guy, hello hitchhiking again!

It was Monday morning, and it seemed that the Route 66 traffic was pretty heavy. As we stood on the side of the road, this dark blue '48 Plymouth sedan came by. It was full of teenagers, and they were yelling at us to "get out of town." This activity went on for at least an hour. On one pass, the driver pulled over and said, "If ya' ain't outta here by sundown, we'll take you out of town, and we're not kidding!"

Ron and I walked down to the corner gas station for a bottle of pop. The owner, a big happy-looking chap, asked where we were from. "Chicago, we're both from Chicago," was Ron's reply.

"Yer kiddin'. I'm from Chicago too. What part ya' from? I'm from Foster Park."

We told him about the kids in the Plymouth and their threats. He told us not to mess with them. The driver was the son of the sheriff, and one was a bad-ass Indian. "Last week, a flyboy came through here in his uniform. They told him the same thing. When sundown arrived, they told him to "Get in." They dumped him off about three miles east of here. They're little sons a bitches!" He told us that there was a Greyhound station in town. He strongly suggested that we grab tickets to Chicago. He knew that there was a bus leaving that afternoon. "After you get your tickets, come on back and hang out here," he said, pointing to the sofa. There was an old Jeep seat posing as a sofa in the office of this gas station.

We risked a walk into town. "There it is." Ron had spotted the station on the opposite corner. As we walked diagonally across their main street, about half a dozen of these punks came rushing toward the two of us. Instinctively, we both just clinched our fists and walked right through them. Not a word was spoken. Maybe this was just another warning, or maybe they were just chickenshit, we didn't know. As we were leaving the ticket window, one of them appeared behind us. "What time does that bus leave?" he asked the girl that had sold us our tickets.

"Six o'clock," she replied.

When we returned to "Chicago's" gas station, he seemed relieved for us. "Hey, there's a movie theater down the street. Why don't you guys go catch a flick, and I'll pick you up when I leave here and take you guys to your bus. Just watch for my Merc' from the lobby. I'll be off in a couple of hours." He had a '50 Merc' like the one that I had.

It was now bus time, and what a relief that was. We jumped on that big blue and silver Scene-a-Cruiser. We finally laughed, and we laughed a lot! This was our first laugh since Senior Blues dropped us off at the devil's outpost nearly a week ago. We opened our respective pocket books. Believe it or not, mine was *On the Road,* by Jack Kerouac, *really*!

We finally arrived at our Chicago Greyhound station in The Loop. "Man, look up there, Curt. It's our city. We're home, home from the cowboy and Indian wars, home from the damn desert!" It was around midnight. We grabbed the IC to the good ol' Southside.

"And each time I roam, Chicago is calling me home, Chicago is
Why I just grin like a clown
It's my kind of town" Thanks to S. Cahn and J. VanHeusen

As I tiptoed up those squeaky stairs hauling my massive green Samsonite two-suiter, Mom came rushing out of her bedroom. Nothing had changed. Mom had heard her "tomcat" comin' home late, as usual!

"How was the flight, Curt?" Mom asked.

I had to clear my head for a moment. "Uh, oh, the flight? It was great, Mom, a real great flight!"

No tea tonight. I was out like a light within minutes. My Samsonite was resting on the dining room table. It could wait 'til morning. Morning. Yes, morning on the Southside of Chicago!

JAZZ WAS ALWAYS ON OUR MENU

Curt, Ron & Casey at Chicago's Blue Note ©

One week ago tonight, we were stranded in the Mojave Desert. We're now enjoying jazz at Chicago's famous Blue Note on North Dearborn Avenue. Ron and I have made this our Mecca for our favorite sounds in music. My cool buddy Dee had turned us on to this place during the summer of '56. Count Basie's gang was due to appear one weekend, and Dee knew that Ron and I were big Basie fans.

Dee was one of the most well-rounded guys that I had ever met. The guy could play third base better than anybody that I knew. He and his dad had built a '32 Ford that just plain kicked ass! The cat knew his music from Annie Ross's jazz vocals to the rockin' blues of ZZ Top. Dee never got involved in any fights. He was physically able to handle this kind of a scene, but it just wasn't his nature to be violent. I know a guy that should have used him for a role model! Last, but not least, Dee was a superb photographer, later becoming one of Chicago's most renowned blues and jazz photographers.

Sadly enough, a year from this evening, the Blue Note would no longer exist. Tonight, it was Casey, Ron and Curt getting set for another memorable evening. Count Basie and his fantastic sixteen-piece band were on tap tonight. Joe Williams would soon be belting out "Roll 'em Pete," "Everyday" and my current favorite, "Teach Me Tonight." Mr. Basie's band was like that of an All-Star baseball team.

"At One O'clock, the party starts jumpin'." This was the Count's opening theme. The party was on! For the next five hours, we'd be sippin' something cool and diggin' the great sounds. There was a little service bar on the far wall on the east side of the room. As I look back, big Joe bought me my first scotch and soda at this very bar on a subsequent visit.

The restrooms were in that same corner. The band members would use the same restrooms as the guests. Often, Joe or the Count would be in there having a smoke of some kind! Joe was never aloof and always willing to shuck 'n' jive with the hipper cats. We must have qualified, 'cause we had no problem with our questions and comments.

Joe Williams once responded to my question about the band's ability to always perform with such enthusiasm. He responded with a question: "Are you a baseball fan?" I said, "Sure am!" Joe explained, "These cats are like a baseball team that comes out to win every night. Mr. Basie and the whole band really care. They really care, man!" He went on to say that it was not a band of individuals, but a team. The rhythm section was second to none. Freddie Greene was on guitar, Sonny Payne was on his hot set of drums and big Eddie Jones was slappin' the bass. There were other cats like Frank Wess, Frank Foster, Thad Jones, Joe Newman, Charlie Fowlkes and more!

This particular night. I had promised to get Joe's autograph for a little Aquinas High School chick. He said, "Catch me after the last set. I'll take care of it then, man."

About two in the morning, the last tune was played. Joe went first to the service bar for his Scotch and then directly toward us. He walked to an empty table— most were empty at this time. He asked the waitress to please clear it so that he could sit with his friends, referring to us. The waitress nodded a "yes" and proceeded to another area. She came by again. He asked politely again. No response. Joe was a big man, so he simply laid his long arms in the middle of this little café table and swept everything to the floor. "Sit down, guys."

Looking at me, he asked, "Got something for me to write on?" He was about to accommodate my earlier request, asking, "Who am I signing this to?"

"Mary, it's for Mary. Thanks, Joe!" He sat and finished his toddy with us, then off he went.

The three of us went for coffee so that we could review our cool evening. Of course, Ron and I had to do a rerun of our crazy west coast trip for Casey too.

Sunday morning, Ron and I were still gloating over our return to our Southside base. We want to get back in our groove. He calls about noon. We had to catch some zzzs after the Basie scene the last night.

I have often been asked if I play a musical instrument. My response is always the same. "Yes, I play phonograph!" That was my plan for this afternoon.

"Hey, want me to bring over some sides?"

"Yeah, how 'bout that Wynton Kelly jam, some Miles and maybe some Basie that I don't have. Would ya' grab me a pack of Luckies at Julie's on the way? I'll pay ya' back when ya' get here."

We sit in my crib (if ya' ain't hip, that's a bedroom!) with my Grundig hi-fi goin' all afternoon. Mom is always sticking her head in the door to see if we want some coffee. She's also diggin' some of the cool vocals. We're spinnin' some Sarah, a little June Christy—and Old Blue Eyes, of course! Joe Williams's ballad LP, "A Man Ain't Supposed to Cry" has been almost a nightly session since Ingrid split the scene last summer.

Ron stands up and leaves my room to go visit Mom in the kitchen: "This album is nothing but heartbreakers. I need a break. Want some coffee?"

The Blue Note was our main haunt, but Ron, Casey, Dee, Vince and I spent many other evenings at the local jazz joints. We had Robert's Show Lounge, The Crown Propeller Lounge and The Pershing Lounge. We were fortunate enough to see many great artists live and up close. Many afternoons I would visit the local bars up and down 63rd Street. This gave me the opportunity to see some informal sessions with the likes of Gene "Jug" Ammons, who was the son of the immortal boogie piano artist Albert Ammons. Muddy Waters spent some time in a few of these joints too. The black cats in these places used to refer to me as "the cool gray boy," "angel eyes" or "the blue-eyed cat," although I have brown eyes. It was just their way of saying "a cool white guy." There was a joint on Cottage Grove just north of 63rd Street called The Cotton Club. The first time I had heard the "gray boy" thing was there at The Cotton Club. I was eighteen and underage as I walked in with Jessie, my black friend. The bartender knew Jessie and remembered me from a previous visit. "It's okay, he's a cool gray boy, he's okay." Though I was underage and white, from that time on I would always be served a cold one and was never charged. It seemed to be a silent and mutual respect.

A couple of memorable meetings were with Sarah Vaughn and with my favorite vocalist of that era, Roy Hamilton. We had gone to see The Mastersounds and Sarah at the Blue Note. Early in the evening, I caught

Sarah sippin' something cool at the service bar. We talked about Errol Garner and his great "Misty" tune. Errol seldom glanced at the keyboard and never learned to read music. I asked "Sassy" to do "Misty" for me.

As closing time approached, we had moved up to a front table. Sarah had surely forgotten me. She hardly glanced my way through several sets. She was wearing a mauve brocade evening gown. With her mike and cord in hand, she gracefully vamped down the two or three steps from the stage. I could smell her floral perfume as she approached our table.

When she was practically in my face—*"Look at me, I'm as helpless as a kitten up a tree ..."*— with a big smile. She finished with a heavy accent on that last line, *"Look at me!"* virtually face-to-face with this overwhelmed kid! Then, as she began to turn, she softly touched my right hand—the hand that was now sweaty and gripping my beverage very tightly. I was overwhelmed! Pretty cool I thought, and so did Ron.

Now, the Roy Hamilton thing was very different. The producer of a local TV show was the son of Mr. and Mrs. Gottstein. They owned the Hot Dog Pit on Stony where we spent many days and nights. Stan worked at his folks' place part time. He knew that Ron, Casey, Vince, Pepsi and I were big music fans. He asked me, "Curt, who's in town that would be worthy of an appearance on our show this week? Anybody exciting?"

Without a second thought, "Yes, Roy Hamilton is here, if you can get him."

Stan was pleased to have this opportunity to show us his clout. "If we line him up, you guys are coming to the show."

He did book Roy for the show. Vince, Ron and I were there with bells on! We were sitting in this small live audience when Stan waved our way. "Come over here, Curt." He put his hand on my shoulder and said, "Roy, if it weren't for Curt here, you would not be here this evening. He is your biggest fan!"

Roy reached out with his big hand and gave me a most sincere shake. Roy had also been a boxer, and undefeated by the way! "How are you, Curt? I'm glad to meet you. You know we're at Robert's Show Club tomorrow night. Do you go there?"

This was a very good question because not many young white kids did go there. "Yeah, we'll be there tomorrow!"

Before walking back to the set, Roy autographed Vince's copy of "Don't Let Go." Appropriately, he signed, "Don't Let Go, Roy Hamilton." I'll betcha' Vince still has this precious memento! He went about his business doing a couple of numbers, "You'll Never Walk Alone" and "Unchained Melody." He also did a rather lengthy and informative interview. As the show ended, his manager, Bill Cook, came over to us and suggested that we ask for him at the club the next night.

Robert's Show Club, Friday night, Roy was just amazing during his first set. His performance of "A Mother's Love" was absolutely stunning. As the song gained more and more reverence from the crowd, Roy's stage lowered to a sub-level, portraying his own reverence. It was a most rewarding sight.

During this set a young waitress came to our table and asked, "Curt, are you Curt? Mr. Cook wants you guys to come backstage. Come this way."

Backstage, Mr. Cook, a short man and a dapper dresser, greeted us with a big smile. Mr. Cook also discovered and managed Brook Benton. "Hi, guys. Roy's changing for the next set. Come on, he wants to see you."

As graciously as we had expected, Roy moved toward us, still struggling with his cufflinks, and shirt wide open. Yes, he was preparing for his next set, but this was also his chance to take a little breather. "Thanks, fellas. I'm so glad that you could make it." We chatted about his hits and not so hits! I modestly admit, he was amazed at the fact that I could name all of his 45 rpms and their flip sides. I remember his one-word comment, "Wow!"

During our visit, Vince was not at all shy about talking to one of the 1,233 ladies back there. Actually, there were quite a few chicks in that room! Roy noticed that I was ogling his cufflink collection. "I collect the darn things. Curt, why don't you pick a pair for yourself? Be my guest, please." I shyly refused his offer, twice! I didn't really feel that I should take them—wish I had!

I did, however, make a request: "Roy, is it possible for you to do 'Everybody's Got a Home but Me?'" He did perform my request and knocked 'em out with his dramatic version of this emotional tune.

Roy passed away prematurely in 1969 at just forty years old. In retrospect, I believe that his most heartfelt tune was, "If Each One Would Teach One." When and if I ever make it through those pearly gates, guess who's going to request another performance? God bless ya' Roy!

Stan was kind enough to invite me to future shows. I had the opportunity to meet Johnny Ray, a quiet man with a wonderful voice and a style like no one else! Another guest was Chico Hamilton, the famous West Coast jazz drummer. Chico was instrumental in the birth of "cool jazz" on the West Coast as a leader and member of several fine groups. Chico was so funny. They had given him a full link of Sinai 48 Salami, a token gift from one of their sponsors. As we sat side-by-side for the remainder of the show, he asked, "Curt, do you want this damn thing? I'm flyin' home."

"No thanks, Chico. I'm not flying home, but I'll be out late and don't need any baggage."

After Roy's last set, Vince, Ron and I decided to take a ride on the IC. Lionel Hampton was playing at the Blue Note.

"Airmail Special" was pouring out on to Dearborn Avenue as we approached the stairway to our jazz Mecca. With it being a bit late, we landed a table right up front. I had heard Hamp's groaning as his mallets were flying many times on my records. This was something—we were just a few feet away. The sweat was flying, and he was groaning like a man who was being whipped. "He is one emotional cat!" was Ron's in-a-nutshell description of this jazz giant!

The letter! – Sometime during the first week of August, I received a letter from Ingrid. I was having coffee and rolls with Mom and Percy. We were in the back of the store in Percy's pad. The ol' cow bell over the store was clanging. It was the mailman with today's bills and such.

"One for you, Curt," the mailman called as he was scurrying back out the door. I hurried back to Percy's kitchen and dropped their mail on the table. As Mom and Percy checked out their mail, I walked over to the kitchen sink. The window faced out on our big green and spacious yard. As I opened this letter, postmarked Sweden, I felt something strange come over me. Within the first couple of sentences, I knew that something was up. Due to my audience and my somewhat euphoric state, I really didn't completely grasp the main message.

I ran upstairs to my bedroom and set the letter on my bed. The day went on as usual. I helped Percy in the store for awhile. I ran Mom to the Kroger at 86th and Cottage Grove so that she could do some shopping.

"Curt, want some Bay's muffins?"

"Yeah, Mom, that's great. Let's grab a pound of that thick-sliced bacon too. We can make some sandwiches for you and me, and Pepsi if he's around."

Later that evening, Ron and Pepsi were in my room with me. The window off of the alley was wide open, and it was raining like hell. I sat on the edge of my bed as I checked the window sill. "No rain comin' in," I kind of whispered to myself. I picked up the letter and began to decipher it as I read each line. In essence, it was saying, "I won't be coming back," and more personal verbiage. I crushed the letter in my right fist and threw it on the floor. Pepsi and Ron were both very perceptive guys. They knew who this letter was from.

"Wait, Curt. Where ya' goin'? Come on, stay here."

"Let go of me. Get the hell outa my way!" I grabbed my rust-colored suede jacket and like a cannon bolted down the back stairs. I never wore this jacket in the rain. I loved it! With nothing but a pair of Levis, no shirt, no shoes, I ran through the yard and out the front gate. If it were not for the rain, I might have caught fire! I was as upset as I had ever been. I walked extremely fast down Harper with nothing but anger fueling my pace. Puddles were like lakes, the rain loud and unrelenting.

As I reached 82nd Street, that unwelcome smell of damp sod was present. No, this was not the smell of this evening's rain. I felt the soft touch of a large hand on my left shoulder. I turned quickly. Nobody was there. I had never seen Luther nor felt his presence any other place than 1540. This would be the last time that I would be visited by him, anywhere!

It's New Year's Eve. Ron and I are on the IC train heading for the Blue Note. Duke Ellington always returns to his favorite Chicago spot on this special night. As we clickity-clack through these Southside neighborhoods, they each seem so special, each home with its Christmas lights shining and family activities in full view. Ron's eyes are glued to the passing scenes. Quietly, he says, "It's especially fascinating tonight seeing all of the holiday spirit, isn't it? By the way, are you still going to try to talk with Ellington?" Ron knows that I like meeting these cats. It's as though I'm notching my rifle as I meet each of our heroes.

"Oh yeah, man. After I sip a couple of Manhattans. Then I'll catch him between sets. Watch me, man!" We never tire of this Mecca.

Here it is. Another New Year's Eve, and we're climbing that legendary stairway. Drum riff, the tinkling of the piano keys and a few short toots from Cat Anderson's trumpet. As we reach the top steps, we hear the sound of cocktail glasses rattling. The cigarette smoke is as thick as a storm cloud. Now we know that we have arrived at The Scene!

Ron is lucky enough to get his request played during the first set. Paul Gonsalves wails on his tenor for over twenty choruses of "Diminuendo and Crescendo in Blue."

"What a gas man, what a gas!" Ron is absolutely elated.

I approach the piano bench as though I'm on a mission, because I am! Just as I'm about to speak, Duke says, "Watch; this chick is going to bring me coffee or tea. I ask for a cup of hot water, but they always bring tea or coffee. All I want is hot water. That's what I drink, hot water!"

Edward Kennedy Ellington—This man spoke like a very hip English nobleman. He reeked of class! He was, without a doubt, a hybrid—jazz, blues, classical and pop, a master of them all.

Now, my nerves are as loose as a goose because Duke spoke to me first. "Duke, is it true that Billy Strayhorn was only seventeen when he wrote 'Lush Life'? Those lyrics are so deep." He taps his hand on the piano bench, as if to say, "Sit down." That I do as he responds with a positive to my inquiry about Strayhorn.

To this day, I am amazed as I listen to these lyrics from the pen of this seventeen-year-old boy! If the opportunity ever presents itself, listen to these incredibly mature lyrics.

> *"The girls I knew had sad and sullen gray faces*
> *With distingue traces*
> *That used to be there you could see where they'd been washed away*
> *By too many through the day...*
> *Twelve o'clock tales."*
> *Billy Strayhorn*

While I was in the audience of the Duke, Ron had struck up a conversation with his DJ idol, Sid McCoy. As usual, we closed that joint in the wee small hours— Happy 1959!

Curt – Twentieth B-Day - Hat & Shirt – Thanks to Ron! ©

Ron and Mom were extra good to me on my twentieth! Ron gave me a cowboy hat and a black shirt with crossed racing flags embroidered on the chest. Mom suggested that I roast myself a Long Island duck. I glazed the duck with a cherry wine sauce. With a quart of Heilman's Old Style beer and my Gramma's old turkey platter, I sat down to play Robin Hood. As I was devouring my feast, I said, "Mom, would you like a nice slice of my duck?"

Ron snickered as he heard my offer. "Gee, man, you're all heart. A whole slice, you're going to give your mom a whole slice?"

I laughed and quartered the duck, giving Mom a choice quarter!

These were two of the greatest people in the world to spend time with. They were both so damn honest! We had many, many candid conversations on many, many subjects.

Jazz, beaches and my own record store? No, this was not to be! At the request of Senior Blues, I have returned to Los Angeles. It's January of '59, and it appears that I'm about to manage a new record store in Compton, California. Senior tells me on the phone, "It'll be the Frank Sinatra Record Store! I need you to come out here so these guys can meet with you."

I called cousin Peg the morning of my arrival. I didn't want to be there and not tell her. She thought that I was calling long distance. I said, "Get that damn coffee pot on, girl!" She began crying immediately. She always had been an emotional chick! I grabbed a bus and had what was to be my last visit ever with this wonderful woman. Some things are just meant to happen.

This was the dream that seemed to be before me, but not for long! Senior supposedly had a couple of big-money cats to back this venture. It did appear to be coming to fruition as I attended several meetings with his friends. The site was chosen, and more than enough cash seemed to be available. I was asked to attend a Sinatra recording session at the Capitol building in Hollywood. It was for the "Come Dance with Me" LP due out that year.

As fate would have it, I had promised to spend some time with a young lady that I had met at the little taco stand across from Senior's apartment building in the Beverly area—a little Irish girl, of course! This was not just a coincidence. I had witnessed some stuff that didn't set well with me. I really wasn't sure if I could handle their whole scene. So, I opted to spend some time with my "taco" girl instead. She had coal black hair and such fair skin. This petite girl had the most honest and light hearted laugh that I had ever heard!

Two days later, and another call from Senior. "Curt, Peggy Lee will be doing a session today. I'll come back to the pad and pick you up." I copped out again, although I really wanted to see Peggy in person.

In the few days that I had stayed at this apartment, some things seemed very strange. His roommate fried up a bunch of pork chops one night. By now, I was a pretty damn good cook, and I detected a strange smell and taste. "What's that smell? What's cookin'?"

"Drew is frying the chops in oregano. He loves to cook Italian." The next morning as they left for work, he pointed to his chest of drawers. "If there's anything that you need, it's in here."

Not having a clue, and somewhat wary of his friend, I just shrugged an "okay"! Shortly after they departed, I checked that drawer. Half of the damn drawer was full of pot, aka marijuana! Now, I knew what the chops had been "seasoned" with. I have a helluva sense of humor, but I don't like being played with, and I don't like being lied to!

That next evening, one thing became very evident to me. This "roommate" was actually Senior's boyfriend! I now knew where Curt would be living: on the Southside of Chicago, where he belongs!

Fortunately, my big brother Cary had moved to Inglewood in '56. They were living over near Peg and Bill's house. Without a word to Senior, I called Cary and asked him to come by and pick me up, posthaste! He was there within the hour. I simply told him that "things were not working out" with the biz deal. There seemed no need to go into the details. I had dinner and a couple of beers with him and Rhoda. Cary had to be at work in the morning. He was kind enough to take his beater car to work. He left his Buick so that Rhoda could drive me to the Greyhound station. A Greyhound bus—does this sound familiar?

Our Buddy Is Gone – Tuesday, February 3, 1959, Ron, Pepsi, Vince and I are walking down to Wee Mac's for our evening coffee and bull session. It's cold and slushy on the Southside. As we approach the corner of 87th and Stony, an eighteen-wheeler catches the stoplight, eastbound on 87th. With the light red, I make a wager for coffee. "Betcha' I can run under his trailer before the light turns green. Hurry, any takers?"

"No, Curt, don't be stupid," is coming from Ron.

I rush to the truck, go to my hands and knees. Before anybody can accept my bet, I'm out and on the other side.

"Very funny, man. Just real funny." Ron and Pepsi were not laughing at my dumb move. Vince just stayed neutral, at least vocally.

Our favorite waitress, Bertha, was pouring our coffee before we hit the booth. After my stunt had lost its fizz, Bertha came rushing back with the news. She had turned the volume way up on the radio behind the counter. Buddy, Ritchie and The Big Bopper were dead! That was the terrible news on this cold Tuesday on our Southside. There was very little said the rest of the evening, just quiet accolades for Mr. Holly.

Frankly, I really don't remember where this fits in chronologically, but it is worthy of note and maybe a chuckle.

I was seeing this girl from the Jackson Park area, on a very casual basis. She had a tall and very pretty Japanese friend, Lily. I was a bit smitten with this young Japanese lady. As I often did, I lobbied for us to go visit Lily. Her grandmother was always there, seated in her crossed-legged, Buddha-like position on this little raised area in their living room. You almost felt as though you were in a temple. "Grandma" never spoke, but somehow you just knew that she knew more than we knew!

We were trying to decide what kind of food to go out for. "Let's get some Chinese, or does anybody want some fried shrimp?"

Grandma finally spoke, just one word, and I'll never forget it— "*Pizza!*" I never heard her speak again. And we did have pizza that night. Who could argue with that proclamation?

Beaches and palm trees are calling once more! One of our baseball and gas-station buddies was home on leave from the Navy. Bob was due back in Pensacola in just a few days. "'Glad ya' didn't stay in LA, Curt. Now you and Ron can take the trip back to Florida with me!" Mention of a trip to anywhere always seemed to be the magic words for Ron and me. "You guys can hitch a ride back, or you can always take the trusty Greyhound." This, of course, was in direct reference to our summer trip in '58.

Now, with the convincing behind us, we packed for another uncharted territory! Ron and I each had the heart of a schoolboy, always lookin' to see what we could stir up. Ron, as always, was thinking cars. "Bob's quick little black and white '55 Ford Vicky should be a fun ride, Curt."

State by state, we find something to laugh about. The fried clams and shrimp are damn good! Coincidentally, Freddy Cannon has a song in the top ten called "Tallahassee Lassie." Bet your fanny that song is getting its share of play down here.

It seems like the snap of a finger and we are suddenly sitting in the Greyhound depot in Pensacola. Our bus is due any minute when Ron says, "Ya' sure that you don't want to hitchhike? Just kidding man, only kidding!"

The bus is another one of those Scene-a-Cruisers with the little upper deck. "Wow, Ron, how could this bus be so full? We're down here in Florida, at the bottom of the world. I wonder where all these people are coming from?" The upper deck was pretty full, and there were no two seats together. "Oh well, you might as well grab that seat up there, Ron. I think I see my seat!"

"Yeah, sure, I see her too, Romeo!" Ron snorts back.

I grab the aisle seat next to a very attractive blonde, about my age. "Excuse me, anybody sitting here?"

"No, it's not taken."

This little chick has the cutest southern drawl as she says, "I'm Judy. I'm goin' back home. I've been with my grandparents for a visit." This little lady is not shy at all. She is a virtual plethora of information.

"I'm Curt and I'm headin' back to Chicago, the Southside of Chicago."

Judy was wearing blue jeans and a red cardigan sweater. If Homer High would have had chicks this pretty, this casual, and friendly I'd have stayed awhile longer. It was late but neither of us slept a wink. We talked all the way to Lexington, Kentucky. The southern sun brought a new day and the bus was alive again with the buzz of the other passengers. Judy was home, darn it! Her folks raised horses and my assumption was that it was a sizable spread. The offer was extended to "Stop and visit sometime!" We exchanged addresses and phone numbers. I left her with these lyrics;

"Anyplace along the line, I'll forgive you if a stranger puts your little heart in danger, if his face resembles mine. Whenever your head hits that pillow, whatever the hour may be, Don't dream of anybody but me." – Bart Howard & Neil Hefti

Another love lost. We never made contact.

ALABAMY BOUND

George W. & Curt ©

That morning sun is baking me again as I awake on this hot Monday in May. As is my habit, I light up a Lucky Strike and gaze out my window. "There's that red Ford semi-tractor. It's been just sitting there for days," I thought as I puffed on my smoke. In a short while, I was down at the Gulf station to investigate this vehicle's reason for being there. There was a rather tall black guy having his smoke.

"Is that Ford yours?" I asked him politely.

"Yeah, been waiting for some parts. Been here for days."

"Yeah, I know. I live up there," pointing to my room.

We shot the bull for a few minutes and then he asked, "Hey, do you know where I can get a couple of bottles of Kentucky Tavern whiskey?"

I'm thinking, "Do I know? Silly question, yeah, I know!"

He goes on to tell me, "My wife, back home, loves it and we can't get any there."

"Where's 'back home'?"

"Oh, Alabama. I live in Montgomery, Alabama."

"Hang on. I'll see if Jessie will let me borrow his wheels!"

Moments later, we were at Bubble's Liquors so that this cat could make his wife happy. As he jumped out of Jessie's Dodge, he asked, "Want me to grab anything for you while I'm in there? I'm buyin'."

"No, I'm cool. Thanks anyway."

Upon our return, he went on to tell me about his mission. He stuck his hand out. "By the way, I'm George, George W. Temple. I know that you're Curt and I see your last name on that big wall. Man. I wish I had that "Cash" name. Is that your Dad?"

I told him a bit about Dad.

"Anyway, as soon as they get this truck ready, I'm headin' down to Clinton, Illinois to pick up a load of corn. Then I'm headin' back home to Mama!"

My mind clicked into its wanderlust mode. "Is there any chance that you could take on a rider? My brother is down there in the Army at Fort Rucker."

He quickly responded with, "If you'll help me drive."

"I don't know how to drive this big thing."

"It's easy, I'll teach ya'! Greg says that my rig will be ready to roll by mornin'. Wanna go?"

"Bet your ass, I'm goin'! What time do you want to leave?"

"Be down here at seven in the mornin', and we'll take off then."

The news is broken to Mom, and I throw some things in my bag. "Can I call Luke and Johnnie's house so that I don't shock them?"

"Yes, and be careful, please be careful. And call collect when you get to Luke's."

"Mornin', George, I'm ready if you are." I'm now wearing my burnt orange, all-wool Stetson. I traded Sean some music for this precious lid. I recently had it cleaned and blocked down at Swan Cleaners on Stony. I'll have to tell you, George fell in love with this brim as soon as he saw it. But he ain't ever gonna own it! He immediately dubbed me "Tex."

The first day, about two hours out, George stops his rig on the shoulder. "Okay, Tex, let's see ya' give it a whirl. I'll show ya' 'bout the airbrakes and all that. It's easy. It's like a five-speed, only it has two sets of gears. Actually, there are ten speeds, but don't worry, you'll get the hang of it real quick."

Soon I was toolin' down the road. You'd almost think that I knew what I was doing! After a short while, with my hands perspiring like a summer cocktail, I passed the baton.

We were stopped in Urbana for out-of-date tags. George had to wire his boss for the fine money. While George was heading for the courthouse, I was kicking back in the cab. Along came a local cop telling me that I can't be parked here, it's a city parking lot. With my hands even moister than earlier, I had to maneuver the damn thing out of this little lot. I parked it in the first gas station that I saw and locked it up. As I walked back to the courthouse, I met George coming toward me. We left that berg singin, "Goodness, gracious, great balls of fire"!

We arrived in Clinton just a little too late. The grain elevators had closed for the day. By this time, we had switched hats for a joke. I was now wearing his Greyhound driver-looking chauffeur's cap. We grabbed the blue-plate special at the local diner. George spotted a flashing blue neon sign: "Pool Hall." "Hey, Tex, wanna shoot a game or two?"

"I don't know, George. That might be kinda' touchy here in this farm town. You and I don't exactly look like these white brothers! But if you're game, I am!"

We stroll into this cavernous hall. This had to have been a warehouse in past years—it's large! Most of the walls are covered with tin signs and old farm tools and, it seems, anything else that can possibly hang. If you can sniff it, dip it, chew it, or smoke it, there is a sign touting it. Milk Duds to chicken feed, it's one massive bulletin board! With all of the white farmer kids from the area watching, we rack 'em up! George gets off a break that can be heard all across this joint. Nothing is said as a lot of these young guys wander over.

"Where you guys from?" this tall blond guy inquires.

"I'm from Chicago and my buddy is from Montgomery, Alabama. We're pickin' up a load of corn down at Brumley's in the morning."

The blond kid nods to his buddy and asks if we want to shoot some doubles. We never use this term on the Southside, but I say, "Sure, let's lag for the break."

The other guy that's to shoot doubles against us is immense. He has just one tooth up top. "Snaggle-tooth" is how George refers to him as we talk about these two later that evening. No money is gambled, which I'm kinda happy about. Gambling can sometimes spoil the fun!

George and I get comfortable in the cab with the radio lulling us to sleep. At the break of dawn: "Tex, those farm kids from last night just came to work. They're open!" Within half an hour, we have that thirty-five-footer loaded with Illinois feed corn. With our corn loaded, our friend Snaggle-tooth helps us tie down the canvas tarp.

George is ripping through those gears 'til we reach a nice cruisin' speed. The radio is still blasting, as we come to this conclusion. He loves a lot of the white cat music, and I'm jigglin' around with every R&B tune that's played. I know that I can't sing any better than Elsie the Cow, as I begin a little sing-a-long with Brook Benton. *"Someday, some way, you'll realize that you've been blind. Yes, darling, you're going to need me again. It's just a matter of time."* Likewise, George does his sing-a-long with Johnny Cash.

Just south of the Kentucky border, we stop at a good-sized truck stop for fuel and lunch. While George is filling the saddle tanks, I ask this unfriendly guy, "Where can we get a bite to eat?"

"Who's we?" he inquires.

"George," as I point to him, "and myself."

"You can eat over there. The nigger can go 'round back to the kitchen."

"Hey, can't you see, I'm a 'nigger' too? Now, tell me, where can we both eat?"

He snarls, "Both of you niggers can eat 'round back!"

Conversation over—now we can eat! I don't go into the details with George. It doesn't matter, he heard it all. George pays for the fuel and parks the rig. He grabs me by the back of my neck with his sandpaper hand. "Let's go see what's ta' eat, Tex!" We swagger our way to the kitchen door. "Oh my, somethin' sure smells good in here, ma'am!" George is quite at home back here. I'm convinced that we would not have been served half as much up front. We sit on a couple of sacks of dried beans. The back door is wide open with a cool breeze gently drifting in.

"This is just great, ain't it George?" This heavyset, happy-go-lucky black lady serves us massive portions of bacon, eggs, biscuits, grits and butter, and then more eggs and bacon! All this is washed down with some nice strong chicory coffee. I ask her if I was a common sight coming in here through the back door.

"No sir, ya' shoo ain't, not ofin a white folk ever come in here."

As we pull out, our gas attendant buddy is scowling at us. I can't resist: "Hey, smiley, be careful. I think your sawdust is leaking!" as I point a finger to each of my ears.

Still singin' and laughin', we enter the state of Alabama. "Tex, I know that we've had some laughs so far, but it might not be too cool to pull that trick down here. It would be downright dangerous, man!"

As the hunger pangs become too much to handle, we decide that we must eat somewhere. Up ahead, on George's side, to the left, I spot a little pastel green building. "Negro Motel and Café," the old tin sign reads.

"All right, Tex, you tried it in your joint. Wanna try it here?"

"Hey, Belly, it only seems fair. Let's give it a shot."

I had learned during our chats, that he was called "Belly" by his friends and family back home. He is tall and slim except for a bit of a pot belly.

This is an experience that is almost as vivid today as on that May day! As we jump down from the cab, I am still astonished at that sign. This is the style of building that I had seen so often in Southern California, almost an adobe look, only a mint green! Entering the building, George simply says two words, "Be cool!"

About a half a dozen guys spin their heads as we sit at the counter. The guy who you'd expect to be standing on his feet, as is the norm, is stretched out on an Army cot behind the counter. No doubt, we are an inconvenience to this cat. He rubs his eyes and slowly stretches his arms. Then he pulls his grayish T-shirt into place. Before he can speak, George attempts to soften the blow. "Howdy. My friend and I are mighty hungry. Watcha' got back there?"

The man silently flips this grease-stained, handwritten menu across the counter. Just one menu is offered!

"Hey, George, I'll have what you're havin'."

He gives our host the order. "We'll each have a bowl of chitlins and the chicken fried steak. Some coffee too."

After a few moments, old smiley face slides a white porcelain bowl in front of each of us. I hesitate and watch George's first move. He begins to ingest this nasty-lookin' stuff. I wiggle the bowl a bit and almost puke. This white slippery stuff looks more like bait to this Southside kid.

"Sorry, George, I thought that I was tough. Guess I'm not! I'll just pass on the guts." With all thoughts of hygiene now driven from my brain, I simply attempt to survive the next few minutes.

George reaches for a quarter and heads for the Rockola jukebox in the corner. By now, we have one hundred percent of the attention from the clientele in this strange place. Bobby Darin begins belting out his "Dream Lover" tune. George strolls back to the counter while giving a dead stare at some of his viewers. "How's the chicken fried steak?"

"Um, oh it's just hunky-dory George, just like Gramma used to make," I reply with a chuckle!

"There's a couple more tunes to pick on the juke, Tex. Your turn, man!"

"*Personality, you've got personality,*" shouts Lloyd Price as I select my last choice, "Summertime Blues," by Eddie Cochran.

With our festive dinner behind us, we slowly walk out the door toward the truck. Looking back, every eye in the joint appears at the window as they watch our every move. George, being a cocky sort, starts to untie every tie on the canvas tarp over our corn.

"C'mon, George, don't push our luck. C'mon, you're just messin' with 'em and they know it."

Paying no attention to my request, "Tex, you get the ones on your side. I'll get these."

Soon, we're toolin' down the road again. "Man, that was funnier 'en about anything I ever done. That was just great!" George is crackin' up thinkin' back on the events back there at the now-memorable; Negro Motel and Café.

There's this big mountain near Birmingham that they call "Big Red." About half way up, in a lower gear, we spot an old white couple on the side of the road. They have a '54 Plymouth with a small trailer hooked up behind. Steam is pouring out from under the hood. "Tex, don't ya' think that we should help the old folks?"

George pulls onto the shoulder and trots back to the couple. "Anything we can do, folks?" We realize that the only hope is for us to pull them up Big Red and to the next service station. George and I crawl under each vehicle and chain 'em up. George says, "Just sit there, Sir. Don't touch the wheel, brake or anything. We'll get you up the hill." These two old-timers never once break a smile. Maybe they're in shock—don't know.

Soon, we spot a service station. George pulls in with his added cargo. George and I finish unhooking the Plymouth and their trailer. By now, my hands are as dark as my buddy Belly's. The old guy approaches me and asks, "What do we owe you?"

"Don't know, Sir. Ask George; it's his truck."

"How much is fair, son?"

"Like I said, Sir, ask George. That's up to him."

The old girl reaches into her purse and pulls out a buck and hands it to me.

"Hey, George, here's your half," as I tear the bill in half and silently walk away from these unappreciative humans.

I still have my half, forty-seven years later!

Finally, Montgomery is on the horizon. George maneuvers his rig down this unusual little street. "Here 'tis, Tex. This is where I work. I'll just lock it up here in the yard and we're done."

With the truck in the yard, we make our way down the dirt street. The only way that I can describe this street is that it looks much like the *Porgy and Bess* local, "Catfish Row." It was as though I had been transported to the Gershwin musical.

"You're only about two hours from your brother's place in Newton. Let's walk down to the bus station. I'm buyin' your ticket."

Once again, we're receiving some very unfriendly looks as we walk the short way to the depot. "I've never seen a car with a "Jitney" sign on the top. What's that mean, George?"

"That's a taxi, man. A jitney is a taxi down here. I'll be right back, Tex!"

"Hold on, I'll go with you George."

"Ya' can't. I'm goin' in the colored area. You can't come in here!"

I look up, and sure as hell, there's the other area. "White Only" is what the black and white porcelain sign reads. George is out in a flash. "Only six bucks, Tex. That ain't bad, and your bus leaves in about an hour. I'll call the Mrs. and tell her that I'm home. I'd like you guys to meet before you get away tonight. If I can get her to come back, I'll see you in awhile. If your bus shows up, just grab it. And thanks, it was a helluva ride, Tex!"

It was after eleven and my bus was due in just a few minutes, and still no George and Mrs. I never saw George again. On subsequent trips, I looked for this friendly and funny guy, to no avail. I never had any luck. Even with today's computer technology, I've never been able to find George W. Temple!

Y'all ain't never been down south 'til ya' been to Newton, Alabama! After a week of crazy times with Luke and Johnnie, it was time to head back home to the Southside! How did I get home? I'll let ya' guess! The ol' thumb was ready for the challenge again! This past week had included a very fast and risky speedboat ride on the water moccasin-infested Lake Tholloco. This was a pretty dumb idea considering that none of us could swim the width of the average pool. Luke's wife, Johnnie fed me plenty of her great pan-fried cornbread. Luke and I put down plenty of Busch Bavarian brew at the going-away party for his best Army buddy "T-Tap." T-Tap was a big laughing machine that had no "off" switch. There were no dull moments!

Mrs. Balcomb, Luke's landlady, charged my just six bucks for my sleeping quarters for the week. Mind you, I slept on a big goose down feather bed. There was about a half dozen beds in her immaculate attic. This area had two large windows, one on either end of the attic. A heavenly breeze drifted through, all night long. Everything was painted with shiny grey enamel, every bit as tidy as a military quarter.

"See you guys in a couple of months," I called back as I began my next journey of unknown events.

Within an hour, two young construction workers pick me up. "Where ya' headed buddy?"

"Chicago. How 'bout you, how far ya' goin'?"

"We're goin' up to Huntsville. We'll take you that far. We've got a big job to do up there. We'll be there for several weeks. Huntsville is up at the northern border of the state. That should get ya' off to a good start. Want a beer?"

"Hell yeah. I haven't had a 'Dixie' since I've been down here. Thanks!"

These guys are both Cardinal fans, so we have plenty to talk and bicker about. "Tell me about this guy Stan Musial. Is he much of a hitter?" I almost lose my beer rights with that one!

"This is where we turn off, "Chicago." I'll drop you at this junction. It's pretty busy. Good luck, man!"

After a rain-soaked day of thumb-in-the-air begging, a guy finally stops. He's a little blond cat with a DA haircut. He's driving a red and white '55 Chevy rag top. "Chicago, huh? Well, I'm going to Whiting, Indiana. Do you know where that is?"

My bike trip with Luke comes flashing back. Do I know where that is—silly question! I'm thinking, "I can probably walk home from there."

The blond cat reaches over and throws the door open. "Hop in!"

"Cool. Thanks man, thanks a lot!"

Not more than twenty minutes later and absolutely no conversation, he says, "Feel like drivin' for awhile?" I soon realize that this neat lookin' little convertible is only a six-banger. What a waste of a good-lookin' set of wheels! As soon as the quiet man nods off, it's pedal to the metal for me. I drive for an hour or so with my foot buried in that floorboard. That little red bomb never tops seventy miles an hour. I drive for the remainder of this leg of my journey. Mr. Talkative snores a helluva lot more than he talks.

Lever Brothers and the big soap box is now on the horizon again—almost home! One more short ride, and maybe I'll be home at good ol' 1540 and my bed. A rotund man with a big stogie in his chops pulls over. "Hey, kid. Where are you headed?"

"Chicago, Sir. How about you?"

"Yep, me too. Jump in. Where abouts in Chicago are you going?"

"83rd and Stony Island. Y'know, Route 30!"

"What's there? Do you live there?"

"Yeah. I live above the camera store just west of Stony."

"Cash Erler's. Are you Cash's kid?"

"Yes, I sure am. Wow, this is just great!"

He talked more in these few miles than that last cat probably did all of last year. "Curb service, Curt. You're home!"

Newton, Alabama
1959

Lon, Curt and Luke – 1959 – Newton, Alabama ©

Alabama once more! This year's travels are far from over. As the summer is upon us, so is Luke's discharge from the Army. His little Alabama wife Johnnie is in that delicate condition. They would be parents in a just a couple of months. I had promised Luke that I'd get down there and help him with the drive home.

Pepsi has heard all about my recent Alabama adventures and finds a way to slip away from work for a week or so. For years, I have been kidding one of our best buddies, Lon about hitchhiking down to Amarillo, Texas. Why Amarillo? I guess, just because we had never been there and the name fascinated us. Well, if not Amarillo, let's get Lon to take this trip. Like most young cats around here, he has never been further from home than 130th Street!

Luke gives us his target date and we pack up Pepsi's cool little '51 Ford. Buddy Holly is jumpin' and hollerin' as we pull away from 1540. *"Maybe baby, I'll have you ..."*

Our trip is not as complex as my last journey down south. We add New Orleans to our route to perk up the itinerary a bit. As we are getting closer to NOLA, we pull in for gas and receive a "shortcut" from the attendant. This shortcut will take us through the swamps for many, many miles. Pepsi had left on this little sojourn immediately after work. He has had no sleep to this point.

"Pepsi, why don't you catch some shuteye and I'll get us to New Orleans while you regenerate a bit." Lon, like Pepsi and me, loves music. With Pepsi sawing logs in the back seat, we're enjoying some of the hits and some stuff we have never heard. Outside, we keep hearing these strange noises in the swamp.

"I ain't ever heard anything like this, Curt! Let's turn the volume down for a minute."

I pull off to the side of the road. Gators, weird birds and bugs are serenading us with their eerie sounds. Just then, Martin Denny's haunting tune "Quiet Village" begins to play on the radio. It's around midnight and there's very little moonlight. It's damn dark! I turn off the lights and the engine. With the sounds of the swamp accompanied by "Quiet Village," we call out, "Pepsi, Pepsi, wake up. We don't know where in the hell we are!" Pepsi jumps up to witness what he probably thinks is hell on earth! He only fumes for a moment before he breaks into a hearty laugh. After all, we all came for the fun, didn't we?

We had a short stay in Newton, Alabama. Oh yeah, we laughed a lot and found time to down a few suds. I enjoyed Johnnie's fried cornbread again. The ride home, now with two cars, was fairly uneventful. Johnnie enjoyed all of the new sights. She had never wandered so far from home. Luke was a civilian once again and he was singing more than normal, something about – "Sweet Home Chicago"!

Cary – Curt – Pepsi – Luke ©

With Luke back home we were now able to get back to our favorite indoor baseball activity, our Cadico Ellis All-Star game. Things are lookin' good again!

Luke takes this All-Star game very seriously! ©

OUT OF OUR SAFE ZONE

You'd have to know Jessie to really know Jessie! "Curt, wanna go for a taste?" Jessie calls up to my bedroom window. He works next door at the Gulf gas station. He's a big, cool-lookin' black cat. Jessie's job is actually supposed to be a car washer. Jessie does that and much more for this gas station. He can turn a wrench as well as most of the mechanics there. The clientele love him and he is a true buddy to me. No BS from Jessie, at least not to me. Try to conjure up an image of Gershwin's "Porgy"—that's Jessie! A broad-shouldered man, maybe thirty-five, maybe more and one big-ass smile, always! He's wearing his old, faded, red work shirt. It has turned to a shade not unlike a barely ripe tomato—maybe a brick red, not sure. It is always starched and ironed. His wife "Baby" ensures him of that. The truth is, I want a shirt just like it, but where do you shop for a faded red work shirt?

This "taste" that Jessie is referring to is an after-work pint of Kentucky Tavern bourbon. The same stuff that George W. Temple's wife dug so much. This is his idea of happy hour! To those who may frown on this scene, have you ever heard of two "suits" meeting at some chez martini joint after the office closes? Sometimes, we are too quick to judge another's culture or habits. You talk about more bang for your buck— Jessie will spend two bucks and the suits maybe twenty.

"Hang on, Jess. I'll grab a shirt and my kicks!"

We take the old Dodge and run down to Bubble's Liquors at 91st. Most booze stores have little paper solo cups that are free for the asking, so I grab a couple. Just as cool as those chez martini glasses to us!

We return to our cocktail lounge behind the Gulf station. With all windows down and the summer breeze slidin' through, we tune in one of those stations down on the far end of the radio dial. *Living with Vivian* is on station WBEE out of Gary, Indiana. She's playin' some Spaniels, El Dorados, Moonglows, Flamingos and other cool groups.

Jessie's brother-in-law, George, sometimes drives him to work. On those days, we sit in my dry-docked '50 Merc', just a few feet away. No music on those days; no battery, no music! *"Crazy Little Mama' knockin' at my front door..."* is soothing my spirits as we sip our after-work cocktails. Just another day on our wonderful Southside!

Hoy-Toy was the Chinese restaurant down at 86th and Stony. Jessie loved their BBQ-style pork and the sweet sauce.

"Hey, Curt, I'm poppin' if you'll run to the Chinese joint. See if your little lady friend will throw in some extra rolls, okay?"

I grabbed the old green pickup with the "Gulf Gas" logo on the side and boogied down Stony.

"Hi, camera boy, what ya' have today?"

"I know how to get those extra rolls," I thought as she continued with her greeting. "My, my Pearl, you're sure lookin' pretty this afternoon. I'd like to have two orders of your delicious BBQ pork to go, and could you please throw in a few extra rolls?"

"Okay, got it, camera boy. Extra rolls, and anything else?"

"Nope, just your big smile, Pearl! What does 'Hoy-Toy' mean, Pearl?"

"'Hoy-Toy' mean lucky, very lucky. 'Hoy-Toy' good luck. You rub his tummy and you have good luck. You want hot cup of your jasmine tea while you wait?"

"That would be great, Pearl, thank you. See, I'm lucky already!"

"Hey, Jess, let's go next door and eat in the yard."

Jessie just loved this. "Sure, I enjoy that big green yard, and your Mom will call down and say 'Hi,' I just know she will."

I believe that he felt privileged to be sitting in this big yard in an all-white neighborhood.

"Hi guys, how about some iced tea?" Mom calls down from her always busy kitchen. "Thanks 'Msss Erler', thanks so much."

Out of nowhere, Jessie says, "Curt, wanna borrow the shirt for your date tomorrow night? I can have Baby wash and iron it for ya' tonight."

I jumped at the offer. "Bet your ass, I do, Jess. Yeah, I wanna!" I was taking this six foot-plus chick to the Jeffery Theatre to see, of all things, *Porgy and Bess*. I wore it proudly Friday night, although it seemed to kinda hang on my shoulders. Wonder why?

My most memorable event involving Jessie was a night at his apartment. One Friday afternoon he asked Ron and me if we would like to come to his pad for a party. "Ron, I'd like you and Curt to come over tonight. Baby wants to meet you guys. I'm always tellin' her about your crazy trips and stuff. We're having some neighbors over for a rent party."

Ron and I asked, "What in the heck is a rent party?" It turns out that a rent party is a common event in some areas of the city. It's just as it states, a rent party. The guests kick in a certain amount of bread, like five bucks a head. This would cover some snacks and the drinks and sometimes there would be entertainment. Any profits would go toward the host's rent. Ron and I were exempt from these fees. We were special guests, which was the qualifying term to be used if anyone inquired. Often, the problem with this little tradition was that you had no control over the guest list. This was a word-of-mouth thing and covered the whole block and more! So Jessie and Baby were really not choosing their guests. Ron, as usual, asked, "Should I bring some jams, Jess?"

"Nah, there'll be tons of records there. Baby's got stacks of 78s and 45s. She'll be doin' her DJ thing. Baby loves doin' that."

Ron's reply was, "I hope that she needs some help, 'cause that's my thing, man, spinnin' those sounds."

Jessie lived at 43rd and Indiana, not exactly a Mecca for young white cats. We decided to be ready when Jessie got off of work. This would save us the car fare and would minimize our chances of any trouble. We'd still have to make the journey home late at night. What the hell, we survived the Mojave—we could certainly survive this somewhat more timid Serengeti! Traveling the Southside late at night was nothin' new to these two jazz fanatics!

"I'll bet that this is Ronnie the Cat and you're Curt" is Baby's greeting as she comes down to meet us and help haul some of the goodies upstairs. This is one of those big, three-story high, red brick six flats. Probably built in the twenties. Ron, with his normal good manners, reaches for her hand and says, "Hi, Baby. Yes, I'm Ron, and this is my little brother Curt."

"You're puttin' me on. Ain't no way you guys is brothers."

"Hi Baby. You're right. How could I have this runt for a brother? I'm Curt, and thanks for the great job on the shirt last week."

Before long, the place is packed with people and the drinks are flowing—more drinks than I've ever seen flowing anywhere in my life. There are men and women sitting everywhere. Some are on the kitchen counters, the sink, even one on the Frigidaire! Some have wandered to the back porch. It's hotter than hell and just as humid. There are some cats sitting on the crazy-looking linoleum floor shootin' craps. Others just sitting there for the lack of any other place to roost. Seems that most of the ladies are hangin' out in the parlor. That's what Jessie calls it, his "parlor"!

Ron and Baby are shuckin' and jivin' at her old Zenith phonograph. Like a couple of kids, I hear, them. "It's my turn. I wanna play Joe Turner," is coming from Baby. Ron's lobbying for some honkin' Joe Houston saxer tune. I'll handle this: "Hey kids, 'got any Roy Hamilton tunes over there?" Within a minute, Baby was spinning Roy's big hit record, "Don't Let Go". As Roy's great 45 came to an end, Ron was pretty damn excited with the whole scene as he began singing Bill Haley's "We're Gonna Rock this Joint Tonight"

It's getting late and things are starting to get edgy here and there. Some foul mouths are screaming at each other over food. This one ugly bastard is bad-mouthing Baby 'n' Jessie for not having enough snacks. "Bullshit, we need more chicken and we need some links, man!"

I'm sitting on that silly-looking linoleum next to Ron. This ugly cat seems to be trying to get in my face with his wild antics. It's decided that they'll "dollar up" and throw some cash in a pile. After the little collection, someone will make a food run. He throws a dime into the kitty and says, "Let them white SOBs go to Harold's Chicken Joint with George. Let them make the run. They ain't paid nothin' noway!"

I reach across our little circle and whack him on the left side of his face. A pretty good shot considering that I'm sitting and he's barely within arms reach. He bolts out the back door swearing, "I'll be back. I'm gonna get you."

Jessie, who was standing at the sink, taps me on the shoulder. "Come on, you guys stay with me. He ain't kiddin'. He's probably goin' for some heat! He's rushing to his bedroom with Ron and me close behind. Tearing through his chest of drawers, he comes up with a gun. It appears to be a .45, an automatic—I don't know, I'm not a gun guy! He slaps a clip in the handle and says, "Follow me!" Down the stairs we fly. Jessie looks both ways for big-mouth. He's nowhere in sight. Jessie is sure that this guy will be back soon, and armed! Jessie instructs us: "Go down to 43rd and grab a bus. I'm stayin' here to cover you. Buses are not too frequent this late. Just hang in there."

Following his plan, we hustle down to 43rd. Within a few minutes a bus appears. Not another soul on it, just Ron and I and the very stunned driver. As we start to head east, I begin to feel a bit guilty. Jessie is takin' a big risk for us. Neither of us is saying much, just watching the Friday night action on almost every corner. Home sounds pretty good about now.

First thing Monday morning, I'm watching out my bedroom window, waiting for Jessie to pull up behind the Gulf station. I'm just hoping to see his big-ass smile any minute now. About 8:00 AM, Jessie pulls in, looks across the alley and gives me a big thumbs up! Tearing down the back stairs, I'm anxious to get the scoop.

"He never came back, Curt, but Sunday mornin' one of my neighbors told me that you sure messed with his face! Hey, man, don't sweat it. Before it was all over, it turned out to be a good place to get a fist in the eye. Pretty rowdy crowd, man! By the way, Baby really liked you and Ron!"

Bob, Ron, Curt and Roger – Gulf Station – 1959 (Bob is now gone, Ron's in Heaven, and Rog' was killed as he slept, in Viet Nam) ©

As Christmas arrives, I seem to have a different perspective than in past years. It's funny; I'm always reaching for something special as each Christmas season approaches. This year, more than ever, I have begun to realize that it is nothing tangible. We all know the true meaning of this wonderful time of the year. We certainly know that it's not Santa's birthday! It's the celebration of the birth of Jesus Christ. Beyond the religious aspects of the season, there also lies our love for each other. It's also the beautiful memories of Christmases past that make it all so very special today. *"God bless us, everyone!"* Thanks to Tiny Tim and Charles Dickens.

My Birthday date this January 29th was Kathleen M. Roberts. This was that pretty little girl that I had met back in the spring of '58 on Euclid Avenue. While almost two years had passed, I maintained contact with the hope that she would eventually come around! This was no easy task. Kathy had her ways and wasn't easily convinced of my charms!

I was now twenty-one years old! I borrowed a '54 Caddy ragtop for this very important event. The agenda included Italian dinner at Frank Sylvano's on Stony Island. This landmark restaurant served as some proof of my worldliness. Kathy was a wonderful date. The conversations were excellent and allowed each of us to gather some insight into the other. I stole my first kiss that evening.

"Lords" Lon, Sean, Vince and Curt – Spring 1960 ©

I now have a Gulf gas station at 83rd and Baltimore. This is not only my business, it's also my home—for awhile, anyway. Brother Percy has finally pushed my patience to the boiling point. The T-Bird–Caddy deal has never been resolved, and he is becoming far too dominant with Mom's business and property. In retrospect, I suspect that Pepsi and I were becoming a threat to his "monarchy." Anything that will leave him in total control will suit him just fine.

"To hell with it, I'm leaving!" This was the morning after he had his clock cleaned in a family poker game. Buck wiped him out to the tune of around a hundred bucks and his portable TV! I had Percy for another hundred but was feeling his pain. By design, I cut the cards, "double or nothing" until we were even. Percy wasn't even noticing, or didn't give a damn, that I had lost all of my cash. This cash was needed to pay for my gasoline delivery in a day or two. Fortunately, my *Porgy and Bess* movie date loaned me the cash for the gas load. You remember, the six foot-plus chick! He was ornery as hell toward everybody the following morning. Mom was even feeling the effects of his anger.

"Mom, I'm going to build a bedroom for myself over at the station. I'll stop by to see you every day or so." I pored over my closet trying to decide—what stays, what goes? I opted for my favorite threads. I took all of my black, white, gray and red shirts and slacks. No, I didn't have any red slacks! My portable Motorola phono and a few LPs were also making the trip. With my bags packed, I walked away from 1540. As they say, my heart was in my mouth.

Sean and Lon ease my pain considerably as they work at the station with me. Sean and I have been buddies now for almost twenty years. We seem to understand each other in almost any situation. We have a lot of laughs and never let the slow days get us down. Hey, when it gets too slow, we just converse with the lovely ladies as they pass our way! Lon has the demeanor of a large teddy bear. Big and strong, yet one of the most mild-mannered guys that I have ever met. Vince is "chasing" for a couple of the tow truck outfits in the area. If there's a traffic accident anywhere in our area, Vince is there with his transmitter and receiver tipping off his two tow buddies, Ace and Reggie.

Sean @ Baltimore Ave. Gulf ©

Now, I need to see Kathy more than ever. Her loving and compassionate side is now surfacing. I like to think that she is growing fond of me, too! We have our songs, like most couples do. I cut a hole in the wall between my "bedroom" and the pay phone. Each night that I don't see her, I call and we chat for awhile. This is always the right time to play "Telephone DJ"! *"Scotch and soda, jigger of gin, oh what a spell you've got me in ..."* was often played. "Night," by Jackie Wilson, is the tune that really fits the bill for me. *"Night, here comes the night, another night to dream about you...".* Actually, Jackie is doing a little spin on Mr. Tchaikovsky's score. "Stuck on You," by Elvis is another appropriate record for this now very close couple.

My Kathy at a Frozen Lake, Michigan ©

"It's now or never,
come hold me tight ....
When I first saw you
with your smile so tender
My heart was captured,
my soul surrendered ...."

Pepsi has been in a bad accident! It's Friday, May the 6th, just a day after his nineteenth birthday! Pepsi and two of his buddies have hit a light post on Doty Avenue at a high speed. It has been raining, and Pepsi's '59 Buick convert' lost traction and spun out of control. Pepsi was rushed to the Roseland Hospital. The other kids were okay, but Pepsi suffered some severe head and hand injuries.

Pepsi's Buick ©

With nobody here to hold down the fort, I lock up the station and drive to the hospital with one of Pepsi's girlfriends. "Thank God!" is the simultaneous statement from Judy and me as we first lay our eyes on our Pepsi. Yes, he is badly injured, but he is smiling. Somehow this doesn't surprise us! Pepsi's big white Buick is totaled! It had actually wrapped around that post. The impetus threw Pepsi and the left door completely across the oncoming traffic of the northbound lanes.

As any good Erler will do, Pepsi took his therapy very seriously. He worked very hard to get his hand back in shape. On the lighter side, I sure wish Judy hadn't sat on my cool Buddy Holly shades and their blue lenses on our ride to the hospital! (See Kathy's picture. She's wearing them before this incident!)

My Kathy © "*I could write a book, about the way you look ….*"
Baltimore Ave. Gulf Station – Spring, 1960

Kathy needs to hit the jazz scene! For far too long now, Kathy has heard all of us guys talking about our jazz venues and adventures. It's time to show off my "Baby" to our jazzy crowd.

"Hey, Kathy, are ya' up for some cool sounds this weekend? Chris Connor is at the Tradewinds on Rush Street. How 'bout Friday night? I might even buy ya' a cocktail. Is it a date?" We had a great table, right up front. Chris put on a helluva show. Kathy is now one of the full-fledged members of our little jazz society!

Just a few days later, poor Luke walks into the backyard with his face looking like an old catcher's mitt. "What's up Luke, what happened?" I'm heading toward him, shocked at his badly bruised face.

Trying to keep his spirits up, as well as his pride, he explains, "Oh, this guy at work, he hates me. It's because of my position. He resents me since I came back from the Army. He mutters comments to his buddies when we're shootin' pool at the bar. I guess I kinda bumped him out of his job. Anyway, he was waiting for me in the parking lot. Without a word, he just tore into me. He had me over the hood of my car, just pounding on me!"

Now, my heart is beating like a hammer. Luke is near tears, and it just doesn't seem right because Luke is such a peaceable cat. "Take me to him, I'll kick his ass. Come on, let's go to that bar, maybe he's there!"

"No, Curt, it's not your battle. It wouldn't help a bit. Let's just have a cold Old Style and forget it. I just don't want Johnnie to see me this way."

"Are ya' sure about the bar? We could just drive over there. Just give me his description. Maybe I'll accidentally have a disagreement with him and I'll punch the crap out of the jerk. Wouldn't that make you feel a little better?"

"No, Curt. Just grab a tray of ice cubes and bring us a couple of brews, and we'll see if we can get me looking a bit more presentable before I go home."

Mom's Favorite View ©

Sunday, June 19th, was Mom's sixty-fourth birthday. This means that it's time to pull out the old Sears grill. We are all out in the yard at my new home—1540! I had moved back shortly after Pepsi's accident. Thank God, Percy now has a "pen pal" and is acting civil again.

"I'll take a quick run and pick up my surprise guest," I announce to the family. I had asked Kathy to spend the afternoon with the family. Mom has already met Kathy and really likes her. "I'll be back in a half an hour."

As I held that white picket gate open, I could see the eyes focusing on my "Little Irish Treasure"! Let me tell you, Kathy looked like some chick in a '40s movie. It was a scene right out of *State Fair*, or was it *Meet Me in St. Louis?* Her blue gingham summer sun dress, a straw hat and white mules. If I had any damn foresight, I'd have this picture on my desk as I write this today. Geez, a camera family, and yet nothing for posterity! Later in the day, we grabbed a seat in the red swing away from the crowd.

"Ya' knocked 'em dead, Kathy-O, you really did! I'm one very proud guy today, thanks to you!"

There seems to be no doubt, Southside Kid is in love with this pretty little Southside Lass! In spite of statements like, "I'm not going to get serious. There'll be no marriage for me. I'm stayin' single!" the inevitable was about to happen!

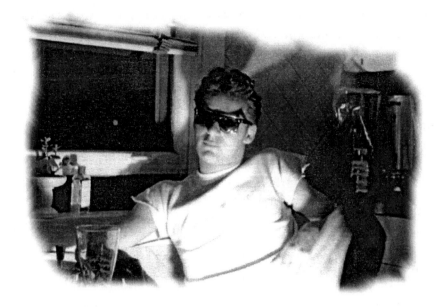

Still Pondering this Love Thing! ©

Here comes that love thing again! Sometimes, love comes rushing by—you hardly touch it, and it's gone! It may linger, but it is gone! Love isn't something that you can put in a box and simply remove the lid as you desire it. It transcends all material things. I have felt so many kinds of love—a word, a touch, a simple gesture, the smell of someone's skin, a shy revealing smile, the wink of an eye, a nod of approval. Love doesn't come in sizes, styles and colors. It comes as love. Maybe ….. those precious words at that needed moment—"I Love You!"

"There's a somebody I'm longing to see.
I hope that she turns out to be
Someone who'll watch over me.

I'm a little lamb who's lost in a wood.
I know I could always be good
To one who'll watch over me."
Gershwin & Gershwin

Kathy's folks are planning a vacation in Hot Springs, Arkansas, later this summer. I know already that I'll be missing her at that time. The summer has been just great.

We're all sitting in the yard—Ron, Kathy and Kathy's best friend, Liz. "Summer Place" is coming from the kitchen window. "Can things get any better than this, Ron?"

Ron, with his subtle wit, rolled his eyes toward Liz, then back to me. I knew what he was saying with his little, telling grin. He was never much for being "fixed up," and this situation was beginning to have those earmarks. Now, a whisper is coming from Ron. "Yeah, man, they can get better." "Curt, would you and Ron like to accompany us on our trip down south?" Mr. Roberts was actually asking Curt to be with Kathy on their family vacation.

"Well, yes. Yeah, I'd love to. Ron and I could follow you in his new Volvo. I have a job to finish up first, but there's plenty of time. I'll be ready, and Ron's got vacation time coming." It was travel time again for the Wanderlust Boys!

Soon after this wonderful day, Ron and I were laughin' and singin' as we tooled down the highway. Our accommodations were somethin' else! The Lanai Suites at the Majestic Hotel, a classy joint for sure! Ron and I took Kathy to dinner on one of the evenings. Southern hospitality was ever-present at this establishment. After dinner, I was so happy I jumped in the pool. Now, this doesn't seem too unusual, but I was wearing a white dress shirt and black slacks. Furthermore, I swim about as well as I dance! In any case, we woke up some patrons, as it was kinda' late.

The trip home was a little different. Ron and I had much to discuss. You see, I had proposed to Kathy while we were there. Ron really liked Kathy, but I know that he was very concerned about our plans. My employment record did not exactly dictate a rosy future for these two young kids. "Curt, what in the hell do you think Mr. and Mrs. Roberts are going to say? They're going to be livid, man!"

"I know man, I know. They're really gonna flip, no doubt about it!"

Ron's New Volvo ©

As the summer went on, Kathy and I began to firm up our plans. Kathy was still only seventeen and enrolled in Chicago Teacher's College for the fall semester. Ron had introduced me to his good friend Ed over the summer. Ed knew my situation and did some checking at work. He was working afternoons as a rate clerk at a freight company somewhere near 23rd and Western Avenue.

One evening while we were sitting in Mom's yard having a few Old Styles, Ed asked me, "Curt, how would you like a steady job?" He had jumped at the opportunity to help. He fixed me up with a nice Teamster's job working on the docks, unloading trucks. Now I had a steady income, and Kathy would be eighteen in November. We firmed up the date. It was decided that November 16th would be fine. Kathy would be of age, and this would give us a little time to save some money.

Later in the summer, Percy's pen pal was to be visiting us here at 1540. Not knowing anything about his distant friend, we kind of figured this to be a mail-order-bride deal. As it turned out, his "mail-order bride" was a guy. As television's Berretta used to say, "and that's the name of that tune!" No further comment here!

Kathy and I rented a real neat place on Dante in the 8800 block. Ron, Kathy and I spent the evenings painting and preparing our new home. One night after we had worked fairly late, Ron was getting ready to go home. He announced his plans for the next few days. He was taking his mom down to Rock Island in the Volvo so that she could visit her family. We wished him well as he was slipping on his gray suburban coat. I can see him standing in that hallway as though it were yesterday. We never saw Ron alive again.

BLOW GABRIEL, BLOW

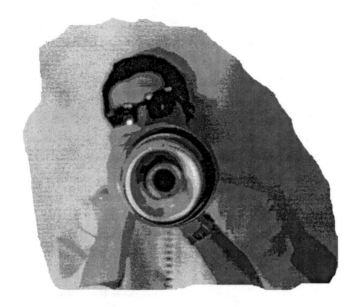

Ron could blow a mean trumpet …. and I know where he's
playing now! ©

Ron hadn't come home, and it was getting late. Ron's dad called late on the evening of Friday, October 28, 1960. "Have you seen Ronnie? Is he with you? We haven't heard from him and we're very concerned."

"No, Mr. Laffey. I've been working. I have no idea where he is. Have you spoken to Ed?"

Ed had no idea either. His folks and I knew how conscientious Ron was about staying in touch. The norm would have been that Ron and Curt were somewhere! With my unpredictable work schedule and Kathy and I making our wedding plans, this wasn't the case this evening.

I tried to console Ron's dad, but I was extremely concerned as well. I realized that Ron had just learned to drive last spring. He had purchased that new 1960 red Volvo in April. He didn't really hang out with anyone other than our little group. There were just a few of us. Casey and Sean were both in the Army now, and Vince was seldom, if ever, with just Ron. We all had a lot of common interests—music, cars, sports and, of course, the girls! With two of our gang serving Uncle Sam, the other logical thought would be, maybe he's with Ed, but that had already been answered—he wasn't! Not having any idea of where Ron had been since he got off of work, I was stymied!

My bed was flush against the window above the alley. I can still recall standing on my bed just staring out east toward Stony Island. I was whispering to myself, "Ron, where are you, where can you be? Why haven't you called home, or called me? Please, Lord, take care of Ron and let him be safe, please dear Lord." With no more contact between his folks and me, I tried in every way to rationalize his virtual disappearance. I'd like to describe the feelings that I experienced until morning. The truth is, I have very little recall of when, or if I ever, fell asleep.

Saturday, October 29th, approximately 8:00 AM, Mr. Laffey phoned. "Curt, I have some news. It's the worst news, Curt. Ronnie is dead! He was in an accident last night. He suffered severe head wounds, and they couldn't save him." He had been informed that Ron had attended a party with some guys from work. The assumption was that Ron had been homeward bound. He was driving on a winding road out in Willow Springs. His car hit a tree at a high speed, and Ron was thrown from the car.

From that moment until the first evening of his wake, I do not recall much at all! Ron's many friends and family there were also in shock. As hard as I tried, I just couldn't find the right words for his mom and dad. All three of us were in a walking trance. There were some guys from work there, but I didn't want to ask them too much. Down deep, right or wrong, I wanted to blame somebody. It was not a good idea for me to stir anything up, not there! Dean, in his maturity, stepped up with a thought. "Curt, would you like me to talk to these guys? Maybe they can give us some more information." Again, I don't really recall how I responded to Dean. The truth was, Ron was gone. I was in total shock, and nothing was going to bring him back.

The evening that Ron was buried, it was cold and pouring rain. Kathy and I sat in the dark in Mom's living room. The room resounded with the sound of the rain pounding on the roof above. I knew in my heart that Ron was not where we had left him, but I couldn't stop thinking of what had transpired that morning at the cemetery. I was speechless, and Kathy was in a very tough situation. It was obvious that I was truly lost without Ron. Kathy asked me if I would like to put off the wedding, saying that she would understand. Now I spoke: "That's not what Ron would want us to do, and we have our own lives to live. The sixteenth will be our wedding day!"

Thank God that Ron had introduced Ed and me. We had so much in common. We both loved our sports, music, humor and good food. He stuck with me like a big brother during these hard times. When Kathy and I had set our wedding date for November 16th, Ron, of course, was to be my best man. I approached Ed with a very tough question. Would he be my best man? Ed responded with, "Curt, I could never fill Ron's shoes."

"Ed, I'm not asking you to fill his shoes, ... I understand. Be my best man, okay?"

Ed accepted the challenge and became my right arm during the two weeks leading up to the wedding. Without the incredible support of Kathy, Ed and Mom, I wouldn't venture a guess at what my fate might have been. I have often stated that Ed was my gift from Ron. I truly believe that it was Divine intervention. Ron had brought Ed into my life almost as though it were on cue!

Ed – Best Man ©

"Ron, you will live forever in my heart. I know where you are. I pray that my own roadmap can lead me to you. I miss you, every day of my life. Without your subtle humor and constant companionship, I have realized a very large void. God bless you, Best Buddy!"

TWO SOUTHSIDE KIDS BECOME ONE!

Wednesday, November 16, 1960. Today, Kathleen Mary Roberts becomes Mrs. Curt Erler. The weekday crowd at St. Felicitas was sparse and tentative. At least it seemed that way to me. The little Irish priest was so nervous that he dropped the rings. There had been much discussion in the previous weeks about Curt not being Catholic, ... and about Kathy being too young and not ready for marriage. There were, however, the few faithful in attendance on that sunny November afternoon. It was a big privilege for Kathy to have her younger brother, Jackie, as one of our altar boys.

As we walked down the aisle, Kathy was singing softly, "*I Love You a Bushel and a Peck* ..." We didn't have much money, but we knew that we had the most important ingredient! Love is all you need!

"I Do, I Do," a kiss, and on with our lives we went!

A Bite of the Wedding Cake ©

As the reception was winding down, Sis and I made eye contact. It was time to go. As planned, Kathy and I began "our dance.". Sis had cued up our closing number. "Old Blue Eyes" began to croon:

"It's the last dance, we've come to the last dance.
They're dimming the lights down, they're hoping we'll go.
It's obvious they're aware of us, the pair of us
Alone on the floor.
Still I want to hold you like this forever and more.

It's the last song, they're playing the last song. The orchestra's yawning,
they're sleepy I know.

They're wondering just when will we leave, ..." Cahn & Van
Heusen

As the tune played on, Kathy and I danced out the back door. We
laughed as we walked right down the middle of Dante Avenue. Within
two blocks, we were home! Our new apartment—well, our new half of
an apartment—was now home for the newlyweds. With just twenty-two
bucks between us. **We say a little prayer and we share a kiss.**

EPILOGUE

Monday evening, **December 5th, 1960,** a call came over the loudspeaker system. I was working the second shift at Viking Freight at 23rd and Oakley Avenue as a dockman. "Erler, hey Curt, you have a phone call!"

It was Todd. "Hey, kid, would you like to become an insurance agent?"

"No thanks, Todd, that's not for me. I'm not a salesman."

"Yes, Curt, you sure as hell are!"

I met with his district manager, Mr. Longworth, and all went well. On December 19, 1960, I left my blue collar at home and wore a white shirt and a tie to work!

"Thanks again, Todd!" As you will notice in the following photos, 1960 ended on a high note!"

New Year's Eve Couple ©

New Year's Eve Kiss ©

Fifteen months after our wedding day, Uncle Sam came a calling. Kathy was expecting our first child. What surely seemed to be a devastating blow turned out to be a great lesson in life and love. After completing basic training, I was fortunate enough to be stationed in California. I was able to come back home and retrieve the future Mommy, my dear wife Kathy. Our first of three daughters, Cassandra, was born in Paso Robles, California, that fall. I made it all the way to the mighty rank of E-4 (that's like a corporal, not a general!), and I soon became the chief clerk in charge of a large equipment pool at Camp Roberts. We finished our hitch with Sam while learning a million ways to cook beans, rice and hamburger.

G.I. Curt ©

1964 – I returned to the white-collar world. The next thirty-three years were spent in management positions with two major corporations, as well as my own marketing entity.

1997 – I had a bout with cancer and major surgery. After a very successful marketing career, it was now time to retire. It was time for family and friends, as well as my writing and other hobbies.

I've sampled the local fare, from reindeer sausage in Fairbanks to gumbo in New Orleans. Chorizo con huevos in San Diego to chowder in Boston. Fish 'n' chips in Canada to the cantinas in Mexico. Luaus in Hawaii to Hoppin' John in Bermuda. The cable cars in San Francisco, the wine train in Napa. I've enjoyed so very much, from the famous river-walks to the corporate towers. I've done my time in Vegas and Reno and have met my share of famous folks. I've actually been blessed by Pope John Paul II.

Yeah, this Southside Kid with the ninth-grade degree has had a ball, biplanes, Lear jets and all!

A FEW LAST MINUTE THOUGHTS

S ome folks say that we shouldn't live in the past. I don't; I just enjoy a visit now and then.

Unable to find a time machine, I have built my own. You're holding it in your hand!

I'll never know who or what Luther was, or is! I do, strangely enough, include him in my prayers every now and then.

I don't know what my Uncle Rex looked like. I know that he did hang himself in the attic. Sometimes, when Luther appeared, I would wonder, "Is there, could there be, any link, any link at all?"

Cigarettes? Oh, that didn't last long. Kathy and I haven't smoked for over 40 years.

Whenever I think of heaven, I think of the old Southside neighborhood. Just a tiny dot on the globe, but it was heaven to so many. Longitude 87.58559, Latitude 41.73391 — that's where you'll find it on any globe. To my family, it was 1540 East 83rd Street, Chicago 19, Illinois, USA.

1540 was very much alive. It had a heartbeat and a temperament of its own. It got sick, it got well, it worked hard; it was powerful and yet so relaxed. It was home!

For those of you that lived here and had similar Southside experiences, I offer the following trivia:

Friday night movies at the library / Bounce or Fly & "500"
Wanzer Milk / Mrs. Hackles
Zooma the Man from Mars / Fudini and Pinhead
Tavern Pale / "I Want to Give Them Away but Mrs. Muntz Won't Let Me"
Bireley's Orange / The "Shoe-Car" on Stony Island
Uncle Mistletoe / Golden-rod Ice Cream / Sky-King
Five-cent winners / Push Ups and Squeezes
Red Goose Shoes / Super Burger
Cushman Motor Scooters and "Whizzers" too! / Cartoon-O
Cyclone Anaya / Bert Wilson / Purple Cow
"Whispering" Joe Wilson / Mr. Bluster / Super Circus
WBKB / Popsicle Pete
Jim Moran the Courtesy Man and, ...
"Be Keen, Be Keen; Drink Chocolate Flavored Ovaltine"

Bibliography

Chronicle of the 20th Century, published by Jacques Legrand and Chronicle Pub. Mount Kisco, N.Y.
The Baseball Encyclopedia, The McMillan Company,1969
*Thorndike Century Junior Dictionary, Copyright, 1942
(*This was my grammar school dictionary, used for eight years at St. Felicitas grade school. If it's not in there, we don't need it.)

Music Credits

(Thanks. Without you, we would have nothing to sing about!)

"A Bushel and a Peck" – Frank Loesser
"Christmas as I Knew It" – Johnny Cash
"Don't Let the Stars Get in Your Eyes" – Slim Willet, Cactus
Pryor & Barbara Trammel
"Don't Dream of Anybody But Me" – Bart Howard & Neil
Hefti
"Don't Sit under the Apple Tree" – Lew Brown, Charles
Tobias & Sam H. Stept
"Earth Angel" – Jesse Belvin, Curtis William & Cleve
Duncan "Goodnight Irene" – Leadbetter & Lomax
"Misty" – Errol Garner & Burke
"Great Balls of Fire" – Jerry Lee Lewis
"Heartbreak Hotel" – Mae Axton & Elvis Presley
"I Could Write a Book" – Rodgers & Hart
"It's Just a Matter of Time" – Brook Benton, Belford
Hendricks, Clyde Otis
"It's Now or Never" – Eduardo Di Capua, Aaron Schroeder,
Wally Gold
"Let it Snow, Let it" – Sammy Cahn & Jule Styne
"Lush Life" – Billy Strayhorn
"Mairzy Doats and Dozy Doats" – Milton Drake, Al Hoffman
& Jerry Livingston
"Music, Music, Music" – Weiss & Baum
"My Kind of Town" – S. Cahn & J. Van Heusen
"Night" – Lehman & Miller & Tchaikovsky
"One O'clock Jump" – William Basie
"Only You" – Buck Ram
"Scotch and Soda" – Dave Guard "Sentimental Journey"
– Bud Green, Les Brown & Ben Homer
"Shoo Fly Pie and Apple Pan Dowdy" – Sammy Gallop &
Guy Wood
"Soft Winds" – Goodman & Royal
"The Last Dance" – S. Cahn & J. Van Heusen

"Times Two, I Love You" – Fulton & Steele
"Yankee Doodle Dandy" – George M. Cohan
"Young at Heart" – G. Leigh & J. Richards

"Ghost Riders in the Sky" - "You Belong to Me"
"You, You, You" - "Jezebel"
"It Only Hurts for a Little While" - "Love Is Strange"
"G.I. Jive" - "Tear Drops" - "A Man Ain't Supposed to Cry"
"Roll 'em Pete" – "Unchained Melody" - "Slow Walk"
"Don't Let Go" - "You'll Never Walk Alone"
"A Mother's Love" - "If Each One Would Teach One"
"Everybody's Got A Home But Me" - "Personality"
"Dream Lover" - "Cry" - "Chances Are" - "Here In My Heart"
"I Was the One" - "Diminuendo and Crescendo in Blue"
"Lush Life" - "Tallahassee Lassie" - "Party Doll"
"It's Just a Matter of Time" - "Summertime Blues"
"Quiet Village" - "Maybe Baby" - "Crazy Little Mama"
"Rumors Are Flying" - "String of Pearls"
"Night Train" - "The Long Black Veil"
"Till The End of Time" aka "Chopin's Polonaise"
"Fever" - "Money Honey" - "One-sided Love Affair"
"Day by Day" - "Don't Be Cruel" - "Too Much"
"Playing for Keeps" - "Jailhouse Rock" - "You Send Me"
"Whippoorwill" - "We Go Together" - "Stuck on You"
"Airmail Special" - "Dance with Me, Henry" - "My Prayer"
"Song for a Summer's Night" - "Red Top" - "Rebel Rouser"
"Mule Train" - "Who's Sorry Now"
"Times Two, I Love You" - "Too Young"
"Dragnet Theme" - "The Little White Cloud that Cried"
"Wheel of Fortune" - "Rock the Joint"
"Crazy Man, Crazy" - "The Twelfth of Never"

Web Sites
http://www.historyplace.com
http://www.m-w.com
http://www.timeanddate.com
interactive2.usgs.gov
http://www.chicagobus.org
http://www.baseball-reference.com
Don't miss the Chicago / Southside book by my dear friend
Caryn Lazar Amster (Link below)
http://www.chicagospiedpiper.comcaryn@cmapublishing.net
http://www.southside-kid.com

Contributors

Cover design – Honey Stetson
"Luther" sketch – Cassandra Erler Posladek
Web-Site Design – Nicole Erler Bryant
Baseball grip photos – Modeled by Brett and Brooke Posladek
Editor – Rod Traff

Special Thanks
Ed Newell – For being there!
Jack and Mae Roberts – My wonderful in-laws.
Casey, Sean and Vince – For their lifelong friendship.
Anna Newell – You are a buddy!
George W. Temple – My Alabama buddy.
And to all of you – For reading my book!
*Note – Your questions and comments are always welcome at;
southsidecurt@cox.net
http://www.southside-kid.com

A Brief Description of the Main Players
Dad, aka Cash (born 7/29/1891 – Rochester, N.Y.)
Mom, aka Winona (born 6/19/1896 – St. Louis, MO)
Kathy – Loving and dedicated Wife and Mommy!

My siblings (all born in Chicago, IL)
Cary – Tall, handsome, with a self-serving personality
Buck – 5' 7", muscular & athletic
Percy – Tall, rather opinionated fellow
Todd – Tall, handsome and extremely athletic guy
Luke – Good-looking, articulate guy, rather introverted at times
Sis – Pretty and smart
Junior, aka Pepsi – Handsome kid with charm and wit
Ron – Handsome, with that "Black-Irish" look, incredible humor and integrity and, most importantly, My Best Buddy!
Luther – A grim-appearing, big man, wide shoulders and large hands. Always wearing blue jeans, suspenders and a plaid shirt. An occasional visitor from … ?
And too many other interesting characters to list. Watch for them, they're all here.

Love 'n' God Bless!

More Photos;

Kathy at Lake Tahoe ©

Three Beautiful Daughters / Nicole ~ Honey ~ Cassandra ©

Kathy & Curt @ Cubs Game ©

Curt & Ed – '90s ©

Curt &Vince – August, '81 – YEP August! Vince really digs his tree! ©

Cary – Curt – Pepsi ©

Da' Gang ~ Almost 60 years later !

Friendship! ©

Yeah, … RIGHT!

544708